BACKGROUNDS OF
THE DIVINE COMEDY

A SERIES OF LECTURES BY

DINO BIGONGIARI
former Da Ponte Professor, Columbia University

(INCLUDING FOUR LECTURES BY HENRY PAOLUCCI)

EDITED BY ANNE PAOLUCCI

Library of Congress Cataloging-in-Publication Data

Bigongiari, Dino.
    Backgrounds of the Divine Comedy / Dino Bigongiari ;
supplements by Henry Paolucci ; preface by Anne
Paolucci
        p. cm.
     ISBN 1-932107-12-6
     1. Dante Alighieri, 1265-1321. Divina commedia,
I. Paolucci, Henry. II. Title.

PQ4390.B62 2005
851'.1==dc22

                                            2005046212

Published by
GRIFFON HOUSE PUBLICATIONS
for
THE BAGEHOT COUNCIL
P.O. Box 252
DOVER, DELAWARE 19903
griffonhse@aol.com

CONTENTS

PREFACE

The lectures contained in this volume were delivered by Professor Dino Bigongiari, Da Ponte Professor at Columbia University, in the Fall of 1953, as the first half of his graduate course on Dante and Medieval Culture. My husband had already taken the course when I first came into it; we both continued to audit it for several years after that, while working on our dissertations. During that time, we both took verbatim notes, collating them into a single text every evening, after class (well into early morning), while the words were still vivid and fresh.

My notes were in shorthand (learned expressly for the task), my husband's were in longhand. Coming to Columbia after several years as a navigator in the United States Air Force and from a rich background of readings undertaken on his own for many years prior to his work toward the Ph.D., Henry Paolucci brought to the project a maturity of experience and a solid acquaintance with many of the basic texts Bigongiari cited or quoted in class. His was the anchor needed to insure accuracy.

Three different sets of notes were taken and preserved, with Professor Bigongiari's knowledge. We had hoped to have them ready for publication soon after that and actually began the editing process several times. Each time we did so, we realized that we would need a block of uninterrupted time — much more than we could spare, once we started to teach — to edit the notes properly.

Difficulties loomed large every time we took up the project. Bigongiari's delivery in class was — not

1

surprisingly for those who knew him — altogether different from his writing style, which was always direct, terse
and unadorned. In class, he riveted the listener's attention with his Socratic nudgings, his frequent questions
and often witty pronouncements, meant to elicit some
kind of response from the students, often interrupting
himself to go back to something that he felt needed more
explanation. He never lost his train of thought, even
after providing a long "footnote" to clarify an idea or a
statement made much earlier.

The lectures were always personal as well, for he
never shied away from his own judgments of authors and
works, never minimized criticism of those writers he
believed to be untrustworthy sources, providing at the
same time the evidence needed to sustain such judgments. His voice came through casually, but with the
authority of someone at home in the materials he put
forward.

He was fluent in Greek and Latin and most of the
modern European languages. He said once, to emphasize a point, that he never commented on texts he could
not read in the original — a statement that reinforced the
awesome impression one had of his wide reading and
well-grounded knowledge of source materials.

A graduate of Columbia College (1904), he was
quickly recruited for teaching at the College, later in the
Graduate School, where he remained for almost fifty
years, until his retirement. He was soon recognized by
his colleagues as the most brilliant Greek and Latin
scholar in their midst. His reputation grew over the
years. By the time he retired, he had taught in a number
of departments at the Graduate School and had earned
the respect of colleagues all over the world. His love and
knowledge of modern literatures, as well as his ease in
other areas of learning (including history, poetry, mathematics and physics, astronomy and psychology) was

clear enough even to a casual observer.

In the classroom especially, he commanded attention, even when the subject was beyond our immediate grasp. He would aim higher than where we could reach, hoping to provoke questions that would bring us into the Socratic exchange so dear to him.

Without notes of any kind, Bigongiari would delve into his immense store of knowledge, his long acquaintance with Greek and Roman texts and authors (as well as more modern ones) to give his students the backgrounds he thought were basic to an intelligent understanding of Dante's *Commedia*. The result was a mosaic made up of precious shards, arranged in a pattern which was vivid and provocative. He followed his own format — highlights in a modified historical sequence, emphasizing writers he thought important for the discussion, often returning to them more than once. The continuity was not so much the directness of a written text but rather a spiraling forward, often with reminders, on different levels, of what had already been said. Repetitions, when they appear, turn out to be restatements, in different contexts, meant to further illuminate an unfamiliar subject. He was a master of this kind of exposition, which not only proved effective in class but commands respect, also, at a distance, just as a mosaic gains fluidity and clarity when we are somewhat removed from it rather than up close.

Often, he would interrupt himself to ask what we knew about this work or that, this author or that one. If no one answered, he would himself address the doubts most of us were too embarrassed or too shy to voice. Not many of us suspected his casual observations were anything more than that; I certainly was one of those who, at the time, naively enjoyed his "asides," not grasping until much later their importance and relevance as resonances of the main theme.

Much of this comes through in the lectures my husband and I took while students in the course. Reading the text of those lectures today, I can still hear the voice of the master, see his eyes searching the room for the kind of response he craved and solicited in different ways, with a variety of questions. Those of us present felt privileged to be addressed in that way, in spite of our inadequacies. Many of us took in and, later, as teachers ourselves, often unconsciously applied his methods in the classroom. I know my husband and I did. I still lecture without notes. I also remember my frustration, listening to Bigongiari, at the poverty of my own preparation, wanting to know more, wanting to make more sense of what I knew, trying to keep up with someone I could trust to give me the directional signals needed to cross new and unfamiliar territory.

All of this created a dilemma every time my husband I turned to the task of editing the lectures. Each time we returned to the typescript of what we had collated from our separate notes, we found it almost impossible to reach decisions about how to proceed. Other more immediate professional tasks contributed as well to our inability to bring the project to conclusion. It was not until after my husband's death in 1999 that I decided to approach the project again. Too much effort had gone into it for me to ignore or abandon it. More important, in final analysis: I didn't want Bigongiari's unique contribution to Dante studies to be lost.

Still, without my husband's keen knowledge of the texts and his sharp and unwavering instinct for detecting errors, the task seemed formidable. Nonetheless, I was determined to see it to completion.

The first thing I had to do, as an editor, was to delete all the unfinished sentences, the many questions and intrusions aimed at getting students to respond. Such interruptions simply would not work in a book.

Where questions were on the immediate subject, I integrated them into the ongoing discussion; where they referred to earlier material or called for long and detailed response, I introduced them at the end of each lecture (or chapter), so as not to disrupt the continuity of the core presentation.

Most of the Greek words and phrases have been retained, to give some indication of Professor Bigongiari's command of the texts he cited or quoted. Any errors that have crept into the spelling of such words are mine.

I have made no effort to restructure the discussion more rigorously, or to strike out what seem to be repetitions. I felt that the unique method of circling around the target rather than approaching it head on — Professor Bigongiari's special talent for holding the disparate parts of a discussion together without losing any of them in the process — should be preserved.

Completing the project was well worth the time and effort that went into it. The difficulties seemed to recede as I explored again the exhilarating world of ideas, which only a truly great teacher can map out. Although the exciting immediacy of the lectures is gone, the book provides Dante students with excellent materials for research and offers the reader an authoritative introduction to Dante's world and the philosophical backgrounds that found their way into his great poem.

The *Appendix* contains four lectures by Henry Paolucci, given at the request of President Nicholas Butler of Columbia and Professor Bigongiari, when the latter was forced into a brief absence because of illness. In them, Professor Paolucci expands on Aristotle and the Greek experience, as well as the fall of Rome and the appearance of Christianity.

ANNE PAOLUCCI
May 2005

1. DANTE'S PLAN: THE LADDER OF LOVE

What is behind Dante's plan, what was his intention in writing *The Divine Comedy?* Like almost everything else that came out in Western Europe between 300 B.C. and the late humanistic period, *The Divine Comedy* was shaped by an ethical interest to find a solution to the problem of what constitutes happiness or beatitude and how this beatitude is to be reached — a problem that has been plaguing the universe from the time of Zeno down to our day.

Different people have looked for happiness in different things. Some, like the Stoics, find happiness in the performance of duty, in the practice of virtue for its own sake. They make that the object of their pursuit. Some others, like the Epicureans, look for happiness in pleasure. Most of us today are Epicureans; we look for happiness in pleasure — although we should remember that for the early Epicureans pleasure meant intellectual pleasure as well as the other kind. Still, they were not concerned with the intellect for itself, just as the Stoics were not interested in duty or virtue as ends in themselves; both were concerned with those ends for the pleasure they could give. The Epicureans followed an intelligently controlled pursuit of pleasure. The Stoics tried to get out of obligations of duty as much as possible, and were willing to give up pleasure only if circumstances forced them to do so. These two groups — the Stoics less and the Epicureans more — constituted a force inimical to the public good, to organized society.

A third group of people — the one to which Dante

and others like him belong — hold that pleasure is not beatitude, that man was not put in the world for that. Man was distinguished from other animals, they say, was given a specific form — reason — for a very different end. By his very nature man can be happy only if he struggles to attain the truth. What does this mean? To understand it, one must recall the first line of Aristotle's *Metaphysics*: "All men," says Aristotle, "by nature [not by education or by accident, but because they are so made] desire to know." By nature man has in him an unquenchable desire to know; not as a guinea pig, not as a rabbit, but as a *rational* human being. By nature, he can be happy only in the pursuit of knowledge.

The question then arises: is there an end to this quest? Is there an absolute to be reached? Or — put another way — is this quest for truth or knowledge an infinite series, as we think today, or is there an end to it? The answer that Dante and men of his century give is that it is a *finite* process. This process of the satisfaction of our human nature is a quest for knowledge that leads to absolute knowledge. How do we go about attaining it? What did Dante and his contemporaries think about it?

Dante envisioned the process the way St. Paul did or the Platonic way, as a ladder — a certain kind of ladder going up by rungs — and then, finally, by a leap (because the ladder is not complete), up to the highest, the absolute truth. In other words, God created the universe, not on a basis of equality (this whole system of equality as we have it today has no place in Dante's universe) but on the basis of an orderly grading of *more* or *less*. Everything in the universe is ranked; the whole constitutes an *ordo* or grading. God has indicated by the imprint of value He has left on things whether they are high or low on the ladder; and He has given us a mind and a heart, a comprehension and a desire, to look upon things and evaluate them and see whether we will rise up from one rung to the next and to the highest, or move down lower.

This is, of course, a commonplace of Dante's day. Man is born with this desire for God, to see the *invisibilia Dei* — that's the famous quotation from St. Paul — and man reaches Him by moving up gradually in this upward climb through the visible things. In one of the most beautiful passages of *The Divine Comedy*, Dante tells us how God created the human soul, how our soul touched divinity for an instant and then fell, came down to animate or inform — as the men of Dante's time used to say — this body of ours. When that happened all was forgotten of the divinity except the desire, the yearning to try to recapture what was lost.

This yearning is what we ordinarily call "Love." Dante tells us how the little boy, still carried away by the memory of that bliss of the instant he had touched divinity, loves first something about his mother, something about food, and then perhaps some toy, and then some kind of a little animal or pet, and so on. Then, finally, he discovers this yearning to return to God leads in stages up to the highest material body (we must remember that in Dante's universe and also in Provence, the feminine element is a special thing) *the beautiful woman*. This is the way by which God has decided that we who have come from Him shall rejoin Him.

At this moment, the ladder ends, and we leap into a new dimension. The possibility of seeing the Absolute is not within the limits of our reason. The approach is what the ancients called supernatural or a *praeter*-rational. At a certain point this *scala Dei*, this ladder abandons the intellectual approach, ceases to be rational and discursive, and becomes a *vision*. This is not to be mistaken for what we ordinarily understand by "mysti-

cism." It is not that kind of mysticism where we say to
ourselves: I shall pray and shut my eyes and fast, and
perhaps God will appear. It is an intellectual vision, this
vision of Dante; it is not the vulgar mystical approach,
but the approach that has been called "plotinian." After
you have exhausted all the resources of the intellect and
reason, you are ready to move beyond them. We get
there — to this point where the leap is made — by a
temporal process, as a result of reason. The angels, as the
Christians used to say; the *intelligences*, as the Moslems
say, see without effort. They have an intuitive comprehension of what for us poor mortals is discursive. There
is a light that comes to illuminate the mind, that enables
it to think discursively, to pursue the laborious path of
reason; there is another kind of light — and here Dante
departs from St. Thomas — an intellectual light that
enables us to see, not discursively, but as a vision. We
can see and follow step by step the demonstration of a
geometrical theorem. But there is another kind of intellectual light that enables us to see, not step by step, but
immediately, the whole of the theorem, as in a vision.

This ladder of love, one rung mounted on another,
from less to greater, in Dante's *Paradiso* takes on a
special form, an astrological or astronomical representation and structure because according to him all things
that happen in this world — the very fact that I can move
my hands or that the grass grows — must be traced back
to principles, first principles, and those are found in the
stars. In other words, the causes of all things are in the
stars. And it is this gradation of the *causae rerum* that
Dante presents as the stepping stones to God in the
Paradiso. Here Dante brings out all that pseudo-scientific and also scientific scheme of things which from a
general point of view we must say was a mistaken
account of things, but which was there and we have to

consider it.

What does Dante have to say about Justice, for example? How does Justice come into the world? It is the radiation of the planet Jupiter. How does man become a meditative person? The contemplative character of the soul comes from Saturn. How is man made brave? This comes from Mars. These, or most of them, were common views. Justice as connected with Jupiter comes from Greek philosophy. The connection of Saturn and the contemplative soul is not quite such a commonplace. Indeed, it occurs only once: in the work of Proclus. In the *Paradiso*, the quest for beatitude is graded according to the casual principles inherent in the different stars.

The stars themselves, as mentioned earlier, are moved by *intelligences*, which the men of Dante's time called angels. It is only because of the presence of these intelligences, which are somehow connected with the heavenly spheres, that these spheres move at all. And here Dante follows that strange figure who for a long time was said to be a convert of St. Paul: the pseudo-Dionysius, who is really a Neo-Platonist, and who has left an account of this celestial hierarchy of intelligences, full of strange conceptions, but full also of much true platonism. It is the conceptions of pseudo-Dionysius that Dante utilizes to describe the active power of his heavenly spheres. How does he apply it?

It is through the causal principles and *intelligences* that inhere in the stars, in various gradations, that man moves toward the full attainment of happiness. He does not move spontaneously from one gradation to the next, from Mercury to Venus, and so on. This new movement, which is the external picture of this process of proceeding from one virtue or causal principle to a different one, involves another element, that which is always present in Dante's works: *Beatrice*. She furnishes the motive power whenever a change of level is called for.

Again and again, Dante remarks that what he is doing in the *Paradiso*, this rising up through the heavenly spheres from the bottom upward, is contrary to the force of gravity. How is it, he asks, that this man, Dante, this heavy body that should be falling, is rising instead? How is he able to do this by a kind of effortless impulse? Man — who has all sorts of desires and who practices virtue not through an impulse ordinarily, but through a certain feeling of obligation or duty — how is it that he can do this? What he's talking about, of course, is that special character of the soul, which Aristotle and the Platonists spoke about so much and which was especially dear to some of the romantics: the "beautiful soul" that does good, not for pleasure but for the sake of goodness.

How does man come to find pleasure, Dante asks, in doing things that others consider a duty, and do so laboriously? The preparation for this changed condition is described in Purgatory. Man by nature, by the human nature implanted in him by God, has an invincible desire to return to the point from which he has come, from which he has gone astray in this world. The question is: how is this *anima nobilis* reconstituted, so that instead of straying it moves directly upward, to God? How is this *anima nobilis*, deteriorated by the fall and further spoiled by all that man has built upon the impulses that derive from the fall, made whole again? The answer is found in *Purgatorio*. It is symbolically represented at the end of the second canticle in a somewhat pagan picture of two fountains. One carries away all memory of evil — the idea is ancient; it is found in Pythagoras and kept miraculously alive by a few Christian writers, and here recaptured by Dante. The waters of the second fountain (whether an orthodox notion or not is uncertain) completely restore human nature. After the process described at the top of Purgatory, Dante is in the condition Adam was in before the fall. His nature now functions without the incrustations of sin. But, in order to be able to drink this water, bathe in the waters of Lethe and Ennoe, Dante must again go through a crisis of conscience which is very difficult to understand, except that Beatrice once more is brought in for the finishing touches in this process of purification, which is the final act on the top of the mountain of Purgatory.

What is this process of purification, consecrated by Beatrice? All through Purgatory, Dante describes the monotonous process — perhaps I shouldn't say monotonous, for Dante in the *Purgatory* challenged all people of all times after him, showing how very varied monotony can be — at each level he gives a picture of the vice to be purged, opposed by its contrary virtue, and then he introduces examples of souls that have purged and washed away the vice, and pictures of what happens to those who are lost in the vices. And then at each step after all this he shows the corresponding beatitude. At each step Dante hears miraculously a voice cry out a provisional beatitude — not a permanent happiness like that of the *visio Dei* in *Paradiso*, but a provisional, contingent happiness, a moment in the process of purification. Here again the motive power is love. Dante at all steps in this process, by implication and outright pronouncements, is concerned with the conception of ethics and morals, not simply a matter of precepts. In the *Purgatorio* we see how following St. Augustine he makes ethics a practical aspect of love.

Dante is, of course, orthodox in his approach to Purgatory. We don't get there because we deserve it — we get there because God wants us to get there. And that takes us to the basis of this process of purification; it takes us into Hell. What is Dante doing, what does he

think he is showing us when he shows us Hell? He is
showing us that before you can begin the process of
purification you have to have reduced your soul to ashes.
When something is wrong morally, what do you do? Do
you ask the doctor what is wrong with your soul and have
him remove it? Do you try to find out what the law has
to say about it? Dante always wants you to be in a moral
mood about such matters. The situation is not so much
an act of reason, but a sense of fright, a sense of horror
before the spectacle of sin. The spectacle of the world
creates in us a sense of horror at its wretchedness, a
sense of horror that moves us to seek our own salvation
as human beings, and moves us to get out of this world
as soon as possible.

I'm not a preacher, I'm not an evangelist talking
for the Salvation Army — although I have great admiration for it — I'm not telling you what I believe or
recommend, but what Dante was doing. He was showing
us how horrible these vices of ours are: he was trying to
show in the *Inferno* how ugly sin is. It looks so beautiful
when you start off from an act of half-creditable lust (if
I may use the phrase) such as that of Francesca da
Rimini. But as you move down the spiral of sin, you move
to lower and lower depths to the base act of treachery.
Once you find yourself at the bottom of the spiral, in a
dungeon, then you find it very reasonable to want to
move out; then all the suffering that is to come with the
process of purification comes as a very welcome bless-
ing. Of course, this is only one scheme, one outline of
the process. There are two or three hundred other
schemes besides that of Dante. The important thing is
the flesh Dante puts on this scheme — the poetry with
which he describes it. It is one thing to say that lust is the
least of the sins in the spiral, to talk of an almost
creditable lust, and quite another thing to read the story

of Francesca in the fifth canto of the *Inferno*. In other words, all this we have been considering has little to do with Dante's power as a poet.

Finally: even in the *Inferno*, Dante's scheme is built about the axis of love. He portrays sin as nothing more than the erosion or destruction of love. He shows that the worst in man is simply a matter of the gradual extinction of love. For Dante — and for the Catholic Church, for that matter — it is impossible to say such a thing as evil *is*. Evil is not *anything*; it is the absence of something that should be there, a privation. To give you the example that used to be given to elementary school children of the thirteenth century: blindness isn't anything; blindness has no essence, it is the absence of an essence, it is the absence of sight. Our distorted free will blinds us in a certain way; and the more crippling the blindness gets, the more severe the privation.

Dante builds his great poem on these philosophic, pseudo-scientific, and scientific ideas.

2. DANTE'S AGE

A review of the ideas and development of the cultural history reflected in *The Divine Comedy* must begin with the scientific and philosophic development associated with ancient Greece and Imperial Rome, as well as ancient Hebrew spirituality — how all these are transfused into Christianity and how subsequently, after Christian culture has thus been formed by adapting and rejecting and transforming these elements of the ancient world, it is given injections from other civilizations or other nationalities, especially the Germanic. We want to know what formed the thirteenth century, out of which grew this beautiful flowering, this magnificent plant that has drawn so much attention through the centuries. We want to know something about the soil in which it grew, something of the days in which Dante lived; what was going on then, and what really led Dante to write the way he did and expound the ideas he so eloquently represented.

The atmosphere in which Dante wrote, the time in which he lived, was one of internationalism, or supranationalism. Dante was one of the greatest expounders of the idea of a universal or world state. He has been given credit for this not only by literary people but also by political philosophers and political leaders concerned with the problems of international relations in Europe. He was a great enemy of nationalism of every kind, and most especially the nationalism of his own people. But in considering Dante's role, his position on world rule, we should know that the thirteenth century was overwhelmingly international, culturally and in every other respect, *except* political.

As cultural internationalism was flourishing, the great monarchies of Europe were being formed. Dante had great contempt for this nationalistic development and had many fine ideas about international government. But the fact is that history since his time has gone nationalistic, and ideas have gone their own way. This nationalism was developing in France, in England, and in Italy too, but in a special form: that of the Italian communes, which were a characteristic phenomenon of the thirteenth century. Even a century before Dante's time there were political philosophers who were concerned with this nationalistic development and who philosophized about it in terms which were the very antithesis of those of Dante. The greatest of these, Marsilius of Padua, stands at the very antipodes of Dante. So, the first thing we can say about Dante's age is that it was a very international century, culturally.

Quite otherwise in politics. Already there were beginning to develop those ideas in practice, and to a certain extent, even in theory, which were later to be characterized by Machiavelli under the conception of *raison d'état*. That's a French phrase for something for which Americans — or the rather the English — don't have a word, although they have the thing itself. They *do* what it means but they don't like to call it by its name. The Germans have a word for it, the Italians have a word for it, the French also — but what is it? It is the justification of things improperly done in the name of the common good. In other words it is the transgression of morality for political reasons.

This idea begins to become more and more explicit and the conviction begins to be held more and more strongly that the business of the world goes on primarily by *raison d'état*. It wasn't an entirely new idea.

St. Augustine had thought of it before — but indeed, what had he not thought of before! And he had stamped it as a *stain* — quite unlike Machiavelli — as a *stain* brought on as a consequence of sin.

But whatever you may say about the political situation, in all other aspects Dante's age was a period of cultural internationalism. If you keep in mind the development of Catholic Christianity you see that it was then that it most magnificently affirmed itself. The Catholic church, which means a universal church, affirmed its catholicity and brought about a truly universal culture, by means of the Latin tongue of the time. One language was used, in business as well as philosophy, a Latin which was well disciplined, between two extremes: on the one hand there was the early medieval Latin which was a degenerate form of classical Latin, uncontrolled, deprived of rules and bereft of polish; and on the other, that terrible thing, what I should call the attempt to write the way Cicero wrote — that futile attempt to revive classical Latin, Ciceronian Latin, which professors even down to my day insisted upon. It was this other extreme that eventually killed Latin.

This Latin language, in Dante's age, is *one* and education is *one*. And that's another aspect of the internationalism already mentioned. It was a wonderful thing, the ease of movement of students and of professors — from London to Paris to Bologna and elsewhere. St. Thomas, born in Italy; St. Bonaventure, trained in Italy, lecturing in Paris; Albertus Magnus, the German, also at Paris. Students and professors moved freely all over Europe. And the subjects were the same. People not only spoke the same language in a philological sense, but also in an intellectual sense. And this was true not only in the universities, but everywhere. The church at this moment, in this particular century, and after many political contests, was the controller of education. And it is as the controller of education that she spreads cultural unity all over the Christian world.

For a long time universities were under the control of the Pope, they were papal institutions. This had come about for several reasons. Perhaps the most important is the rise of the mendicant orders — the Domenicans, the Franciscans and the others. It is a very impressive phenomenon: these monks who had shut themselves up in the monasteries, away from the world, to study and pray, now came out into the streets and squares to preach and teach. Dante tells us about a very famous Domenican whom he heard in Santa Maria Novella, discoursing on the topics of the day — and the same thing was going on in Santa Croce in Florence. They went everywhere, especially wherever there was trouble — strikes in Umbria, for instance — to calm the people, as arbitrators and mediators, to settle strife between city and city and country and country. Their coming out from the monasteries had a great effect on everything. Of course there was an ugly side to it. Boccaccio has drawn it for us — about interference in the home life, among other things — but then Boccaccio was the least fair of all men, although he was the greatest short-story teller the world has ever known. The important thing for history is that these monks — these Dominicans, Franciscans, Benedictines and Augustinians — took over the universities, especially in Paris, which was the intellectual capital of the world, as Rome was the religious capital. St. Bonaventure, a Franciscan; Albertus Magnus and St. Thomas, Dominicans; the Benedictine order and the Augustinians were all represented — the latter by the figure so influential in French politics: Egidius Romanus. Thus it was that the church, through these orders, succeeded in bringing about the internationalization of culture.

Another aspect of Dante's time to consider here is what was going on in the commercial sphere. Italy has never been again so international commercially as in the time beginning with Dante and extending for a century and a half beyond him. The great merchant guilds of the Italian communes had warehouses everywhere — including Scotland and Portugal. There is nothing more impressive than how the Lombards — or however one calls them — internationalized trade, through banking, first of all, and then the distribution of goods. Florence grew rich on one kind of activity especially, that of the Calamari, an association of merchants that bought second rate fabrics from Scotland and from the Balkans and from the Eastern shores of the Mediterranean, worked them over, polished them up and sent them out again all over the world, with of course an added value of 5,000 percent. The business world and international trade are subjects that are bound to come up again and again — the Guilds too, which were already well-established corporations in Dante's time.

The spirit of internationalism was much greater at this time than in the later renaissance. Of course, this period too, Dante's, was a renaissance. What goes on in Europe after the moment of cultural fall, whenever that was in Europe, was a series of what can be called *renaissances* — a gradual recapturing of ancient culture. This happens all along the way. What we call the renaissance after Dante was an *artistic* renaissance, when people held that all that is beautiful is beautiful to the extent that it is modeled on the blueprints and examples left by the Greeks and the Romans. The people of Dante's time also were schooled by the Greeks and Romans, and went on to do works not inferior to the works of those who imitated the ancients, and indeed often matching and surpassing the works of the ancients themselves. By the side of Botticelli you must remember there is a Della Robbia, who worked not by imitation but by the spirituality in his own soul. And there is a Beato Angelico, who could surely do without the example of the ancients.

The renaissance of the fifteenth and sixteenth centuries is primarily artistic and not cultural in the more general sense. Italy invaded France and England and Spain with its art, but, by then, the broad cultural basis for internationalism was gone. The artistic renaissance touched only an elite, who found themselves united in what was really a very fictitious world, a world that contained such men as Michelangelo. For the people of that world, all those cultural ideas which were operative in the thirteenth century, in theory if not entirely in fact, had become objects of ridicule. The idea of an empire, which was, after all, a truly supra-national conception, was gone; and the Catholic Church had knocked down its great antagonist, the Hohenstaufen dynasty, to be confronted by a great reaction to its bid for temporal power that brought the Church to the lowly state it was in at the time of the Renaissance. Instead of being *universal* the Church became one of many. The worst offenders were that series of popes, culminating in Leo X, for whom ancient art was much more important than Christian theology — until a great pope, Pope Adrian (who succeeded Leo X, and who was ridiculed because he could not recognize a Corinthian capital) came on the scene. There was also that great political figure, not an emperor, but a great political figure, St. Louis of France, for whom the world was indeed one and who held that politics must be identical with morality, and who tried, who really tried to show, against his advisers, that he could sustain the position "My country right: Yes!, My country wrong: No!"

The thirteenth century was a splendid period. If cosmopolitanism did not triumph historically, it did inspire our great poet, who made for it a magnificent monument. This spirit of internationalism inspired everything that Dante wrote and did. He is really a martyr to the international ideal, the greatest of the citizens of the world.

What is this unified culture that nurtured him? What is it that was familiar at Cologne, Austria, and everywhere in Europe? What brought it about? What held it together? The first thing we can say about it is that it represents a complete return of Aristotle. All these countries are united because they are all taught by one man, and that one man is Aristotle. Those of you who are familiar with the history of philosophy know that before this time, whenever the church needed a philosopher, it went to Plato. This was a result particularly of what St. Augustine had done. Plato was the official philosopher of the Church because of the definitive stamp put upon him by St. Augustine in establishing the line of continuity from the Greek or ancient world to Christianity. In the twelfth century the centers of Platonism were many, and one of the greatest of these was Chartres. The school there is known to many in connection with the name of Abelard, or perhaps he is known better for the famous letter to Heloise.

A great deal had been done with Plato. There were many important works on the history of philosophy; but of Aristotle there had come through only what had to do with logic, with Aristotle the dialectician. Then, inside of fifty years, Aristotle becomes the master of all who know in all the things that are worth knowing — to paraphrase Dante's words. All of Aristotle comes back, in one form or another — and, when I say all, I mean *all*. For a while they said that the *Poetics* hadn't come

back, but already we have found three major translations, and who knows how many others there are still to
be found in the libraries in a form not easily recogniz-
able.

The important thing is that in Dante's age that
entire political philosophy, that whole period of thought
in the Church that stemmed from St. Augustine came to
an end. Here we have one position, that of the great
Gregory VII, who argues that kings are not made by God,
but are chosen by the people. He represents the social
contract theory distinctly about 1080: the relationship
of ruler and subject is a contract. As long as the king
abides by it — and no longer — need the people who enter
into that contract feel bound by it. On the other side is
the view that God has decided to distribute power along
two lines: spiritual and temporal. The emperor rules by
divine grace. He is by divine grace the vicar of God on
earth, as the pope is the vicar of Christ in spiritual
matters. We hear the emperor Justinian say: *I, made by
God what I am, and in consequence of what God dictates to me
personally, decree the following laws.* Now, as a consequence of the recovery of Aristotle, a new doctrine of the
state emerges: the state is not by contract nor by divine
delegation, but as a *natural* development. The state is a
necessary development, given human nature. The minute
you say "man" you mean a gregarious or social animal,
and that means the state.

So, after the period of initial criticism, we have
Aristotle back, this pagan philosopher who repudiates
the idea that God created the world. The world, he says,
existed forever — and surely the idea of creation is
essential to Christianity, if any idea is. This pagan
philosopher rarely mentions God: Aristotle is less poly-
theistic than Plato but also less theistic. Of course at first
the church is very hostile. But St. Thomas works with

him, taking what he can, leaving some things undiscussed, rejecting some others, uses him to show philosophically the inner meaning of Christianity. He is the prime example of the triumph of the schoolmen in the middle of the thirteenth century.

People realized long before Bacon that you don't get very far in science by discussing abstract universals. They realized that you have to use Aristotle for the very thing that detaches him from Plato. The *universal* is the form of the individual, but it cannot be the object of science. Before the thirteenth century was over, the necessity for studying individual things took over. Already at that time we are approaching the nominalistic interpretation of Aristotle. These universals are but the *names* of things. We must focus our attention on the things themselves. We must have less of *essence* and more of *quantity*. We must concern ourselves with weighing and measuring. It is these studies, these commentaries of the nominalists on the *Physics* of Aristotle, together of course with the development of mathematics, that provided the material for a new basis for modern science as it developed in the fifteenth and sixteenth centuries. In his great work (which purports to be a work on da Vinci, but which is really something much greater) Pierre Duhem has left us a magnificent study of how modern science is built on these Aristotelian philosophers who studied and interpreted Aristotle along the lines of nominalism — the replacing of essence by quantity.

The importance of Aristotle in this picture of Dante's time is abundantly clear. He may have been obstructive to science in the late fifteenth and sixteenth centuries, but he was surely not obstructive to science at the time the nominalists were studying and lecturing at the University of Paris.

3. THE GREEK INFLUENCE

What does Dante have to say about freedom? In the *Purgatorio*, he introduces as the controller and director of all moral reformation in human life, the man who for him was the embodiment of freedom, that heroic figure of Roman antiquity: Cato of Utica. In all of Dante's other writings, Cato is always the voice of freedom. The nature of freedom is a question which every age has raised and about which everyone still speaks. What do we understand by freedom, and what does Dante mean when he speaks of it?

The first thing to note is that this freedom about which everybody speaks is not a universal category. Whole civilizations have risen and flourished and gone out of existence without any notion of what we call freedom. What must be said about it is that it is one of the great phenomena of western civilization. The first question to ask is: how soon and in what way was psychological freedom distinguished from other kinds of freedom?

Whenever in the history of western culture a stand has been taken for freedom, the figure of some great Roman or Greek — a Brutus or a Cato — comes up. Today some of us are apt to make fun of what some people say about freedom; there are some who, when they speak of freedom and liberty, are talking about the very opposite of what others mean by freedom and liberty. It's nothing new, this different understanding of the meaning of freedom. All you have to do is turn to St. Augustine and you will find that he defines freedom in a way that is likely to appear the opposite of what some of us imagine freedom to be. For St. Augustine, freedom is an obligation; the obligation to conform to a certain line of action. In other words, once you have seen what you have to do and have the capacity to do it, it is obligatory upon you to do what you have to do. If it were not for the contamination of original sin, says St. Augustine, man would be free to fulfill his obligation. He would naturally go toward his proper end, even as the stone, if not obstructed, rolls naturally down toward the center of the earth. We too should go as directly to our end, but, because of sin, we waver. And yet it is possible for us to straighten out. As with a heavy body that is kept from falling, so is it with us: remove the stains and blemishes that have come from original sin, remove those impediments and we will be obliged to go in that direction in which we should go. If we knew where it was that we were supposed to go, who would want to be free to go astray?

Liberty for St. Augustine, therefore, is liberation. It is the liberation from those obstacles which impede our movement in the right direction. Rousseau reminds us: you have to be compelled to be free! There are many other similar ideas on the subject. That's the first thing that needs to be clarified. Then we have to consider the ethical system of Dante, the moral and ethical system of the *Inferno*, of *Purgatorio* and the *Paradiso*. Are we to consider it as followers of Confucius consider the problems of human conduct — everyone ought to do this, or one shouldn't do that — or do we really have an ethical system in the *Divine Comedy*? Are such and such forms of conduct good simply because we find them to be so from experience, or because someone has laid down the prescription? Or do they derive from some rational principle inherent in the nature of the universe? In other words, is Dante really an ethical poet, or is he a prescriptive poet addressing us like a Sunday School teacher?

Howsoever we approach philosophical ideas in Dante — the nature of government, political freedom, scientific theories, moral and ethical considerations — we must remind ourselves that he is not primarily a philosopher or a scientist, or a moralist but, first and foremost, a poet, even if we must follow him in translation. And let's remember that for Dante, and even more, for Shakespeare, not so much is lost in translation as in other kinds of poets; for the more lyrical a poem is, the less of it remains in translation. Take, for instance, Virgil, who disappears entirely in translation, because he is such a great *lyric* poet. The lyricism cannot survive in translation unless the translator is a poet in his own right. But where is the English Virgil? And even then what you get is not the poetry of the original poet, but a new form altogether, the poetry of the translator. With Dante, the poem is important, even in English.

We have seen that, in addition to being a period of internationalism, the thirteenth century was a magnificent synthesis of Hellenism, classicism, Hebraism, and Christianity. But to say that it was a synthesis isn't saying much; this synthesizing was going on all the time. It is involved in the whole history of Christianity, as it meets and deals with each new situation, the problems brought about on the historical scene by the advent of this or that people. We have also seen the triumphant reentrance of Aristotle throughout the western world; and not Aristotle only, but the works of the commentators, the effects of which were often of more lasting importance in subsequent cultural history — not of course in philosophical developments, but in other fields. Now, we must go further back to get some sort of glimpse of classical civilization — to look at its origin and show how everything, practically, has flowered out of certain initial impulses (we cannot call them principles) in the Greek world.

I cannot possibly do justice to that extraordinary moment in history, the dawn of that civilization, that magnificent day which was to last 2000 years, which so often renewed itself, until it finally reached the point where it had to devour, destroy itself — the fount that fed all Western Europe and upon which the western world still feeds. Let your imagination soar, to visualize that moment.

A great deal has been said about the civilizations of the Orient, before the Greeks. We speak of the Ionian philosophers, for example; but what about the Hindu or the Chinese? We talk about Greek sculpture; yes, but what about the works of the Orientals? The thing to stress is that Greek sculpture is qualitatively different from everything else that flowered elsewhere in the world, around 500 B.C., from the things that interest historians so much today. Many of them speak of what they called the "axis." What is this axis? What is the meaning of this term used especially by European historians, but also among us, here?

The axis is that bolt, you might call it, in the history of the world, when all of a sudden extraordinary men like the Hindu sages, the Chinese philosophers, if you can call them that, and the masters of Greek thought, all appeared — a sudden efflorescence in the world. I could name the great men of those oriental civilizations about which I know nothing; but I can tell you the books to read, written by men who do know much about the subject. These men, almost without exception, will tell you that these great cultures developed entirely inde-pendently among the Chinese and the Hindus — and the Greeks in Athens. No doubt there was intercourse, there was some cultural infiltration if you like, but it was only in connection with the most minor aspects of those civilizations. The infiltration from outside into the Greek world had nothing to do with those grand achievements which most interest us. And as we examine them internally, we will see how little they were affected by foreign elements.

Today the Greek model is basic, everywhere: fifteenth century painting, sixteenth, and even thirteenth century art — wherever you go, or even back to the eleventh century — whenever painting or architecture makes a rise, back of it there is always the Greed model. The last great moment was the renaissance of the sixteenth century; but even now there are people dismayed by what is going on, who look back to Greek ideals which were the ideals of an art still connected with reality but at the same time informed by *Logos*, by reason. All one needs to do to understand the more than 2000 years of Greek influence on art in the West is go to the museums and see the works of art themselves, or read the biographies of some of the artists. Picture, for instance, Ghiberti walking along one of the roads leading out of Florence. He comes upon the ruin of a column and stops to examine it. What makes it so beautiful? It is not a cylinder. He measures it. It's fascinating to watch these Italians measure the vestiges of ancient art. He measures what we call the *entasis* of the column. Or follow Nicola Pisano. The great poet, Giosuè Carducci, has written four beautiful sonnets about it. You see him in the midst of a great Catholic celebration, as the sun comes down and its last rays fall on an *arca*, a sepulcher, beautiful and engraved; and at the sight of it Greek art is stamped indelibly on his mind. And he goes on to produce those great pulpits and fountains, and other magnificent sculptures. From these we see how closely wedded Greek culture and Christian feeling and spirituality are. You could write a book, and it would be a best-seller, on the history from the eighth to the sixteenth century, on the return of Greek forms in the West — not only in sculpture and painting, but also in literature.

Or consider Homer. He was like the Bible to the Greeks. The language and poetry of Homer united them. Despite all their harrying of one another, they had in their midst something that united them culturally, and this was their *Iliad* and *Odyssey*, and also their great respect, generally, for their poets, a respect that continued down to the sixth century A.D. — a respect that made of the poet the master of philosophy and of moralists and of scientists. That kind of respect for poets has died; but a century ago there was still a great enthusiasm for poets and their function. An enormous transformation took place soon after — the contrast between what is today the opinion about poetry and what was thought of it back then, when "the republic of letters," which was no rhetorical phrase but a reality, was used to describe ancient culture. The rhetor, as Cicero and Quintilian tell us, is not the man of fine talk, in the verbal sense, but one who knows best of all how to bring out what is finest and noblest in human nature. It is not in science but in the writing of poetry that the true greatness of the human spirit is manifested. That is the lesson that the classical world taught, that the medieval world taught also, when a little light of classical antiquity had come upon it.

For Dante, it was a challenge. Here were these schoolmen, without exception, these great school-teachers scoffing at poetry. We find the great masters articulating and defining the various fields of learning, dividing the sciences, considering the intentional sciences, or what we call the logical sciences, making a list in accordance with the *Organon* of Aristotle. And we find down at the very bottom, at the very end, after rhetoric, poetry. That's what everybody was taught; Dante too. But Dante the poet says "No" to all of this. He tells us: there are two ways to reach the heights of truth: one is the way of systematic philosophy, by logical discourse; the other is poetry raised by love. This view became common thereafter: we find it in a sharper and arrogant way in Petrarch, for example. But of course with Petrarch we are already in that humanistic movement which was so critical of the whole body of great scholastic philosophy. Petrarch had no use for it, neither had Boccaccio. For them it was nonsense of no possible application whatsoever. And if they spared Aristotle, it was only to deride his disciples. But Dante doesn't accept that one-sided extreme against scholastic philosophy. He held that both ways lead to the heights: the way of systematic philosophy and the way of poetry. This was a great thing Dante did, insisting on the exaltation and rehabilitation of poetry. It is a phenomenon of western Europe; its history can be traced back to Homer. Dante himself traces it back there. At the very beginning of the *Inferno*, in that hemisphere of light, he places a school of poets of which he himself was the sixth, and Homer the master.

As for science: the Greeks themselves were aware that what they meant when they spoke of science and what other men in other parts of the world meant when they spoke of science was very different. Others were interested in practical applications: the Egyptians and the Syrians, one Greek writer noted, are proud when they can show the solution to some problems in so many yards that they have measured. We Greeks, he says, are not interested in measuring; we reason about the problem, we postulate some axiom, then close our eyes and reason and come to certain conclusions. Then, if those who like to measure want to verify these conclusions of

ours, you may, and you will find them accurate. We don't
have to measure and verify, for we rely on our reason to
supply us with its own proofs. One thing especially to be
stressed about Greek mathematics is that great formula
that has meant so much recently. It is the great achievement the Greek mind has bequeathed to us: that the
purpose of science is to *save phenomena* or *appearances*.
Unfortunately that phrase, that still down to the time of
Milton had a noble meaning, now has become a description of something quite ordinary, low even.

What did they mean, back then, by *appearances*?
They meant that their object was to avoid two reefs: one,
that of the Eleatic philosopher, who closes his eyes to
everything and devises a system in which there is no
room for change or transformation; the other, of those
interested only in observation, concerned only to see
what happens. Neither of these will do. You must formu-
late first, then go to the phenomena to see how your
formula stands.

For example: consider the brilliant discovery,
unknown for centuries, for which credit is usually given
to Copernicus, that the earth turns on its axis and
revolves about the sun — what is popularly called the
Copernican or solar system. All of that was said and
known in 200 B.C. and elaborated in the next two or
three centuries. It was Aristachus of Sanos who worked
out all the details. How did it come about, this remark-
able discovery?

Here we see the phenomena of the stars every
night circling across the heavens, the sun moving across
the sky, the moon also. But they don't all turn together.
The moon, for instance, seems to move back, as we
observe it rise and set every day. It rises at the quarter,
and then we see it half-way across at the same time of day,
and then setting on the fourteenth day. We observe

these phenomena and the various motions of the so-called planets, but how do we go about *saving* or *explaining* them? The old way accounted for these various motions by positing an outer sphere for the *primum mobile*, moving at a certain fixed rate, and another sphere for the fixed stars and the sun, etc., to explain the diurnal motions, the yearly motions and the various other motions of the so-called planets. And then along comes Aristarchus, who says: I can save, or explain these phenomena by a much simpler theory. Instead of having the sun and the planets move around the earth, I will have the earth turn on its own axis. I will send the earth out into space and have it turn about the sun, and so on. I mention this because it is indeed an extraordinary event in the history of western thought, this achievement, not by observation, but by the reasoning of Aristarchus. The bent of science in the western world derives from the inclination of the Greeks. Mathematics is what it is today not because of what Einstein and others have done, but because of the Greeks. Already in Archimedes we are on the verge of a kind of calculus which is almost what we know it to be today.

Even more significant, but so very elusive, is the effect of Greek civilization on our ways of thinking: how our spiritual orientation has been influenced by Greek culture, by their myths and the way they affirm them in literature. Those myths have become indispensable to our lives — well, not so much to ours, perhaps, but surely to many who came before us and shaped the course of western civilization. Take, for example, the figure of Hercules, the way straight and narrow, the parting of the way; this figure of one who receives commands and performs duties. You could write volumes on the fortune of Hercules in literature. Or think of Ulysses. If I let my imagination wander, as I look upon the events of this world, the image of Ulysses invariably invades my consciousness. But what did this Ulysses mean to others, from humble folk to the great men who have interpreted his life?

Take the most beautiful interpretations of them all, Dante's. (We'll skip the Roman ones, both those who depicted him as a great hero and those who showed him as a kind of vicious scoundrel.) Dante at a certain moment faces a great problem: how far are we to be tempted to go in pursuit of knowledge? Is it good or bad to know certain things? Up until very recently we disregarded such questions, but now we begin again to take them seriously because we are confronted with some awful prospects. But it is an old question; Seneca had brought it up and many others. Here is the world: the church tells us we must not try to know anything about three quarters of it, that we should be concerned only about the inhabited quarter — the *Eucumene* — we should not be tempted to go beyond. And here comes Dante's Ulysses, who didn't know there soon would come the Verrazzanos and Columbuses and Vespuccis, the epitome of the brave navigator, the man who goes forth not for profit but for knowledge. It is a daring thing, and Dante exalts him for it. As Dante represents him, you can't help being drawn to Ulysses — not for the crimes that have brought him to Hell, the lying and deceiving, but for his adventurous spirit which carries him out of Hell and puts him in a kind of heaven. He sails far out, beyond the pillars of Hercules, deep into the unknown quarters of the world, and it is a glorious journey even though he smashes against the antipodes of Purgatory in the end, and goes straight to Hell. Another version, if we stay within Italy, is that of a more recent poet, Pascoli, who gives us the toiling Ulysses — very different from that of Dante. Or Tennyson's. I think there is a doctoral dissertation somewhere that traces the many hundreds of versions, all the various Ulysses of the last 500 years. And then there is a very recent Ulysses in a work which I haven't been able to read but which some of you may have read, that of James Joyce.

Or take another Greek character: Prometheus, the great challenger of the deities, the apostle of those who think that man is self-creative (most of us today believe that), who think of man as having no dependence on a higher being. Whenever a position of this sort is represented, it invariably calls forth the name of Prometheus or the word Promethean.

To do the subject justice, we would have to read the Greek poets, the great tragedies in sequence, and much else. Instead, we'll examine certain phases of Greek culture and follow them down from their origins in the myths; then show how these myths were transformed into philosophic doctrine by those great poets who extracted out of them principles of human values. I am referring primarily to the three great tragedians of the fifth century. But first, we must go back briefly, to the two ways of reaching God: the way of knowledge and the way of love — clarify the connection between love and knowledge.

4. *REALITY* AND *BEING*
THE SEARCH FOR UNITY

Ordinarily in the Middle Ages, and particularly in the thirteenth century, it was generally held that you could not reach God through poetry, although Love and Knowledge were intimately connected. Theirs was a world in which everything is finalistic, everything has a purpose, mankind has a definite end, and the force propelling us toward that end — a kind of appetite by which you rise to that end — is love. But you can't have love without considering the object desired by that love. The maxim to remember is that nothing is loved unless it is known. The act of loving is preceded by an act of knowing. The problem we are faced with is this: you approach God by full knowledge of the things created by him; you rise up from one level to the next in that way. In the last moment of this process, however, you have to fall back, as Dante did, on a mystic effort.

Dante reacts against his generation by exalting the poet, by affirming that man can rise to God along the line of poetry, not only by that of philosophic thinking, which takes us, of course, to the *Phaedrus* of Plato. Dante could fall back on that authority. Whether he did or not is another question. In other words, with Dante, we are entering a universe in which knowledge and love are correlative terms. We must know what we love. To what extent we must know God in order to love him is something else.

The influence of the classical world, down to Dante's time, had been enormous. Even more important is the classical influence on education, on literature and literary criticism as it developed in the late Renaissance. When they spoke of genres, these men were reflecting the classical influence; our critics for centuries formed their judgments from what the Greeks and Romans had done. Everywhere in Europe and outside of Europe, the cultured individual was trained in the classical languages and engaged in the study not only of his own national culture, but, more important, over and above his own, he studied Greek and Latin culture. In one country it was English and Latin and Greek; in Germany it was German and Latin and Greek, and so on. And that, of course, produced an effect on the culture of Western Europe that can hardly be imagined. It was the cause or basis of whatever cultural uniformity was ever to be found in Europe. Of course, one might object: all this did not affect the mass of people, who did not know Greek and Latin. True; but that argument can be applied in all fields. Whatever the area of cultural achievement, there are always various grades, passing from the barest knowledge upward, and it is always a small number of the intellectual elite that gives the stamp to a civilization. They show the way; the others follow.

In the 1800s, it was still classical languages and classical studies that were a sign of culture. A man who didn't know much but wanted to give the appearance of being well-educated would cite the *clichés* of classical learning. Today it is no longer like that. Today it is perhaps the *clichés* of sociology or psychology that are cited. Now, if a person wants to appear educated, he talks of complexes or something like that, and he probably knows as much about it as people in my day knew about the meaning of Promethean. But there it is. That was the stamp of culture then. And that's the reason why the new generations find it so difficult to deal with the documents of Greece and Rome — because their equipment in these materials has become an unknown quantity.

A different problem should be addressed at this point: how are we to assess or explain the writings of philosophical poets? What do we mean by the phrase "philosophical poets"? We can name them: Lucretius, Shakespeare, Goethe, Milton, to begin with. The question is: if we have philosophical poets, what is the use of philosophy? Why can't we just forget about philosophy and consider poetry alone? Part of the answer is that you can't get along without philosophy. The alternatives are not "no philosophy," or "any philosophy," but the choice is rather between proper philosophy and improper philosophy. Every time you say that something is true or that it's only apparent, or that a thing is not real, or when you ask what reality is, or if a thing is moral; whenever you ask about any of these things, you are philosophizing. The question is: are you going to do it in a stumbling way, or are you going to do it with proper guidance?

When we try to approach an author who has tried to give order and meaning to his writing, we must make an effort to learn the language of philosophy — grasp what he meant. In Dante's case, that means tracing the history of the various categories that moved him.

The first thing that startles the reader is his strong confidence, his belief in the reality of something which most of us would call fictitious. Dante called many things true that many today would consider false. For there are in this world, as Dante saw it, realities that are not apparent, not objective to sense; realities entirely devoid of matter. Try to grasp — not necessarily accept — what is meant by the existence of such things. The Arabs called such realities *intelligences*, what we call angels; what we mean when we speak of a soul that continues to live when the body dies, that lives on, separated entirely from matter. When we speak of such things, we are faced with what these men understood as immaterial reality. The best example, although difficult to grasp, of course, is the ideas of Plato. St. Augustine tells us in the *Confessions* — a book everyone should read — why he found it so hard to move away from manicheanism. It was because he found it so hard to conceive of a God who was completely immaterial, of any kind of being that was not a bodily being. He could not conceive of anything immaterial being real objectively, only subjectively.

That needs to be stressed, what these people mean when they speak of a being that has full reality but that can't be perceived by the senses and can only be conceived by the mind. It is important to grasp this, because a lot of nonsense has been written on the matter, especially in the eighteenth century, at times when these categories were not understood at all. In almost every textbook on the Middle Ages, you are sure to find two or three errors. One is that the people in the Middle Ages did not know that the earth was round. Another is that the Greek world was completely unknown and was not discovered until a certain day in October, 1492. And a third one is a question that was surely never raised in the Middle Ages, the one which the manuals sometimes tell us was the favorite question of the time, and that is: How many angels can dance on the point of a pin? Nobody asked such a question in the Middle Ages; it was invented by some smart-aleck in the eighteenth century who had absolutely no knowledge of what men thought and talked about in the Middle Ages. Angels are immaterial beings; no matter how small a space a thing occupies, as long as it occupies any space it cannot be compared with things without matter. And so the question does not make sense.

One could go on and on, pointing out such ignorant errors. The task here is to grasp the reality of non-material things, if we want to understand Dante. The first thing to emphasize is that we encounter this in Plato and also, if you will, in Aristotle — this immaterial reality. Secondly, we must try to grasp not only that there are these immaterial realities, but also that they are infinitely more real than material things — superior to them even. Material things are but shadows of the realities; they get their being by participation, by reflection. This is Dante's view. The world of appearances is the world that appears to our senses; reality is the world brought to us by our minds.

This brings us to the ethical sphere. If ideas are more important than their embodiment, if pure beings are finer than those embedded or embodied in matter, then it is our function as human beings to gradually rise above the world of material things and reach the sphere of immaterial things. This is the moral path set for man, and the way of rising to God is by clinging to the goodness of things. The less material a thing, the better it is, and the nearer it is to God. Love — and remember that for Dante love means moral conduct, for Dante's poem has reduced ethics to an act of love — this love-morals consists of gradually loosening our hold on material things, detaching our affections from things of the body and clinging to things of the spirit. This is the lesson of the entire *Divine Comedy*. Indeed, it is evident in the whole of Dante's life. That doesn't mean that he lived up to this in his actions; we're not speaking of the details of his life (who is interested in the life of Dante as such?); no doubt he committed all the sins that we all have committed, and he probably strayed along the same lines that we have strayed. What is interesting is not what he did, but the path he said he should have followed, and later probably did follow: the meaning he gave to his life.

That life is the story of Beatrice. In that story we learn how and why it was that Dante, by an act of grace, could have risen more quickly than most people, into the world of pure ideas. But to make that process even more easy, Beatrice came into the picture. She asks Dante at the end of *Purgatory*: "Why did you go wrong, why were you a sinner?" And he answers: "I clung too much to the things of the senses, to the things that come and pass, and did not cling enough to the things that are real." "And yet I taught you a different lesson," Beatice reminds him. "In the days of the *Vita Nova* you had already risen to that love of things that unite us instead of separating us, that love which was not Eros but Friendship. And you had reached the point when you were to give up entirely your affection for material things, even for my lovely body, which seemed the highest embodiment of beauty. I was to introduce you to a greater beauty entirely separated from the body, and therefore to help you on. How? By dying."

Beatrice tells Dante she died for the sake of love. She was one of the thousands who died for love, but in this case it is in a very philosophical way. "You had reached in me," she says, "the most beautiful thing in a body; but you should not have stopped there. You should have risen to something more beautiful. When I was dead and stripped of the body, my beauty was increased, but you took no notice. Instead of following me to where I led you, you turned elsewhere. You fell back from one thing to another, back deeper and deeper into the world of matter, where there could be only two results: the anguish of despair or the nausea of satiety."

The story of Beatrice contains a theory of ethical evaluation; the gradations of reality on the basis of materiality and immateriality. Evil does not consist in the doing of material things instrumentally to attain an end. It is not evil to eat, to procreate, or build up stores of goods, but only if these actions are done as instruments or tools to serve as a means of rising to a higher level. Happiness, for man, does not depend on food or sex or wealth.

What, in fact, constitutes reality? That reality which is not objective to sense but to the mind is not only a matter of gnoseology or epistemology or psychology, but also of fundamental ethics — part of a psychological system that makes room for it, whether it be the psychology of Aristotle, or something else. When we speak of how the individual, the being in the flesh, derives its reality from something that is not embodied, we are dealing with the separate ideas of Plato, that is, with platonic material. For Plato and those who followed him, one idea is not juxtaposed against another. For St. Thomas and for Dante these various realities are not distinct and isolated but moments of one and the same thing.

The task, then, is to see how we are constituted, how we perceive; how, by a sudden arrival of a kind of light, we pass from the world of knowledge that beasts have, to the world of knowledge that the angels have — with the exception that, while the knowledge of angels is intuitive and immediate, ours remains discursive. We will examine not only what Dante meant by reality, but also how this is made possible for man, the psychology that makes it possible, which is, of course, the psychology of Aristotle. Which of these positions was right and which was wrong is not relevant here. We must put aside such questions for the time being, let our own predilections rest, if we are to understand the various positions, for we are dealing not only with the ordinary things in life, but also with the notion of God. This is so for the ancients.

With Christianity come a number of complications; but until the moment in history when a complicated thing happens, which is two thousand years ago, what was God? Pure spirit, like the *intelligences* or angels. How did this strange situation come about? To understand it properly we must go back to the sixth century B.C., an important moment in the history of mankind, a point of departure, if you will. Some have tried to discredit it, but they have been inevitably obliged to return to it. It is that moment in history, in Asia Minor, when some men first looked upon the world of things around them, manifold, changing, varied as they are, and tried to find a connection among them. The next step was to tie them together, and — tying them together — to try to establish a unity, to make them all appear as the product of one principle or one source, or, as they said, of one *arche*. In this way they laid down the foundation of philosophic thought as it was to unfold down to our own day.

Under this world of change is a substratum that is not a chaos but something that constitutes its order and unity. This substratum or *principium* only has being. The other is something that is merely becoming. All this vegetable life, all the forms of things we see with our senses is merely becoming; but what is underneath, unifying it all and giving order to appearances is not "becoming" but *ousia*. Those are the two poles of Greek thought and of Roman thought, and of the Middle Ages right down to a certain point when they were replaced by two other poles. One cannot expect to understand Dante or St. Thomas or Boethius without some understanding of this contrast of *being* and *becoming*: the one, "real being," the abiding something which is objective to our mind; the other, "becoming," which is objective to our senses.

With the philosophers we encounter the complete removal of deity from all of this, and that is what makes the essential difference between what comes from the Greek and what comes from the Hebrew world to us. There had been a deity before in the Greek world and in a way that was a preparation for this. Already there are attempts in Hesiod to find a principle of order and direction for the things of this changing world. The effort there takes the form of the genealogical tree. Everything, growing up, even the deities themselves, derive from this principle. At this very important moment, however, the deities are put aside. We witness what can be called the de-deification of culture. It is the moment when the *deus-ex-machina*, which is to account for things, is put aside. For that reason we have to give it a great deal of attention, even if at first the solutions presented are very crude.

What is this *ousia*? The first answer (found in any manual on the history of philosophy) is that of Thales, who tells us: *water.* He, like others who look for an answer, pounces on something that plays a double role, something which itself is a variable and yet has the characteristics of a substratum. Why he picked on water is pretty hard to say: how this water managed to become the creating god of nature. The Greeks themselves, later on, said that he probably saw water rise in a vapor or turning to snow or freezing, or something which Thales himself never contemplated, surely, water under pressure, stone-like and crystal. How much is behind all this we don't know: what led Thales of Milesia and others in Asia Minor, to fix on water as the creative force. Perhaps it was the thought of Venus, the creative force of nature, coming up out of water. Others said that perhaps he saw the rising of land out of the sea, in the Mediterranean area, which is a phenomenon that a man might very well see in the span of a lifetime.

Others said, not water but air is the substratum; still another, fire. One man, Anaximander, saw the difficulty in all this and fixed on not one of the visible elements but what he called the "Indeterminate." He called this Indeterminate, from which all things come, *Ton Theon*, the Divine, thus reversing the process as we see it in all other countries. Others get nature from the divine; Anaximander got the divine from nature. Then comes Empedocles, who sees the difficulty of getting one thing out of another and who proclaims that there is not one element, but four, and these are, of course, the four that have plagued us ever since: air, fire, water, and land. This is the famous Empedocles of Agrigento, who is remembered (whereas the others are not) because of his pronouncements on the subject of evolution — and also because we have more of his writings than we have of the others. Empedocles comes to the fore, heralded as the first to grapple with the problem of the descent of man, the problem of natural evolution. He also re-introduces the deity. Moreover, the others did not know how to get things in motion; they were content to let them stand; Empedicles wasn't. He introduces the famous antagonistic forces, deified hate and love. Dante makes use of these opposite forces in a fine passage where he shows how all things come into existence and then pass away, subject to hate (a centrifugal influence) and a counter-influence, which is love.

This is one way in which the Greeks went about looking for the principle or substratum that gives unity, that gives us not a pluriverse but a universe, which means multiplicity reduced to one. This was the first impulse. It didn't go very far. But in the fifth century another impulse took the place of the earlier one. It came from the Pythagoreans, who tried to put aside the interest in the qualities of things, how one thing becomes another, and cultivated an interest in the *quantitative* constituents of things, to see how much space this or that thing covers, to weigh and measure and determine relationships, and to rise thus from a consideration of things to *law*, the law that will give us the principle of order in the relations of things. With the Pythagoreans this passage, from the interest in the qualitative to an interest in the quantitative, brought us very far along in a straight line to Galileo who, after two millennia, after two thousand years, put the keystone to this arch that was so laboriously constructed.

Before continuing with the Pythagoreans for whom not water nor air nor fire but *number* is the essence, we should try to imagine what these people meant by number. The Pythagoreans were trying to find a certain beginning — a principle to unify and give order to appearances. For them a thing *is*, only insofar as it is *one*. Unity and being are co-extensive to the point of identity. Nothing *is* unless it is *one*. Theirs was as great a discovery as Newton's. Think what this means, for excample, in the development in music. They translated sounds into numbers. Or in astronomy. They looked intelligently at the stars and saw the periodic recurrences, the constant order, numerically established, and felt justified in asserting that the *essence*, or rather the *principle* of being, the principle that gives essence is *number*.

5. ORDER AND UNITY; THE PYTHAGOREANS AND THE MAGIC OF NUMBERS

The early poets, Hesiod among others, conceived *anthropomorphically*, what they called deities, tried to see in nature, in the movement of nature, the effects of some kind of being like themselves but larger, a greater man but with qualities akin to their own. The Ionian philosophers, on the other hand, examined the nature of things, their movement and variety, and decided that there was, below appearances, a substratum everywhere from which all things derived their being and which established unity in things. That substratum is God — not that father, that greater man that man himself creates and then puts up on an altar and kneels before and projects through that image, through human traits innate in nature — but the source of unity: a basic notion for Dante.

For earlier generations it was a habit of thought: one can't think a thing unless it is thought as *one*. Our civilization has gone so far in the opposite direction, developing more and more atomistically, that a danger point has been reached and a strong reaction has set in in some parts of the world. What they said — these men who looked for unity — is that it is impossible to act unless there is unity. There is the so-called arithmetical or numerical unity. Tom is one, Dick is one, Harry is one. Things are one, "numero" in this sense, one by number. If these numerical units want to work or act in a certain way, they can do so only insofar as they are units. A second kind of unity is by species. Tom, Dick and Harry are men; as specifically conceived they constitute one, and that one is the "unum" species. Beyond that we notice that man as a species has something in common with other species, and that takes us to the next unit which is the "genus," the *unum genere*. And so we pass from man one to animal one, from the one by number to *genus*. But that doesn't take us very far. There is also the family, the army, the university; in all these, you have many individuals who act together, and to act together you have to have unity.

Finally, there is the most significant kind of unity: unity by order. Order is made up of gradations, various individuals, each one of whom has certain capacities and qualities for filling certain posts, those posts being necessary to do a certain job that must be done. The State is such a unit; the university is such a unit. According to a theory which Dante espouses, a theory which he borrowed from Aristotle, nature provides what is necessary, sees to it that a man is strong to do manual labor; nature sees to it that another is brave to fight; nature — mind you it is nature — sees to it that one man is intellectually endowed to become a college professor, that another is spiritually endowed and pious. All these are necessary if we are to have a state. The state itself exists by nature and not by convention, not by consortium, as the Epicureans thought in the old days, and which has been thought by so many others in recent times. First comes the state, then the individual; not chronologically, obviously, for chronologically the two would come into existence simultaneously, if anything. The state comes first, logically or teleologically, because the state is by nature necessary to man's purpose, and nature is never wanting in necessaries, as Aristotle said. When nature aims at anything, the things necessary for the attainment of that aim will emerge. Nature is never lacking in what is necessary. There will always be strong people and brave people and pious people. There are such posts that must be filled and therefore there are always the men to fill them. And when you have properly filled these posts you have a hierarchy, which is a political order constituted to perform certain work. It is what the Greeks called *cosmos* and what the Latins called *ordo*.

To the medieval mind one, as an individual, could not exist outside of the *ordo*. The individual alone is like the swallow crossing the high seas alone; he can't make it except with the flock (to use a simile that goes back as far as the thirteenth century). In other words, the individual alone gets nowhere. This — what we call social unification — this unity is by *ordo*; so that we have now unity by *number, species, genus* and finally by *ordo*. The last demands the greatest amount of diversification in view of the various functions that need to be performed.

Having grasped the meaning and importance of *ordo*, one can start by asking why the mind works that way. Why is it that we need to set things in order by unifying? Take the city of New York, for example. Where is New York? We say it is in New York State. Where is New York State? In the United States. Where is this country? It is in the western hemisphere. The hemisphere? It is in that larger sphere which we call the earth, which, in turn, is in the planetary system, and so on. What we are doing when we proceed that way is considering the parts, each part of the whole, and that whole is *one*, the unified whole, which is God. All of this is very important for the understanding of Dante's thought. He devotes an entire book, the *Monarchia*, to political unity and what that means. The argument for unity is the argument by which polytheism was attacked in favor of the one deity. And it was that fervor which resulted in the deification of unity as time went on.

It is the unity by *ordo*, the unity through hierarchy

that leads to a trinity. In the Pythagorean world, trinity meets us everywhere. It is not a conception to be met only in Christianity, or in the Indian world. In Greek thought we pass from the *anima mundi* which unifies all physical phenomena to the *nous*, the mind that unifies spiritually and controls and gives direction to this *anima mundi*. Finally we pass to the highest, which is beyond thought, beyond *nous*, and consequently also beyond Being (something Christians could never accept, this thing that transcends Being). And as they progress beyond thought and Being they pass to the One, of whom it can be predicated both that he *is* and that he is *not*. And that is why this conception cannot fit in a Christian universe; there it presents a certain problem — one of many in the *Divine Comedy*.

This fervor of theirs for unity drove the ancients beyond Being. Already in the *Politea* you have Plato coming out with an extraordinary statement about the nature of the good. He describes the different kinds of knowledge, preparing the reader for *to agathon*, the idea of the good. In the twelfth and thirteenth centuries this *agathon* of Plato's, which means nothing more than the Latin *bonus*, becomes a mysterious deity with heretical connotations, about which much was said, especially by the Platonists of Paris in those days; Socrates speaking of this idea of the good, says that it is beyond Being. That's an extraordinary idea, some critic is bound to comment. Well, says Socrates, yes, but you've driven me to it. It is a very extraordinary idea to profess, this highest good, this good of which you can predicate both that it *is* and that it is *not*. The idea does not arise with the Platonists; it is already in Plato.

A favorite question has to do with possible oriental sources for this notion of Being. A century ago there were two famous books that tried to prove that everything came from the Orient, that Greek civilization was nothing but the perfection of elements coming from oriental civilizations. As far as philosophy and science are concerned, the Greek mentality was entirely different from the Oriental. The others say you must not steal. Why mustn't you steal? Because you mustn't. The Greeks are not satisfied with that. Do not steal? You will have to tell us why you must not steal, they insisted. You will have to show me that the world is such that by the very nature of things I should not steal. This mentality cannot be traced to the Orient. (With religion, it's a different matter.)

The notion of eastern origins for politics and philosophy and architecture does not hold. The Greeks themselves remarked about architecture that the constructions of the east compared to their own are like the imaginings or products of a sick mind. Up until a century ago, most agreed, but not today, except for dolts like myself. When it comes to religion, there have been a number of books that focused on the relation between Plotinus and the Hindus. How successful these theses have proved, I don't know. I do know that the history of Platonism leads inevitably to the idea of something that transcends Being, and that you can account for the idea historically as a development of Greek thought.

The commentary of Proclus on Plato's *Timaeus* contradicts what I have said. He finds analogies in the Old Testament, and avoids the New Testament, except to attack it. When he tries to find the Ten Commandments in Plato, he exaggerates; but the book is worth reading. Neo-Platonism does aim at religious mysticism, and this means a great deal to Dante, in the *Paradiso*. For him it is genuine mysticism. Plotinus said that you can experience this ecstasy, which he says he experienced not more than three or four times, only when you have climbed the whole ladder to the top, only after you have studied hard and know everything there is to know. Then you shut your eyes and you get out of the world; *ex-stasis* means "to get out." Only when you have reached the top are you qualified to get out and in such a way as not to lose yourself, as most would, for you get out only if grace is with you. Of course the Platonists did not use the word "grace"; they had no idea of it. Divine help makes you rise to the *absolute* by ecstasies, getting outside of yourself, but only those can do it who have reached that point by hard work and much study. So much for Eastern origins.

Earlier, we followed the growing light of philosophy to the Pythagoreans. We said they were important for they looked for order, not in the things that pass before our eyes and our other senses, but in something that would stay fixed and at the same time would account for what passes before the nose and the eyes and the other senses. They looked for reality in numerical relationships; you hear sounds, you hear the singing of a song. Back of that song, back of that sound made by playing the flute, let's say, there is a physical law, the law of the length of the vibrating cord. As you vary that length, the sound varies. This was an important beginning: for the first time, people learn that you must not trust the senses — despise the senses and that worst and best of them, the common sense. The absurdity of today will be the sublime truth of tomorrow. Benedetto Croce wrote many fine pages illustrating this. An article, written a long time ago by a Frenchman, scoffed at what the author called the nonsense of trying to produce a vehicle that would run with two wheels in the same vertical plane. In other words, he denied — on the basis of common sense — the possibility of the bicycle! That was long ago — in 1918, 1919. Or take the idea of relativity:

no one scoffs at it now, but when first it was put forward, many called it nonsense.

With the Greeks, for the first time people had the courage to say that the truth was not in what appears to our senses but in what appears to reason. Despite appearances, the earth is not fixed, does not stand still — it moves. The Pythagoreans worked out a system based on that, very crude at first, but developed finally into a system not less complete and adequate than the system re-discovered or perhaps developed by Copernicus, with considerable help from the original.

All this is very important in reading Dante, or Petrarch and others for that matter (although much else in Pythagorean thought might be more interesting in itself) not because they adhered to what we have discussed — that came with later generations and the students of Paris — but because something of this Pythagorean thought struck them. They looked for a principle that gave unity to things, and that principle they found in numbers. And this stressing of numbers made possible their conception of a universe. In other words, they explained what they saw, the *phenomena*, by interpreting things, numerically or quantitatively. They produced a cosmology which Dante accepted, which he adopted from Aristotle.

We also mentioned, earlier, the four elements and how they appeared to an Ionian philosopher — earth and air and so on — and we noticed that on the strength of their quantitative appraisal they put the heavy bodies down, the lighter bodies above, and the lightest of all on top. Earth on the bottom, water and air and fire in that order, and they devised movements for these elements. Dante, we noticed, makes use of such movement, but doesn't follow the Pythagoreans in his cosmology. There is a center, he says. The earth as a sphere has a center; but it is the center not only of the earth but of the whole universe. There is the downward movement of the heavy bodies toward the center; there is horizontal motion; and there is movement upward of the light elements. But is that all? The question is important, not for science, not for philosophy, but for poetry.

Beyond the four elements there is a fifth element, or quintessence, drawn in its popular sense from a kindred science. And this quintessence is the essence of perfect order, where the laws of number operate without exception among the four elements — in meteorological phenomena, for example, with many exceptions. There is no movement of the quintessence like gravity or levity; its movement is a movement that never ceases. It is that essence on which the Christians and Dante build their Heaven. Aristotle also espouses it, but he calls it *ether* instead of quintessence. And that's how you get the word *ether* — not from any medical sense of the word, but from astrology.

Dante used a language that came into existence because of these philosophers, what you might call mathematical ethics or ethical mathematics. There are plenty of examples of mathematical entities that are given moral significance. We speak of *odd* and *even*, of *square* in a moral sense, of right and oblique and of right opposed to left, morally. We use the word "sinister" in the sense of evil, and "right" in the sense of good. We have up and down: we're good when we're looking up, and down — *la bas* — down there, is evil. The Pythagoreans worked out a table of ten contrasts. Why should odd and evil have come to mean what they mean? Numbers shouldn't have such moral significance in themselves. The reason we give such significance to them is a vagary of the Pythagoreans that was recorded by Aristotle, which had been popular in the language of the day, and had been perpetuated by scholarship through the centuries. Other civilizations that have not been influenced directly by Greece perhaps do not have such meanings attached to numerical entities.

More important, though less valuable, and more influential though less useful, has been the semantization of numbers. As early as Aristotle and before him, people spoke of the healing qualities of the sacred seven, and of the divine significance of three, and doctors prescribed cures embodying the magical seven. Why does the week have seven days? The Pythagoreans didn't ask, but we know what these units of time involved: the day and the week and the month and the year. They are all easy except one.

The day is the easiest. It is the length of time that it takes the earth to make one complete turn on its axis, or, as they said, the length of time it took a fixed star to move from east to west in a circle, back to its original position. The month, of course, is the time it takes the moon to circle from west to east. We've all seen this motion of the moon; it is one of the most obvious motions of the heavens. You see the new moon appear on the western horizon, and every night at the same time you see it appear slightly higher — a number of degrees above — until after fourteen days it is not on the western horizon but on the eastern horizon. And the year? You know what that is: the revolution of the sun around the earth. The week doesn't figure in this view. In the world of the gentiles it is the sign of the number seven coupled with observations and regulated in accordance with the motion of the seven planets; regulated as a function of — not as equal to — the order of the planets. These planets are not deities, though they seem to be. They are planets that bore the names of deities, or — the theory that Dante espoused — the planets came first and then the deities took the names from them.

This kind of numerology has infected at all times the significance of numbers. Take the number 13 or 10, that most wonderful of all numbers because it is equal to the sum of the first four numbers: one, two, three, four. Where you have the perfect productive trinity, which means nine, you have trinity multiplied by itself. It is made perfect by the addition of *one*. Dante illustrates this in the structure of the *terzine* and the number of his cantos. There are 99 cantos in the *Divine Comedy*, but he adds one in the *Inferno* to make it a perfect multiple of the perfect number ten.

In the trinity, to return to our friend Proclus, it is not quite the same. The Trinitarian idea falls naturally into certain ways of thinking. There is always a beginning and an end, and the middle that must be there to have these two, gives you three. There is right and left, and between them the center. I would not discredit the qualities of the trinity in comparison to other numbers, but in general there is little of value to be said for this Pythagorean influence that has been present through the centuries and that has yielded all of this. Still, this magic belief that numbers as such have certain values should not be confused with another notion of perfect numbers. And that is, not the perfection of ten but that of six, of which the dividers, that is, three, two, and one, add up to six. Ever since then people have worked hard to discover how many perfect numbers there are, and there have been quite a lot.

The next important figure — and perhaps we will say a word about him now, is Heraclitus, who held that you could not reach any principle, because all things are in constant flux. You cannot step twice in the same stream; indeed, you cannot step even once in it. All things change. No principle can be real; the only thing that is real is the flow, the passage. Can we find the laws of this flow? If you can, then you have the beginning of science, something of which Galileo made much in his time. To speak of *reality*, or to find reality, means to speak of the reality of *the laws of motion*.

6. FORTUNE AND THE HETERONOMY OF ENDS: HERACLITUS AND THE ETERNAL LAW

For Dante, nature, deity and man are not one. Of course, he would have liked very much to do what Aristotle did, that is, to be able to say *Theos he Physis*, or *Theos Kai Physis*. Dante can't do it — identify God and nature. As a Christian he must hold that nature is the instrument of God; but he does raise it up pretty high at times — almost deifies it. For him, everything that happens here in the world of nature — the fact that you can move, the fact that you are what you are, that the trees grow as they grow, everything animal, vegetable, mineral; and in man too, insofar as he is a material being like the others — happens as the result of forces or causes that have their origin in the celestial spheres. That's a hard thing to swallow. It's not quite astrology, which is a crude sort of thing; this is already in Aristotle. The things down here are linked to two motions in the heavens: namely that from east to west and that of the ecliptic.

That is Aristotelian, the notion that the roots of all events are in the celestial spheres. And the coordinator of these initial forces or causes in the celestial spheres, is nature. Nature is the principle of motion. From a Christian point of view it is the long hand of God operating in the world. Of course, Dante goes a little beyond that. He often speaks of a *Natura Universalis*, an order, a hierarchy of forces, and at a certain point at the top of it, at the last level, in the ninth sphere, you have God himself as the Mover. Whether Dante actually maintains this in the *Paradiso* is still a question: there are one or two passages in which he seems to do so. The point is that nature is the principle of motion, and this motion is the realm where you are going to find reality, if reality is to be found: by establishing the laws of motion.

We have this whole subject personified in Dante, or rather the deification of it. Of course this deification goes back to the Platonic world and the neo-Platonic, and through Proclus had a very great influence on Dante and his contemporaries. There were four famous treatises about Proclus known only in translation in Dante's time. The most famous, which was early translated — *De Causis* — was one Dante was familiar with and from which he most often quotes; it was a gist made by the Arabs of the famous *Elementatio* of Proclus. A couple of generations before Dante, the whole work had been translated and commented on by St. Thomas; so that Dante was familiar with the doctrine, although it was not theologically accepted — the doctrine of one transcendent person called the Father; then the *Nous*, which some identified as the *Logos* or *Verbum*, the second person of the trinity (in Greek thought never incarnated, couldn't be); and the third is the holy spirit, which came to be identified with the *Anima Mundi*. The *Anima Mundi*, which was condemned theologically, was, in effect, a phase of nature or, vice-versa, nature was a phase of the *Anima Mundi*. That's really the way to approach it. The *Anima Mundi* is not an orthodox concept. It is a Platonic strain, this soul of the world, but there is a way of keeping much of its content without keeping the thing itself.

A question that is often asked in this connection is how Fortune is related to Nature. It's a very important question with regard to Dante. The story of fortune begins of course with Aristotle, and in particular with the second book of the *Physics*, where the whole matter is discussed. Man looks about him at the various phenomena and attempts to account for them, and one way is by the concept of nature. Nature, you must remember, for the Greeks, for St. Thomas, and for Dante, operates teleologically — that is, finalistically. That had been held for a long time. Then, for a while it seemed as if it had been done away with. We used to say that it was the great triumph of science to have done away with the concept of teleology in nature, but it seems that that is not altogether so. I remember a professor of biology, one of the most brilliant biologists of our age, Professor Morgan, who used to say in regard to this subject, quoting a line of Catullus: *Nec con tecum nec sine tecum* — I can't live with you and I can't live without you. What he meant was, the concept of teleology at times looks like a stumbling block to science, but you find that you cannot move there without it. But there is also free will.

There are things that happen as a consequence of human volition. Beyond these, there are things that happen, not as a result of natural causes, nor as a consequence of the exercise of free will, but by accident. For example, by exercise of my own free will I cross the street; a motorist exercising his free will drives a bus down the street. I get run over. Two lines of volition cross. Who made them cross? Or take the example popular in the thirteenth century, from Albertus Magnus. Here is a branch of a tree that naturally grows and decays; there is a bird who by natural instinct builds a nest on that branch. At a certain moment the branch cracks, the nest falls and the birds get killed. The two lines of natural forces cross: the bird didn't intend that result, surely the branch didn't intend it, yet it happened. What brought these two lines together? You witness all the time examples of the crossing of two lines, sometimes both volitional, sometimes one volitional and one natural. Examples of this kind are easy. I, acting volitionally walk through a forest, a rock falls or a tree, and kills me. Of course the commentators of Aristotle (as I pointed out earlier) have brought out very clearly that we speak of fortune only in a certain connection. These crossings of two lines occur everywhere, but we notice only those that have value, that had they been known, would have constituted a finality. We can take the famous example that Aristotle gives, of the farmer tilling the soil. That's something he does according to his free will. At a certain moment he is digging a well and finds a pot of gold. He didn't want to find the pot of gold, that was not his intention; but the point I want to make is that, in digging, he finds many other things besides the pot of gold. He finds pieces of stick, pebbles, a lot of things. Why don't we notice those? Because we only notice those that are *teleologically* considered.

Fortune is the form of efficient causality. It is efficient causality not known to the beings concerned. Of course the Christians will say eventually that what brings together the two lines is not the will of man, is not nature, not any of the higher intelligences but God; all chance ends in God. Chance is a generic term that includes many forms, what the French call hazard and fortune, *casus* and *fortuna* in Latin. In English you don't have the couplets to distinguish chance operating in the sphere of nature and chance operating in the sphere of man — almost all the other languages have. Latin has it: *casus* and *fortuna*. These two efficient causes are forms of the efficient causality not intended by anyone, except by God. We don't know why, but God does. He knows why I should be killed while crossing the street, or why the farmer should find the pot of gold. Therefore, fortune is, to speak the language of Dante and Aristotle, the form of unintended efficient causality. It is a force — for that's what causes are, they are forces in our language — that for most of us is purely random, but for the Christian it is in the mind of God; not random at all, but the *raison d'etre*. In other words, things happen because of nature, chance and free will. These are the three constituents of reality: *fortuna*, free will, and nature.

The question has been raised: but isn't nature, or rather fortune, responsible for the rise and fall of nations? It's not, properly speaking, a question. What they called *fortuna romana* — the fortune of Rome — was launched on the world by Polybius and has been carried down through all the ages since. It takes us into a sphere that is not Aristotelian or Dantesque. If you want to put some sense into it you have to come down to modern times, to what has been called the heteronomy of ends. One is reminded of Machiavelli and what he says about *fortuna* and *virtù*. But you can't make a system out of what Machiavelli said; he was not a systematic thinker. He was a man of great genius that said many things that had been said before often, but he said them harshly and that always has an effect.

The heteronomy of ends means that men act together with their free will. They have definite aims, and they find the means to attain those ends; but when they get at those ends they find that they are quite different. Sometimes the end is the very opposite of what they aimed at. What does *fortuna* mean? Not too long ago, the United States and other great powers fought a war to prevent one power from gaining control of all of Europe. But what did they get? The great powers that won got the very thing that they had fought the war to avoid, they got the very opposite of what they intended. Or take the Council of Trent. They met to try to form a conciliatory church and not a monarchical one. But they reached conclusions, and things have worked out since then, to make it come to pass that they got a monarchical church and councils have become merely instrumentalities, convened for the purpose of enacting the will of the monarch — the pontiff. If you look at the history of the recent past, you find nations come out successfully, that is, they go through the middle stages successfully, but when they get to the end they find they have changed texture.

This heteronomy of ends is not in Dante or St. Thomas. If you ask them they would say: if men used their intellect as they should, things would come out as they should, according to reason. Aristotle reminds us that the more the sphere of intellect increases, the more the sphere of fortune decreases. If that farmer who found the pot of gold had known all the history of everything up to his time, he would have gone about it very differently and would have found the pot of gold, not by chance, but intentionally.

Is fortune the principle of change, as Dante tells us? Yes! Of course, Dante is quite orthodox in what he says. He falls back on an Aristotelian doctrine. He says that fortune has a kingdom of its own. It does not hold in the intellectual sphere — I am not a good man or a bad man on account of fortune; I don't study or do study on account of fortune. Fortune does have a hold, but where? Aristotle gives it a somewhat wider range. Dante more and more restricts it to the economic sphere, or realm, or what we would call the economic and social spheres. That's why we speak of wealth as fortune. Dante gives fortune a role in the social sphere which also can be brought into relation to shifts in economic or political power from one family to another. This is not primarily a political conception, not even secondary; he speaks of fortune only where there is a passage of economic power from one group to another.

What he says is: if intelligences did operate in that sphere, perhaps wealth and power would be crystallized in the hands of a few. God has provided this force of fortune in order that wealth may be redistributed. In other words, this is a concept of the kind that we may call popular. In the *Paradiso*, he develops it a little better, politically. There he says that it is nature, not chance or free will that sees to it that the state exists by being provided always with those individuals who are necessary to make it exist. Nature does it, and therefore nature produces also the man who is able to rule. Nature sees to it that there is a man capable of governing the state. But nature never goes by dynasties — and this is an attack on hereditary rule: the man fit to rule is not necessarily the son of the same kind. No, the man who will some day rule, or should rule, may be the son of a shepherd or a poor farmer. What brings it about that a man of kingly talent should be born in a hut? *Fortuna*. It is the providence of God that puts him in the hut. Then it is up to man, by the proper use of his intellect, to see to it that not the fool who is the son of that king who is now in power, but the humble son of that shepherd be put in power.

Dante, like so many others of his nationality, didn't believe that nobility was hereditary. You don't get nobility from your father or from your grandfather. It is something that is given to you by yourself and by God. But Aristotle has another sphere or range in which fortune operates, especially in the *Eudemian Ethics*; but it is found primarily in the economic sphere or other spheres in which there is rapid change and in which it is not possible to trace that change back to certain causes. That is why most Latin countries use the word fortune also to refer to storms. Why? Because, contrary to the laws of physics and chemistry, in which spheres you have fixed and orderly movement, there is a sphere where we have clouds and wind and change of all kind — the meteorological sphere — and that is under the control of fortune. The Italians still call a storm by the name of fortune, and the same word is found in French and in the old Catalan. The wisest thing said about it was what Aristotle said: that the existence of fortune depends on our ignorance. Remove ignorance and fortune disappears. It was a commonplace of the schools, that whenever you examine things, you have always to try to reduce the matter to this question: is it happening as a result of free will, or nature, or chance?

Having expanded on some of the ideas discussed earlier, lets move on to Heraclitus, who was glorified years later because he had seen that if there is to be any order you must look for it in the laws of motion. In the period before the Atomic Bomb, when everyone or almost everyone thought war was a normal state of affairs, someone wrote a beautiful article on the statement of Heraclitus: "*Poleimos* — war — is the father of all things." He wasn't referring to the dialectical process that merely reconciles all things. Heraclitus must be credited as the man who really believed that clash — physical clash — is inevitable. Was he right or wrong? As we look at history so far, he seems to have been right. He was also the expounder of many other things that we can't take time to mention here — except one that gains importance later on, especially in the form that it took in the Christian world. I am referring to the fact that for all Christians, man-made laws, or what are called positive laws, are justified only if they derive from or do not contradict natural laws. To understand this you must get away from the conception of law that has a majority of people getting together and saying that whatever they decide goes. For centuries men who thought about this said: No. That kind of law is valid if it is rational and proceeds from certain principles of natural laws and natural rights. What right have we to send a man to jail because he doesn't believe in our economic system? A man steals and is put into jail for it. There are men who want to stay by themselves, who don't believe in the formation of certain communities, and on account of them war results, war that brings about the destruction of hundreds of thousands of human beings. These things happen: are they justified or not?

Only if the principle or laws invoked in connection with them proceed from a principle of natural law. To illustrate in a political context: natural law states that the good must be done, and that the good of many is better than the good of the few. For Dante and for St. Thomas, the safety of the state is a law of nature and justifies all legislature that demands that you die for what you don't believe in. It is a principle of natural law that the good of the community demands the sacrifice of the good of the individual. That's one of the reasons why Heraclitus is important in this discussion, why what he said continued to exert an influence for so long. The Roman jurists said it, and St. Augustine, and after him all Christians.

This natural law is a principle that is born in us. We don't get it by ratiocination; it comes like a flash, it is an axiomatic truth with which we are born. Natural laws, of course, include natural rights. Natural rights subsist only because they can be claimed by individuals under natural law. There is something in the individual, in the human being, that tells him what is right and what is wrong. The Christians say it is something that God has put in us. It is providentially ordained by God, or, as St. Thomas says, it is the participation in men of the eternal law. All things — the stone, the plant, the animal, from the lowest to the highest — have been given an impulse to reach a certain end, and the sum total of all these impulses is called eternal law. Man's participation in eternal law is natural law. It is the impulse to act purposefully first for himself, then for others, and then for the whole community of men. And all for the greater glory of God.

Eternal law is the order by which all things are made to move toward their appointed ends. And the man who launched this thought before the eyes of humanity is Heraclitus. This is the doctrine of the rational order of things, or the *logos*. All human laws are offshoots — that's the word he uses — of this eternal law. If they did not participate in that law, they would be invalid and iniquitous. How do we know that the eternal law of St. Thomas goes back to Heraclitus? There are plenty of documents. St. Thomas, of course, refers to St. Augustine. St. Augustine, Origen and Clement before him, speak of this law as the famous law Heraclitus had conceived and proclaimed to humanity. Therefore at this point in our investigation of Greek thought, we should pause and recall, if we are concerned with the heritage or rather with the importance of that magnificent structure of reality, we must recall that this great contribution of St. Thomas on law is what it is because Heraclitus spoke as he spoke about how law or *logos* operates. That kind of law is a challenge to a purely parliamentary view, the view that holds that when men get together, when they reach a conclusion, that's a law. Not so, for Heraclitus and those who followed him: a law is valid if it proceeds from natural law, and natural law is valid because it proceeds from eternal law.

In a related context, the name to remember in connection with the origins of science in the Greek world, is that of Democritus. In Democritus, the Greeks had a perfect scientific theory, one that could account for changes such as the Eleatics had felt constrained to reject, which discerned or discovered that sounds and smells and heaviness are purely human contributions. Take away man, and they have no reality: there is no sound, no smell. These are qualities we call subjective, proclaimed centuries later as if they were entirely new discoveries. In fact, they had been worked out to the greatest detail by Democritus. He reduced them not to caprices of the human mind, but to invariable atoms that combine to form all things that can be weighed and measured.

What induced the Greeks to abandon this man, to abandon the doctrine of atoms and mathematical discipline, and the rejection of secondary qualities as they were called by Locke, and to turn instead to the platonic ideas (which was very bad or not quite so bad — according to whoever raised the question), and to Aristotle? What was it that make the Greek world swerve to Plato and Aristotle and away from Democritus? The answer lies with the Sophists. Or, put another way: why did the Greeks decide to be humanists? Why had they no respect for the man who thinks that humanity is for science, as many of us do today? From then on, it was science for humanity.

7. DEMOCRITUS AND THE SOPHISTS

The *logos* of Heraclitus, of course, can be found in the beginning of the fourth gospel; *en arche en ho logos.* It can be traced through to Philo the Jew, the greatest of the Hebrew Platonists. It's Platonism deriving from Plato; Plato in turn wouldn't have existed if there hadn't been that development; and that development would not have taken place if there hadn't been the great thought of Heraclitus.

As for the Augustinian conception of predestination and how Dante copes with it: he has to do what every one else does with it. St. Augustine himself tells us, after he had been himself a strong champion of free will, in answering a question posed to him by the successor of St. Ambrose as Bishop of Milano: I started out as a champion of free will but grace won out. For Dante, as for most of his contemporaries, St. Thomas and the others, nothing was more human and therefore more divine than free will. He sees that trait in man as that which makes him most closely resemble God. All freedom, according to his point of view, must be traced back to free will. And this is what animates his representation of Purgatory. Cato is the guardian there, he is the man who died for freedom. But what does one do, then, with the doctrine of irresistible grace? Man is fallen; mankind is in decay because it has come from a rotten root. God, in his mercy, has decided to salvage something out of this *massa peccati*, this mass of sin; God picks out someone here and there to save. He sends out a summons for those he wishes to save. This summons is *grazia irrisistibilis*. He sent such a summons to St. Peter, who was going bad.

God made him right. He could have sent such a summons to Judas, he could have made him right too, but he
didn't. Why? St. Augustine's answer was: it is a *mistero*.
The Church has been very wise on the subject. You can
be an Augustinian, you can be a Thomist, you can be
anything you want, provided you do not repudiate the
doctrine that God is almighty, and yet man has a free
will.

After Augustine, St. Thomas is, of course, the
man primarily interested in this matter. He is bent on
maintaining the dignity of man, and is therefore a
staunch champion of rationality and freedom of the will.
What kind of metaphysics you can get out of his position
is another matter. How to judge St. Thomas as a meta-
physician, as a theologian? He tried to do the job he set
out to do. And it was a noble attempt, something for
which he is not often given credit, something which
many people think began when those semi-intelligent —
or perhaps I should say those non-intelligent — philosophers of the fifteenth century came into the world. He is
the one who exalted *man*, not Tom, Dick, or Harry. He
wasn't interested in the particular man, but in man as
such — he put him so high that compared to that level,
the height to which man was raised in the Renaissance,
was like a mole-hill compared to the Alps. The Church,
of course, follows the formulation of St. Thomas. Naturally, it is proud of St. Augustine, who was by all odds the
greatest thinker of the church, to be put on a par with
Aristotle. If he had not kept on the blinkers of faith he
would have, as a philosopher, done great things that
would have astounded us. He is also a dangerous man.
Look at the number of heresies that have come out of
him, right down to the present time: the Jansenists, the
Lutherans, to mention two only. But as every Catholic
knows, the straying is not St. Augustine's fault. On the

other hand, no heresies have come out of St. Thomas. All this will be taken up more properly, later.

In trying to see how people got to think the way Dante did, that the best way to get to know what is real is not through the senses — for reality is beyond our senses — but through reason, we come to Democritus, the greatest figure after the Eleatics. Democritus appears on the scene after those noble Eleatics had pursued their course of thinking into a series of absurdities. In their attempts to get at stability, something *one* and *lasting*, they arrived at a way of thinking which made of the outer world of nature, something to ignore, and paved the way for that book which we don't have but must have existed which was called *Concerning Nothing*, or *What is Not*. In order to save the object of thought, the object of sense is pulverized. It was time for someone to come forward and take on the great job of maintaining that the purpose of man is to save appearances. And those who did the job, did it so well that when people started on that path again, centuries later, they fell back on their theory, the theory of the atom, which no matter how often it has changed is always brought back to the fundamental fact that in the effort to save appearances, it is necessary to find a constant relationship, a rapport between the data of sense and reason that will remain constant and abiding. And just as Copernicus tried to onceal his dependence on Aristarchus, so was it with the brilliant achievement of the Democriteans.

The people who got on to this theory of the subjective character of the secondary qualities — that, without man, what we call smell wouldn't exist, what we call sound wouldn't exist — had fallen upon a work of Sextus Empiricus. When the people of the fifteenth century began to lecture on Galen, who quotes this theory, they found a way to connect the theory with the

Democriteans — but in such a way as they could claim for
themselves complete originality; so that Italians until
very recently, in fact, still claimed that the theory was
due to the discovery of that worst of all philosophical
minds, Giordano Bruno. The French say, of course, it
was Descartes, and the English, Locke. A recent dissertations had a chapter on this subject. Do we owe the
theory to Descartes or to Locke? Well, it wasn't Descartes,
or Locke, or Giordano Bruno. They all got it from
Sextus, and Sextus, was simply exalting the Democriteans.
A fine study could be made on how much fraud there is
in this whole subject of the development of science.

The achievement of Democritus is better illustrated by something else which is closer to more recent
developments in science. Democritus was looking for a
lasting rapport between the world of sense and reason,
and he found it by saying that this world of sense can
become thinkable only if we subject it to mathematical
law. The way to do so is the mathematical theory of
atoms (which has nothing to do with the Hindu notion
of atoms). This theory says: well, all right, we must have
something abiding. So we have the atoms, atoms which
cannot be physically reduced though they can be reduced mathematically. Physically they cannot be cut,
that is the very meaning of the word. They do not
undergo changes in themselves.

Contrary to Parmenides, who had made of the
world one mass, one monstrous ball, Democritus now
introduced the *void*. And when modern science sets in,
that idea will never cease to be a factor in scientific
thought. So now we have this something abiding which
is objective to the mind. To some, this may come as a
shock, the idea that you don't see the atom, you *think* it.
In other words this greatest of the materialists is a
rationalist. The reality of the thing can be grasped not by

the sense but by the mind. By mixing these atoms you are going to get various things variously composed. Mixed with varying degrees of void between them, you are going to get various things. One ratio of void to atoms will give you color, another will give you something else. This is the theory, although we have only the most meager scraps of the actual writings of Democritus — scraps that hardly tell us how he accounts for that theory, where things of the objective world are reduced to mathematical law by establishing a relation between atoms and weight and the amount of void connected with them. In other words, they, these Democriteans, reduced sensations to mathematical relationships. When they pursued this line, Galileo and his followers recalled the very words of Democritus.

This line of thought was carried to a very high level in Greece, but it was not continued. Plato came and then Aristotle and the others; and for 2000 years, except for a brilliant departure here and there, this doctrine remained almost forgotten. The notion of the atom remained of course — there was hardly a generation at any time that didn't have its poets and other writers who brought up the atom — but what they said about it could have been said about the Hindu notions of atoms: the mathematics of the Democriteans isn't there, and it won't be there until modern times when modern science takes it up again.

In the system of Democritus, as Aristotle rightly says, all is in the hands of chance. After the beginning, everything happens *necessarily*, but there is no causality except efficient causality. There is no finality — no purpose. Later on, questions are asked about this system. How can you have values of any sort? How can there be any moral values in a system of this sort? On the opposite side they would bring up, against this, other

considerations: This is a universe; it has order; there is
some power that sees to it that this order is maintained.
And later on they come up with their measurements of
things. Look, they say, how providential God has been.
Here is water; as it is made colder, the temperature
decreases, it compresses. But then when freezing sets in
the process is reversed. They say: the providence of God
is at work. If it hadn't been so, the world would have been
a chaos and no one wants chaos. When we come to
Dante, we will have occasion to notice the magnificent
description he gives of Providence. If God hadn't provided as he has, there would be no land, the world would
be one huge mass of ice. But the Democriteans would
answer: We must not think that the only possible values
are those that we have today. The atoms are infinite and
space is infinite. If the initial chance had been different
there would have been a different world — and there may
be other worlds with other values. There might well have
been a world of all ice, and the inhabitants of that world,
if you can imagine any, anthromorphically in their way
would have said: Isn't it wonderful what God has done in
such and such a way. You can imagine for yourselves
what might be said by inhabitants of a system of icebergs.

Democritus gave, primarily, a wonderful and
valuable impetus to science and, secondarily, he gave an
impetus to what may be called more or less false opponents of religion. I'm referring to those people who, in
the eighteenth century, raise the theory anti-religiously
but who really have no business touching it. In this
system the soul itself is made up of atoms. The soul had
always been differentiated from the body. Homer himself does so. He talks of the *Nichea*, those squeaking little
souls that come issuing out. The effort was always made
to distinguish the soul from the body. But not here. Man
is here reduced to a photographic camera or a calculat-

ing machine that can measure just what atoms do in relation to the senses, which can themselves be atomically described. This may interest many of us today, but Greek civilization was not bred like that. Any passage in Plato, or any chapter of Aristotle, shows how interested they were in man as the center of things. No doubt they wanted a God, but their gods were very human. And they wanted to create, they didn't want merely to be passive observers; and so they create not only their religion but also art. They were the greatest creators of art.

In other words, the world of Democritus is dear to some of us, and to all of us at a certain moment, but not to the Greeks. All of us like the idea of a great scientific project working toward a formulation in nuclear physics, reaching one formulation and starting upon another in a way that has built the magnificent structure of modern physics. The Greeks didn't like that. They didn't like the idea of someone reducing light to a mathematical equation. They were Humanists. Yes, we want science, we want the state and the laws, they said, but we want them in such a way that man may be man. No one more than the generations after Democritus brought that out. We have reached, in a way, an impasse, in this mathematical way of thinking. Man must be brought to the center of things. And what develops in relation to this new position established for man, gives us Plato and Aristotle and the rest. And the man who brought back this restoration of man to the center of the world was Socrates. But before we turn to Socrates we have to examine the milieu in which, and out of which, he grew — a milieu or climate in which man again asserted himself as the center of things. And that climate is, of course, the climate of the Sophists, or, as some of us like to call it, the enlightenment, because of the similarity to the later enlightenment we all know about

— that of Montesquieu and Voltaire and D'Allamber, and the rest.

In considering the Sophists one must discard the notion that they were greedy pedants, grasping for money and profit from their students. That is something which is inevitably connected with the teaching profession; but, as today, so then, there was something else, and that something else is what interests us. After the Persian wars, things change in the Greek world; there was greater intercommunication among various peoples. Of course it is a futile research to try to account for this phenomenon: why such and such happened, why Dante wrote when he did, and so on. No matter what you say, there are other things that can be brought forward to show that what you say has no value. Anyway, external circumstances changed, and in the midst of the changes something came up, an attempt to completely discredit tradition and throw overboard all values, some of which deserved to be overthrown, and others which did not. The changed circumstances manifested themselves in another way. Until then the pursuit of knowledge, of study, had gone on in little groups, little cliques, and a great part of the fun was in the mystery of it. One could apply here what is expressed in the biblical phrase: do not throw pearls before swine. All of a sudden, everybody wants to know, because knowledge is power. And the kind of knowledge and power they wanted had to do with political activities. And so these teachers, these Sophists, gave to those who wanted it, some knowledge of the criteria of truth and the motives of human action — in other words, some logic and some psychology. But in so doing they did much more than give them merely some psychology or rhetoric.

The precedents for this development are important, especially the work of Xenophanes, who launched a full attack on religion, on polytheism, and who was engaged in a constant effort to get a philosophical religion such as was finally attained in Aristotle. Xenophanes prepared the humus for the Sophists. He said things like:

> If oxen or horses or lions had hands like man and could draw images with their hands as men do, they would draw pictures of gods just like oxen. And so for the other animals: The ox like an ox, and the lions like lions.

This is pretty advanced for the fifth century. Here's another quotation of his:

> When the Ethiopians draw their gods they give them squatted noses and curly hair. Others make them fair haired.

In this next passage he attacks the poets, Homer and Hesiod. This is the first instance that calls for a defense of poetry:

> How many have there been since! Xenophanes says: Homer and Hesiod ascribe to the Gods all the shameful things, the crimes that men do: stealing, adultery, cheating.

Diehls has gathered all these fragments and some have been translated.

Xenophanes is the one who hammers against the idea of a God that is a particular thing. He stresses above all that God is one. So he is ahead of Plato on this matter and on a par with Aristotle.

What is God for Aristotle? He is the *first mover*. But you have to add something else: he is the mover *himself unmoved*. Xenophanes was working on it. These fragments are often quoted, recently directed against the Catholic church. Why, I don't know particularly. A so-called skeptic wrote: It is alleged that God makes man in his own image, while in reality it is man who creates

God in his own image — and then goes on to quote some obscure eighteenth century philosopher, and it turns out to be these lines from Xenophanes.

While there were some who were discrediting tradition, there were many others who held that there was a value to tradition. They were the people who say: my father and grandfather did it; therefore I must do it so. These are the opposite of those others whose reaction is equally unwise. They say: my father and my grandfather did it; therefore I am going to do the opposite. The state of mind of the Sophist world was: let's break the whole system up and build a new one. So they tried to show that there is no value to tradition. These laws have to be smashed. They may be useful — for most people it pays to be honest; honesty is the best policy — but the Sophists smash them.

The way they went about it is reminiscent of what is going on now. Laws are the result of convention. We have one principle of ethics; but perhaps the reverse is just as good. The question is: Is everything conventional or is there something that is not conventional? In other words, they reproduce in the sphere of man the search that had been undertaken and formulated by earlier philosophers in the sphere of nature. They formed a juristic principle, now abandoned, the contrast between nature or *physis* which is abiding, and the other, which we can discard: convention. At first the opposition was between *physis* and *nomos*, but eventually this *nomos* was elevated to a high position, and something else was substituted and the opposition became *physis* and *thetis*, which means *position*. A thing is by nature or by position. Today in law we speak of natural and positive law. The opposite of positive is not negative, the positive is dialectically opposed to nature. Therefore the positive equals the non-positive in religion and law. Natural religion is contrasted with positive religion. Plato writes a long dialogue, the *Cratylus*, on the question: is language by nature or by position; is poetry natural or conventional? Indeed, there isn't a single thing, no compartment of culture that hasn't been subjected to that inquiry. Dante, for example, at one point in his poem asks Adam whether speech is by nature or by ratiocination.

This is the great contribution of these thinkers, a noble one, when we get down to the laws they discredited. Obviously, not all the laws of Athens could be absolutely right, for many of them contradicted the laws of Sparta and other people; but even as they discredited them, they found something basic underlying the differences: social solidarity. Perhaps the most beautiful embodiment of this contrast between laws that change from place to place and those that are by nature abiding is in one of the most beautiful works ever written: the *Antigone* of Sophocles. The Greeks stressed its meaning, and in more recent times it has been cited again and again — rightly so. Not that Sophocles was s Sophist. Still, there was much in the Sophists worthy of Sophocles. What does it mean, to smash things up? Take wealth: is wealth by nature or is it by convention? Does nature command communism, does nature demand slavery? Aristotle was honest enough to say, when he talks against this, that not everyone thinks the way he does. What about the superiority of men over women, is that merely a convention? What about education? Should it be for everybody? In all of this, they are as modern as you can imagine. They asked, for instance: What is *fatherland*? It's a convention. The world is the only fatherland. That man has blinkers on who thinks of himself as an Athenian.

The Sophists smashed all the conventions; but they also constructed, built positively.

8. PROTAGORAS

The Greeks chose to return to man as the center of things, and to God — for Whom the Democriteans had no room in their system. But before continuing this discussion, it might be worthwhile expanding somewhat on the notion of science and natural law.

The word science has many meanings. In St. Augustine, science is opposed to *sapientia*; science or *scientia* is the lower form of knowing, *sapientia* the higher. Whatever you get to know, whatever knowledge you get by starting from the phenomenal world, the things of the senses, is *scientia*. Whatever comes from above, from inspiration, from thought, is *sapientia*. St. Augustine knew a great deal about science, about astronomy and other natural sciences, but he wasn't interested in them. To a question he was asked about the movement of the stars, whether he thought one account was correct or another, his answer was: What difference does it make? What separates St. Augustine from most later Christian thinkers was this believe that every act of understanding is possible only by an act of illumination on the part of God. The whole process of abstraction that you find in Aristotle, that starts with material things perceived by the senses, carried to our understanding as *fantasma*, and in the light of our active intellect stripped of particularity and thus actualized out of the possible intellect, that whole process of abstracting thought from the data of perception, is absent in St. Augustine. We see things *sui generis*, in a kind of illumination of its own. In the *Republic*, Plato compares the physical sun and the intellectual sun (which is the idea of the Good): without the physical sun, he says, it is impossible to see the things that we see with the senses; without the intellectual sun, you cannot arrive at any action of truth. If that intellectual sun were to disappear, your capacity to understand would be annihilated instantly.

As for natural law: from the very beginning you are able to reach conclusions, to understand and reason, because you have in you, innate, some principles of knowledge. They are inborn. Your speculative reason can function because of this inborn endowment. And from that, with your theoretic reason, you construct a whole logical system for the natural universe. These principles of knowledge are called *axioms*. They constitute the principles of natural law. It is so in Aristotle, in St. Thomas and in others, also.

The whole thing, of course, can and has been challenged from many points of view. Still, you cannot get away from the fact that you have to start with something *given*. The beginning is natural, the other part is discursive; the trouble here is that the word natural is used in connection with the beginning. As you begin to deduce from these axioms you can deduce along a purely rational, theoretic line and there you get what they call the *Jus Gentium*; or you can go along the other line, by ratiocination, from those axioms and try to meet certain particular conditions of a country or a group of people. This line of ratiocination gives the *Jus Civile*. All are deduced from natural law; some on a universal basis resulting in norms which are not axioms, yet apply everywhere; the others on a limited basis to suit particular needs in a particular place.

There was no room in the Democritean system for some being who does not perish, as all things perish. In the effort to follow this argument we come upon that extraordinary period which we call the enlightenment, a

period of great ratiocination, a period when man acquires the conviction — which has been a frequent
conviction, and just as false as it is frequent — that man
by himself can solve all problems by reason. By reason
we don't mean the *logos* of Heraclitus or the *nous* of
Anexegoras, but what the French call *raison raisonnent*.
You talk things over prudently, you reason about them,
and things seem to go along, until something explodes.
Everything seems disoriented; then you start up all over
again. No one wants to deny that there is much to
reasoning; it is one of the elements involved. But there
is another, and that is the fact or condition of history, a
power that defeats all ambitious efforts, all efforts at
solving everything by reasoning about it. And that takes
us over to the opposite extreme, what has been called
historismus. These two extremes must be kept in mind if
the discussion is to make sense.

With the Sophists, we are in a very anti-historical
period. These Greeks are going ahead and remaking the
world, very much in the same way that we are going at it
today. We have come far with natural science; why can't
we do the same in other areas? Get rid of wars, depres-
sions — all that sort of nonsense. So it was in this period
we are considering: they were internationalists, femi-
nists, pacifists, anti-slavery, everything you can possibly
conceive, and they held the most advanced ideas you can
think of — but nothing that history had worked out, and
so it all fell flat. Their ideas were beautiful and noble; but
the Stoics too had beautiful and noble ideas, and even
better were the ideas of the Christians, later. But conditions hadn't worked themselves out yet to a point where
anything could be done about them — removing slavery,
for instance.

To better understand, let's look ahead to a time
when people can look back to this twentieth century and

say: those fellows had a system of transportation that involves the murder and maiming of thousands every year. To explain what the trouble was, we would have to say that we haven't gotten to a point yet where we can dispense with this murderous system of transportation. Here we have the destruction of life for the sake of transportation; there they had the enslavement of human beings for the sake of production. It is a frequent pattern, a sort of constant rhythm: first, great faith in reason and enlightenment; and then recourse to the actuality of history. In the one case reason makes the world; on the other side, all that is actual is rational. All is rational that has been actualized and worked out in history.

More important still in this context is the abolition of the gods. This proved useful in a way, for the gods came back, as they always do, and on a much higher level. Of course, we have Critias, the Sophist, who asks: what are these fantastic gods? Some clever politician thought them up. We can with political force scare people from committing crimes publicly, but some crimes are secret. How can we prevent them? So, some clever politician thought up the gods, who see everything and hear everything at all times, but can't be seen themselves. They are located in the sky and they scare people because their place is the place of thunder and lightning. The are also good because their place is the place of the sun and the rain that makes things grow. That's how the gods originated. And from that moment on, the idea of religion as an instrument of government for the prevention of crimes and for preserving the social order, has become a commonplace. Voltaire will say: even if you don't believe in them, the wise statesman should encourage religious belief for the sake of the social order. But Critias said it first. And then there is Prodicus, who tells

us that gods are just a poetical way of interpreting the
great basic forces of nature that act on men. Here is
grain, here is wine, here is water and fire, and out comes
a Phaeton, a Neptune, or a Vulcan or a Bacchus, and so
forth. Centuries later we find Heuemures, who tells us
that these gods were great men who at a certain moment
were forgotten as human beings and remembered as
superior beings.

In other words, gods were no more than superior
men whose manhood has been forgotten. Dante will
draw on this. For the early Christians, these gods were
devils, and Dante, in a very famous passage, refers to
these *dei falsi e bugiardi*, these false and lying gods, an
Augustinian phrase found at the beginning of the *City of
God* and also a description of the devil. Dante gives us an
elaboration of the Heuemuristic doctrine, coupling it
with astrology. Gods are connected with the heavens.
Strangely enough, the gods don't come first, and the
stars after; the other way around. There is Venus, the
planet, and there is Mars. The influx of Venus and Mars
on individuals made them extremely brave or amorous.
And on certain individuals, this influx reached such a
level that they were transformed into pure bravery and
pure love. The man became Mars, and the woman
became Venus. This combination of Heuemurism and
astrology is Dante's way of rejecting the doctrine that
the gods of the heathen world were devils. There have
been other ways.

There is one other Sophist to consider here. He
is important because he has left his impress and thought
on history and institutions. I'm referring to Protagoras,
a man who was always famous but who of late has been
given all the importance he deserves. Today, Protagoras
is a popular man. His significance is that he restored —
more than anybody else — the kingdom of man; and in

that kingdom the individual man is triumphant. Man, the individual man, is the measure of all things. The phrase has become a commonplace. We also owe to Protagoras a doctrine of cultural development, and, in addition, a doctrine of phenomenalism. A third thing we owe him is the idea of democracy. Those who have been upset by Socrates for sounding so anti-democratic, who have been mad at Plato and Aristotle for that same reason, will feel at home with Protagoras, who, before Socrates, did and said the best that could be done and said for democracy. All of this we know from the famous dialogue of Plato, *Protagoras*. You can see there how Plato, who was not very merciful with his opponents, stands before him like Dante before Farinata — hostile but respectful.

Plato tells us all that Protagoras says about the claims of the Athenians to superiority. True enough, men are born with different endowments. This one has a mathematical genius, another can talk well, and when we want a ship built we go to someone who has that special genius or endowment. And when we want to have a teacher, we go to someone who has that special qualification. But when it comes to the conduct of states, there is no specialization required — we are all equally endowed with the virtues that make statesmen — a doctrine that was not dear to his immediate followers. And then comes the famous myth, from which we extract this doctrine. There were men who were very much advanced in culture and the arts, but they were killing each other off because of innate rivalry, the desire to dominate others and to acquire goods. So Jupiter began to worry and came up with a scheme. He called Mercury and sent him down to give men something that would enable them to live together without killing one another. Apparently Mercury's mission wasn't very successful for men still lacked something. So he brought them *Aidos* and *Dike* (difficult to translate): *Pudor* and *Justitia*. Justice is that capacity which by its presence enables a community or state to exist; its absence causes a state to fall. This notion of Justice runs through the centuries. How a great jurist of the twelfth century managed to work it out, I don't know. It was made clear that Justice is the force that makes communal life possible. But Justice which takes care of external relations is not sufficient. There must be *Pudor* also. To control our inner actions there must be implanted in us an instinctive respect for others. We must protect ourselves from the menace that comes from within. We must respect others even if there is no sanction, even if we are not discovered. There should be something in us that gives us a sense of revulsion at the thought of harming others, and that sense of revulsion is called *Pudor* (*Aidos*). Mercury asks: How shall I distribute this? Like mechanical ability? Some here, less there? No, no, says Jupiter, give it out in equal shares, each man must have the same amount of Justice and *Pudor*. Men are born equal and free, not equal in everything, but equal and free in so far as *Aidos* and Justice would have it.

The other doctrine of Protagoras, which, of course, is more famous, is the doctrine of cultural evolution, a doctrine fully expounded already in Democritus and given poetic treatment in poetry by Lucretius. It is one of the two views antiquity held about the condition of man in this world. The first view is that man starts out low, very low, and develops higher and higher. That is the Epicurean view, the view of Democritus and Protagoras. The other and more famous view is the reverse. You start out with perfection and end in decay. And this other is known by the name which has been the same in all countries: *primitivism*. Your find it in Hesiod, in Ovid and in any number of other poets. The particular shape it takes is a golden age when everybody is happy, and then a silver age, and so on, until finally you come down to a situation where man is a thing made of clay with one foot cracked. And so it is in the Bible, too. But these men were too smart to let it go at that. They set about to sustain it philosophically.

Dante refers to it, but he draws the idea from Hesiod and Ovid instead of the Old Testament. Of course, it is perfectly obvious that there is progress. The ancients more than anyone else were aware of it. One of the first utterances of Greek thought — found in Thales — is one that links up knowledge with time. After that comes the statement: Truth is the child of time (*Veritas filias temporis*), and that's how it comes down to Bacon: *filias temporis non auctoritatas.* Perhaps the most beautiful formulation is that of Hippocrates, that great doctor who should be remembered for very many reasons, but primarily for insisting that ethics should never be separated from the medical profession or practice. Hippocrates gives us this beautiful description of progress. We come into this world and find that our ancestors have left us a body of knowledge. It is our duty to add to that body of knowledge and to take that body of knowledge we have increased and hand it down to our descendents, who, in turn, will add to it and hand it down to theirs.

No one better than Hippocrates has given us a notion of progress on a moral basis. It is a duty and an obligation and a debt of gratitude that we must pay. There is no Greek author who is not aware of this progress. When it comes to the Middle Ages things of course change. The primitives knew about it. Seneca knew about it. But what is it exactly? What can we say about it? They said what many of us are saying today:

Mankind, after liberating himself from all sorts of slavery, is now the slave of the machine, the slave of
technology. It dominates our lives. If you try to break
any strand of it, you're gone, beginning with the toaster
in the morning, and your car, and so on. Seneca did not
have a situation quite like this, but he is fully aware that
happiness diminishes as science increases. In other
words, he is aware of the truth of that biblical statement
that says that knowledge can be carried so far that it
becomes destructive.

Finally, the third point to emphasize is that this
great relativist, this great individualist who went too far
— asserting against all the efforts of his predecessors who
insisted that knowledge of reality was possible — this
man tells us there is no such thing as intellectual reality.
There is nothing beyond pure sensuous perception. Not
only the data of smell and of the eyes, but also the data
of pleasure and pain is the result of a transient meeting
of two motions: the motion of the thing that I see, and
the motion of my perceptive capacities. The thing that I
see changes, and my perceptive capacity changes; so
that, at any given moment, what I grasp is true only for
that moment, it lasts that one moment and then is gone,
and I cannot expect anyone else to have that same
experience.

Memory is the treasure-house, the storehouse of
these moments, the projection in consciousness of the
*res.*What there is behind this projection will remain an
eternal mystery. Memory itself is not a thought process;
it is simply an accumulation of individual perceptions
that do not enable us to generalize and are therefore
purely subjective and relative; they reveal something
unknown, not reality but a *noumenon*, to use Kantian
language, worked over in sensuous perception.

For Protagoras man is indeed the measure of all

things, not man as a species — one could have no objection to that — but the individual man. That's what makes the doctrine *skepticism*. Of course, there were those who challenged him, answered him even — Socrates for one. Socrates questions all this. What is the point of this position of Protagoras? It is that man can never have knowledge, will never have knowledge? That all he can have is this passing instantaneous perception of something he has created himself? Socrates comes up with a truly magnificent response. Man must be good; man must have virtue, and to be good, man must have knowledge of the good. How are we going to know it? Through something called *logos*, or reason; the objective mind. You have a subjective universality, that is, we can agree inwardly, but only providing we have also an objective universality, external to us. How do we get this objective universality? We know that this thing differs from that, and one moment from the next; but if we examine them all, we see that they have something in common, and that something is the stamp of the *logos*. We must seek it out, this common element. The purpose of man is to rise to this *logos*. Through the dialectic, through *dialogismus* we rise to *logos*. We have to search out what things have in common, and that common thing is the *concept*. In other words, the process, carried out later by the Stoics, is this: that a thing is true when you get universal consent. All that remains is to take this concept out of psychology and put it in ontology and you have the ideas of Plato.

But we've leaped ahead, with Socrates. Here, the thing to remember is that there is no room for any of this in Protagoras. One last point: does Protagoras mean to say that we cannot communicate? Not at all. And this is another great title of glory for Protagoras, for he works out a whole doctrine of pragmatism. We don't know what's right or wrong, but we can consider those things good or right according as they turn out well or not. In all this world of passing things, of convention and of relativity, there is one fixed goal that can serve as a criterion for pragmatic judgment of right and wrong: social solidarity. And for that he worked out the doctrine of democracy already discussed.

9. THE SOPHISTS AND THE DOCTRINE OF INDIVIDUALISM

Protagoras has a place in this discussion, not for the sake of erudition, (erudition is a curse and useless if it cannot be integrated historically, and history makes sense only when it is the present) but to stress the political significance of his theory. Most of us today are politically-minded, as my own generation was. Schiller, a very capable man (not the poet Schiller, but the later one, the scholar, Ferdinand Schiller) is good reading in this connection, particularly his essays on humanism. They are very interesting and particularly enlightening on this subject — on the emergence of individualism. Goethe also is good reading on the "pragmatism" of Protagoras. Long before people used that phrase, there were those who already had remarked how eloquently Goethe had expressed the idea. The Italians in the nineteenth century thought much about it too, never imagining that at some time it would become the official philosophy of this country, the United States, and then be imported again into Europe. A good brief account of the subject, in German, is the last volume of Ueberweg. He has, at the close, several fine pages on the history of pragmatism.

For Protagoras, man is the measure of all things. He gives us the doctrine of complete individualism. In time, excesses emerge, and critics of these excesses lost sight of what the others had done, what they had attained culturally: that man determined himself and did not let himself be determined by anything outside of himself. What that means is that man is determined by *moral* law — *religion*. If you aim at really freeing man, if you really want to liberate him, you have to do certain things. A full statement of a widely exaggerated individualism is found in the first book of the *Republic*. Man operates in complete independence of religious teaching, moral laws, and tradition. Are the Epicureans individualistic? What did Lucretius say about God? If he exists, well, he's far off somewhere and is not concerned about us. And what about the state? To avoid having to go to prison, yes, you should concern yourself with affairs of state; but under no other circumstances should you entangle yourself in such business. What about law? Natural law? There is no such thing. Laws are the result of a social contract. There are no such obligations as those defined by natural law. The instinct of man is to seek pleasure, and these pleasures can go to excesses. Some people have the means to go so far in pursuing pleasure that others suffer and are crushed. There is a great deal of pleasure in harming others.

The Epicureans were certainly individualistic. They had thrown overboard all kinds of what we call today — for some reason the word has come to be so widely used — *regimentation*. These individualists were not religiously, politically, or morally regimented. To explain the fact that you have to live in society, under social laws, they developed a very neat social contract theory. The good you get by doing violence to others in pursuit of pleasure, and the evil you get in consequence of others doing violence to you, do not match. The pain of the one greatly exceeds the pleasure of the other. So they reach an agreement; you stop annoying others on condition that they stop annoying you. This is the theory — much older in origin, but taken up and developed by them — of the social contract.

But their materialistic doctrine forced them to

try to find happiness in connection with external things: joy, pleasure. How are you going to get them? We all try or have tried to get them. Where does it take us? The pursuit of pleasure makes you a slave; — a slave of wine, women and song, or whatever. Therefore you are not a self-determined being, you are not free; you have a god above you just like the rest. Only the man who liberates himself from them is free; and he is the cynic. What does Diogenes of Sinope do? He didn't want an electric machine to toast bread in the morning, or a fancy air-conditioned apartment. He wanted only a cave, a stream of flowing water, and a cup. After a while, he decided to throw away the cup and drink the water with his hands. It can be done, this liberating oneself from pleasure — the cynics did it. But some of their successors began to see that when you do that, when you throw away the cup to be completely natural you destroy not only the cup, but something else that was done to the cup: the orna-mentation, its beauty. The cynics were destroying that which was the most glorious achievement of Greek life. They were destroying devotion to beauty and ornamen-tation. In this context, one should note that the Greeks had not reached the point of thinking that beauty is best realized in a cube or some kind of match-box, or what some used to call the station of Rome, a tomato-crate. Theirs was a devotion to beauty, to ornamentation, not as an *appliqué*, but as a realization, an exteriorization of what is highest in man: that which approaches divinity. That, if anything, was what gave meaning to what Greek civilization was and what the cynics would do away with. Of course, there had to be a remedy.

What is the relation of personality to all that has been said about individualism? What do we mean by personality as distinguished from individualism? When he has liberated himself as such, an individual is a pretty small thing, until he adds something, until he becomes a moral individual, or artistic one. When you add cultural values to that substantial individualism, it transforms it into *personality*. That is the idea that prevails in Christianity. It takes individualism to a higher level, but a higher level that does not repudiate the lower. And the highest level, the highest form of personality is, of course, God.

Those who did the most to raise up individualism are the tragedians: Aeschylus, Sophocles, and Euripedes. Someone has tried to explain it etymologically. It's hard to accept it in those terms, unless you assume that there is wisdom in language, that there is purpose operating in its history, like the chemical processes that operate in the human organism in such a way that we are not conscious of it. Where does the word "personality" come from? It comes from Greek drama. What does "persona" mean? Persona means the mask.

It was the explicit end of the Epicureans to make themselves self-sufficient. The word for self-sufficiency is autarchy. We talk about this country being autarchic, and about Great Britain not being autarchic. We have kept the word, but we have kept it with an egregious blunder, connecting it, by retaining the "h" in its spelling, with *archein*, so that we have the same spelling for self-sufficiency and self-rule. The Italians and the French have done the same thing. But the Germans always distinguish the two, reserving the "h" for self-rule (*autós* + *árxein* = *autatxía* = self-rule; *autos* + *akkein* = *autárkeia* = self-sufficiency).

Hedonism is a form of regimentation. The Epicureans may have been all wrong in this, but some of the things they said which are often recalled for us today, have some value in them. But, of course, when you go to extremes — Gassendi, that greatest philosopher among the *litterateurs*, and greatest *litterateur* among the philosophers (which may or may not be a compliment) stressed this fact very much — and we can stress it today: there is nothing more oppressive imposed upon us today than our desire, even when we really don't want to be pleasure-seeking, to enjoy ourselves.

One thing more, and this is significant. It came up recently in a brilliant editorial about one of the great achievements of modern times — a doctrine supposedly unknown to antiquity — that we do not punish evil-doers out of a spirit of vindictiveness, but out of a desire to improve them. Of course this is in St. Thomas, and it's already old in his time. The first we hear of it is in Plato's dialogue, *Protagoras*. We find there the statement, and there is no reason to doubt it for it accords with his general line of thought, that this was Protagoras' view on punishment — a view which is still very present today. All history is *present*. And it is the present that gives significance to the past. That sounds paradoxical, but as a great Roman said (I don't mean that nonsense of Cicero about history repeating itself, but the truly great thought): what memory is to the individual man, history is to mankind. It is the recollection of what we have been, a recollection of what life has meant to us, the enrichment of our capacities, and in that sense a norm or line that helps us to meet present conditions.

The Sophists, though not Protagoras, pushed this self-affirmation — the independence from moral norms — to extremes. Not Protagoras, for he did say very clearly that we *are* bound by something: by justice and *pudor*. All one has to remember, therefore, is the first book of the *Republic*; where you find an almost identical situation — not a situation, for the situation always prevails — but a theory. You have that same theory almost 2000 years later in Machiavelli. All that you find in Machiavelli, every single thought, you have already in the Sophists — above all in those speeches of politicians, created perhaps by Thucydides. There you have, on a much higher plane, everything that Machiavelli proclaims. Sophism is Machiavelli philosophically conducted. Machiavelli accumulated certain norms and observations, expressed them in a paradoxical way, with no consistency, so that he often contradicts himself. Why then, does he enjoy such great prominence? Well, first, he said these things very wittily, and second, the times were right, and third and most important, the people who were frightened by him, and those who later approved of him and praised him, were totally ignorant of the course and facts of history. Most of the books written on the originality of Machiavelli's thought can be ground to pieces by even an elementary acquaintance with history.

The perfect Sophist of the Thrasymachus type is the man who says that all those things that are called vices — the natural man crushing others in pursuit of pleasure, transgressing all so-called moral laws — are really virtues. They accord with nature, and therefore should be lived up to, if it is true that what counts is the individual. The reason you have laws is one of two: either it is the result of the weak who bound together to restrain the strong, or it is the result of the powerful individual, the strong man, becoming a hypocrite. Instead of saying what he knows to be true — that the strong should crush the weak, as happens among wolves — he decides it is better not to say that, for it might awaken a reaction; he therefore, hypocritically, formulates certain laws. The man today who comes to mind when you recall this ruthlessness in the doctrines of the Sophists is Nietzsche. His theory is that nature aims at forming supermen. But of course there is something much nobler in Nietzsche's conception: ideals of nobility totally absent in those others. (After all, the superman of Nietzsche is someone we wouldn't mind having at the table with us.)

Well, all this that we call *raison d'etat*, which means the repudiation of moral values for political purposes, begins with the Sophists. This doctrine became very important in the middle of the sixteenth century, but long before then it had been worked out in every detail: the fact that we find it necessary and right to drop the atomic bomb and kill thousand at Hiroshima, the fact that we have to have two scales of weights, one for measuring deeds on our side and another for measuring the deeds on the other side; all that we found worked out in that greatest philosopher of Christendom, St. Augustine. If you want to speak the language of the sixteenth century, or your own language, you can say, formulating St. Augustine's thought, that the worst consequence of the fall of man, the worst phase of original sin, is that we are obliged to say "my country right or wrong." It is terrible, but necessary. Only St. Augustine didn't say it that way; he used the Roman phrase: *salus republica suprema lex est.* You see the full import of that; the safety of the state is the supreme law. It means that every other law becomes invalid when the state is in danger.

---

1. There are two distinct views of the way history runs. One is called the primitivistic, the other the Protagorean or, more properly, Democritean. We call primitivistic the view that posits a state of perfection at the head or origin of history, and then a decline. The other, the Democritean, later expounded by Lucretius, makes it very clear that man starts off as a savage and gradually improves. These are the two views. Later on the Christian philosophers had to take those two positions into consideration. They emerged in such a way

that the solution takes a primitivistic form, certainly. Adam is perfection; you start off with a Saturnian age, with a period when man cannot sin, when man is infallible, a period of perfection, call it a golden age or grace, call it anything you want; then comes the fall. And according to the Augustinian view, the drop was very great, it was immense. Man was reduced in intellectual and moral capacities so low as to be almost nothing. This view enabled Christian thinkers to press very hard upon the consequences of sin. Then, when you have reached the bottom you can go on and pick up the Democritean theory. This double conception fitted in very well with something that was much in vogue — found also in the Hebrew sages — that soon after the fall, immediately after Adam's fall, men, humanity sank so low that even the bounds of elemental nature did not prevail. And for that reason, and this is so for St. Thomas and others before him, God in his mercy, seeing that natural law had perished because of the excessive savagery of fallen man, tried to save the situation by introducing positive law, the law of Moses. That was a solution for Christians.

One must also keep in mind that, from the start, people were very dubious about any kind of progress except scientific progress. So it was with Thales and the others: what progress there was — and there was very little — was in science alone. There is very little if any progress in morals, and, consequently, none whatsoever in any endeavor which gives man any genuine happiness. This is a very old view and is still maintained today by many. Once in a while someone tries to maintain that there is some kind of moral progress. There were some who raised arguments in the nineteenth century that seemed rather plausible then, but the twentieth century has made the plausibility of them rather thin. A great professor of the nineteenth century, lecturing here at Columbia in Greek history, would point out how such and such a thing that happened then would be impossible now. Yet, today we see that those terrible things were not only possible, but events have gone very far beyond. There is scientific progress, but with nothing of the sort corresponding in the moral realm. In connection with this double view, the most popular and most readable and charming of all Roman philosophers is Seneca. You can call him a Stoic, or you can call him an Epicurean (although he wouldn't have liked that). Seneca admits progress in the arts. As a result of technical progress, how much richer external life has become, but how much greater now are conditions for unhappiness! These are the two views: the Democritean (rather than Epicurean), and the primitivistic.

2. Was the *consensus gentium* an idea of Socrates?

The answer is no. The idea is a Stoic one, but the germ of it was provided by Socrates, in the doctrine by which he starts scientific investigation on its way — the doctrine so dear to the later Romans, this *consensus gentium*. The people who at first had said that only a few intelligent, noble men, morally elevated, could ever get at the truth, end up saying that the truth is in nature operative everywhere and that anyone can get at it anytime. And this develops into an idea very dear to most of us, but which is only a fairy-tale: Internationalism. Look at the words of Marcus Aurelius on the subject. The fact that we all have reason, means that our rational utterances must be universally valid. And if our rational utterances are universally valid, it means also that not only what theoretic reason says, is universally valid, but also what practical reason says. Therefore, the norms of morality, rationally proclaimed, apply everywhere; the laws too, that derive from those rational norms, and which are necessary for the preservation of the community have to be enforced everywhere, and the enforcement must be the same; and if that is the case then we must have one government, one world community. This doctrine was not invented by Marcus Aurelius. He was not the first, for it was already in Cicero, but it is important in Marcus Aurelius because, in addition to being a Stoic philosopher, he was also an emperor. He was in a good position therefore to give weight to this theory, and test it in practice. And the germ of it does come from the view found in Socrates.

3. The idea of individualism is also found in the myth of

Giges. That's the standard example.

4. Did Machiavelli emphasize the claims of the state over the political freedom of the individual?

He emphasized the fact that for political success, moral restrictions did not count. In other words, he was laying down the doctrine that was later formulated as *raison d'etat*. It's a theory that says that when the higher interest of the state is at stake, when the interests of the state demand it, moral considerations have no value. He's not emphasizing state's rights over individual freedom – that's not quite right. It isn't state's rights, it is the right of the ruler, of the individual ruler. It's totalitarian, if you want to call it that, but not state totalitarianism, but government totalitarianism, for the sake of the ruler and not for the good of the state. After all, we have to bow our heads before *raison d'etat*, don't we? It is cruel certainly, but it is noble; it is cruel for the sake of the whole. This has no place in Machiavelli. The ruler, in order to come out personally victorious, may have to kill his best friends, repudiate his wife, do all sorts of wicked things, because anything immoral goes in order to guarantee the success of the ruler. That is very different from *raison d'etat* – very different from *salus republica suprema lex est*, or, as some put it, my country right or wrong. After all, there's a great deal of nobility in that, and a great deal of historicity. But not in Machiavelli. The comparison holds to this extent, that in both cases morals and politics are disconnected. Machiavelli disconnected politics from ethics. The Sophists, disconnected politics from ethics all along the line, and politically the result was that it yielded such noble people as those we find speaking in Thucydides.

5. How does Livy become connected with Machiavelli?

Machiavelli wants to prove some unsound theories of his, and turns to the first ten books of Livy, and does to them what no sophomore ever did to Xenophon. But, of course it is all well written and smart. Why was he so successful? Well, people get tired of goody-goodies. They may listen for a long time to some goody-goody saying: why, we built up a beautiful empire, rich and powerful, and never touched a hair on anybody's head. But sooner or later they are going to get tired of it and will be pleased to listen to someone spilling out the nasty truth. We have had a long line of thirty or forty great thinkers who have worked out the sad necessity of *raison d'etat*. Take war, for example. No matter how good you are, if you go to war, you must be ready to do everything the enemy does, and then go him one better. That's what we have done, isn't it? Everybody has to do it. People close their eyes ostrich-like for a while, but then they get impatient, and then it's "God Bless Machiavelli." You need a Machiavelli to say to Valentino: you did well to kill so and so, and all that. Of course, Machiavelli too closes on a different level. In the last chapter of his famous book he says: look at the sorry mess Italy is in. Some leader should come up and set things right. And to attain that end he will have to do all these things.

10. DANTE'S LOVE POEM AND THE MORAL PHILOSOPHY OF SOCRATES

The first thing Dante would say about *The Divine Comedy* is that it's an ethical poem; not simply moral, not merely prescriptive, indicating various actions that you might call good, but back of it all is a philosophic theory, a moral philosophy.

Socrates said that we get at the truth by working together, with reason. And the only way to get to the truth, is through dialogue, by means of dialectic. The word is still used in English, French, and Italian; it was used from the very beginning, and we still use it, in the sense of an exchange of thoughts, a dialogue, but not simply that; an exchange of thought that brings out what is common in all our thinking as something that must be true because we all agree on it. That's one meaning. When we come to Plato, we find him using the word very much in the way we find it used in modern times. It is a proceeding to conclusions by an examination of opposing positions. But as far as we are concerned, in the Middle Ages, for Dante and the others, the word dialectic meant logic, that part of logical investigation that is not apodictic, that has not to do with absolutes, but with a problem.

How does dialectic or logic come into play in *The Divine Comedy*? Dante says it's a love poem because its allegory is inspired by his love of Beatrice, and also because the universe centers about love, which holds it together. The latter is more important than the former. It is a love poem when we give to the word "love" the meaning and scope Plato gave to it. Somehow or other,

Dante got wind of that beautiful dialogue, the *Symposium*, but more probably the *Phaedrus*. The correspondences are too great to be pure chance.

It is a love poem also in another sense: the whole purpose of the poem is to indicate how Dante, having undergone a moral transformation, cleansed by moral purification, his eyes opened by an ethical transformation, was able to see the Absolute, was able to see God. After all, the whole purpose of the *Inferno* and the rest is to show how man ought to do what he must do; how he ought to desire the things he desires, from the lowest to the Absolute, to God. Of course, there is in Dante the natural love for knowledge, the natural desire for the good; but that would not be enough to call his poem a love poem. In all stages of the *Paradiso* this natural love, this *élan* toward God operates, but it would have no effect in elevating him step by step, except for a boost that he takes at every important moment, a boost that takes him from one sky to the next, that lifted him to greater comprehension and therefore greater desire; he rises from one desire satisfied to a greater one, until he finally gets to that point where there is nothing more to be desired, where satisfaction is perfect. And that can only be possible when you reach the end of all desire: God. This constant satisfaction of desires, followed by a constant awakening of greater desires, is carried on higher and higher by the power of love, or, more properly, the smile of Beatrice.

The *Commedia* is a love poem also because, through divine grace, Dante has been helped to the highest goal. All men desire to know. That is the first line of the *Metaphysics* of Aristotle. (A learned German scholar wrote somewhere that this line is quoted over 36,000 times in the twelfth and thirteenth centuries.) In addition to natural love, Dante is helped by divine grace and

that help is Beatrice. Personal love enhances natural
love. In this context one must accept Beatrice as a real
person, as far as Dante is concerned, a person that really
lived. Dante says so himself. He makes Beatrice say so,
when she expounds for the first time in its fullness this
Platonic doctrine of love. At the end of *Purgatorio* Dante
tells us what Beatrice lived and died for. In life and
death, she led Dante platonically to God by the only way
one can go to God, according to the doctrine of the
Phaedrus. What is it that comes into this material world
— this inferior world of the senses — out of the divine
plane of truth, where all reality is confined, almost
entirely hidden from us? One thing only: Beauty. All
those other divine things as we see them here are murky
and mysterious.

Beauty alone will lead you back to that divine
plane. Beatrice bravely says that she was the greatest
embodiment of beauty in a world of matter that tends
toward annihilation of beauty. Beatrice explains that she
had a beautiful body, that she gradually transformed her
beauty on earth, or the effect of her beauty, until the
point came where Dante had to be shown that beauty in
the body was an inferior kind of beauty, that truer beauty
is in the mind's eye; and in order to make him cognizant
of that fact, she had to die. I don't know why no one has
bothered to write a *liebestod* on this matter in Dante.
Everything else about Dante has been exhausted, but not
this. The ladder that takes us to God rises so that after
a series of refinements, physical beauty becomes almost
evanescent, and then death comes, and what follows we
see in the *Paradiso*.

Have we any right to doubt the historicity of
Beatrice? Anyone sensitive to reality and poetry will
grasp that for Dante she was a real human being —
whatever she may have died from, whatever may have

actually happened, Dante thought that way about it. Whatever the meaning of those poems, written about Beatrice, one thing is clear: Beatrice changed the meaning of everything Dante had done in life. The first poems of the *Vita Nuova* are entirely transformed. Their meaning is again transformed in *The Divine Comedy*. Which is false, which is true? An event is not what it is when it comes into existence, but what posterity makes of it. If the founding fathers of this country could see what has become of their deeds and intentions, they would explain this better than I can. An event is made by the future. So, answering the question we raised about Dante, those sonnets of the *Vita Nuova* become what they are, really get their meaning, in the *Paradiso*.

So, indeed, *The Divine Comedy* is a love poem — both in a Platonic way and in a personal way. And what's interesting is that Dante, later in life, was able to juggle with those poems based on biographical events to make them illustrate the beautiful theory of the *Phaedrus*. But can a love poem also be a moral poem at the same time? At the very mid-point of the *Purgatorio*, there is a long essay, not a very poetic passage, but it does explain the identity of ethics and love. The passage extends from the sixteenth canto to the eighteenth, heralding at the close of that canto, in a very beautiful passage, the fundamental doctrine of Platonic love.

To appreciate Dante intellectually, we must also accept his poem as a moral poem. Is a series of precepts or norms, a series of commands — thou shalt do this, thow shalt not do that — is such a thing as the *Decalogue* or the statements of Confucius properly called ethics? Does that constitute what may properly be called ethics? What is lacking in a series of precepts? Why can't we say it is ethical? What did Socrates find wanting? Why don't we have ethics before Socrates? Somebody tells you:

don't do this because the gods forbid it, or because our elders have said it isn't good, or have told us how bad it is to do this or that. In other words, why don't you have ethics when you have merely a body of laws or commands? One answer is: you must give voluntary assent, voluntary obedience to the precepts of ancestors. Another is: beauty. Another: you need a broader basis on which to build. In other words, unless you have a philosophy of life first, unless you relate these norms and make them appear as manifestations of that philosophy, you have precepts but no ethics.

Why don't we say there is a philosophy in this naturalism? When a Sophist says these laws are fixed, man's nature is to assert himself by force, might is right, what sort of reaction does he provoke? How can that argument be destroyed instantly? How did Socrates destroy it? The doctrine is always advanced on the assumption that it has its basis in nature. The example they gave was the bull; I don't know how many other animals show that might is right. Might always involves two things: violence or fraud, the lion or the fox. I don't know how early these examples were used, but they go pretty far back. Cicero at one moment talks about them as the old examples. So they are. Man's nature is to crush, the way the lion does; to gain supremacy by force, as a wolf does in the flock — or, if he can't, he goes away and gathers force and comes back to try again. Others do so by fraud. What's wrong with that? Well it's natural, but whose nature? The animal's nature. It's the nature of the lower animals, not man's nature. So the nature in back of the Sophist position is a false nature. It doesn't account for what differentiates man from all other beings. If you are going to have a moral philosophy, a good that is natural, you must think of human nature, human nature or reason. Therefore: if you are going to have a moral philosophy that strives for a natural basis, an abiding something such as the naturalist philosophers look for in the physical world; if you are going to find it, you'll have to find it in reason. You have to establish your actions to be, according to reason, natural, and therefore good. When you have done that, an ethical system may be on its way.

Of course, one is apt to say: why shouldn't we do this? It's natural! We are apt to make the same mistake the Sophists did. Socrates warns us: if a man wants to find his beatitude at the table, that naturality puts him on the level of a pig or a rabbit, far from the human plane. Man has the right to find his beatitude wherever he likes, and if that beatitude is similar to that of the Epicurean pig — that isn't my phrase, that's a Horatian phrase — what is wrong with that? Why shouldn't he follow that urge? After all, our ethics is an ethics of consent, as we said. You can do whatever you want providing that you don't hurt other people; it's a commonplace. Go ahead, do what you like, as long as you don't disturb others. What does Socrates say to that? Why can't I live dedicating all my energy to finding good wines, good food, and so on? What's wrong with that? What's wrong is: you repudiate your human nature by doing so. A few years back I amused myself collecting German, Italian, French and American speeches from great leaders, proclaiming programs for making people happy, providing a bountiful life for man. I gathered these speeches from leaders both from the democratic countries and from the totalitarian ones, and I noticed there was s singular resemblance: they all put forward proposals for the satisfaction of those desires we have in common with the lower animals. That end occupied the greatest part of what they had to say; and they weren't very far from the Sophists in this, and very different from Socrates. How often have you heard the warning voice of Socrates saying: aren't you getting out of your nature when you are doing this or that? Can you do such things and remain a man? How important is Socrates in our daily lives? I don't mean in a philosophical aspect, but in the practical considerations of our every-day life?

Of course, there are those who doubt that there is a human nature as such. That's another matter. In this discussion we must accept it as an axiom, we have to allow at least that it's a postulate for this sort of analysis. From the earliest beginnings, that postulate has been accepted — by Dante, by Descartes, and by countless others. They all assumed that there is a human species which is part of the animal species but which is differentiated by the fact that it has reason. One can challenge that man doesn't have reason or that all the other animals have it as well; here we are dealing with a people who said that man is differentiated from the other animals because he has reason. And therefore, natural action in man must adhere to reason, just as the heavy body adheres to the law of gravity. Ignoring that inborn instinct (and we have this from Aristotle down) that tells us when to eat, drink, that tells us when to copulate, there is a voice in us, given to us about which we do nothing, which is axiomatic; a voice that tells us to follow reason in all these things. That is the central core. We must listen to that voice and work out a system from it. That's what Socrates did, though he never spoke of that voice, which is in you instinctively, ruling and regulating, like the power of falling in a stone, or the power of a magnet.

Throughout so many centuries of thought, there is the acceptance of this — something not to be proved, for it is an axiom given to us when we come into the world. We are endowed as human beings, as members of the species, with an instinct to regulate all those instincts in us that we have in common with the other animals, and we regulate with and through reason. That is fundamental to all these men. The *differentia* is rationality. In the tree of Porphory, what carves out the species and the genus is the *differentia*, and in this case the *differential* knife that carves out the species is rationality. In his teachings on the subject, Socrates emerges as the founder of ethics in the modern sense of the world. He is called intellectualistic, rationalistic. Aristotle could not accept the Socratic view and introduced modifications which went down into the Middle Ages.

What is the act of homage paid by Socrates to reason? Simply this: that all ethical can be reduced to rational. If you reason properly, you cannot go wrong. Sin, if you want to call it sin, is an error in ratiocination. Teach people how to reason properly, and immorality will disappear. Why do we make hogs of ourselves? Because no one has taught us how to reason on the subject. We are befogged by error. Think rationally and you will remove error. The trouble is: *video melior proboque* — I see the better course and approve — but I follow the worse. Reason acts over the impulses democratically, not tyrannically; it rules tyrannically over the body. In other words, the control of the mind over the body is that of a tyrant; but over the impulses, it is that of a constitutional monarchy.

Aristotle will tell us that reason and duty are one: our duty is to perfect our reason. As for reason and beauty: we have to wait for Plato to introduce it in the moral sphere. Socrates has been credited for two things: eudaimonism and intellectualism. We know what intellectualism is. Eudaimonism means: if you reason — contrary to what the Sophists said — you get happiness; and the only kind of happiness a human being should strive for or can have is that of reason. So, the first and most important point in this moral philosophical view, which Dante and so many others accepted, is that there can be no genuine happiness except when reason is applied to conduct. That takes us to the science of ethics.

---

1. Isn't there a basis in religion for the commandments of the *Decalogue*?

The *Decalogue* has dogmatic statements, just as you might find in Homer or Hesiod; but, of course, their importance is infinitely greater than the precepts of Hesiod or Homer, because western civilization has seen fit to become Christian. That means development not only upon the New Testament but also upon the Old. Unless you accept the Old Testament, the New one has no basis. You have a syllogism there of which the major premise is the Old Testament. That's all there is in the *Decalogue*, a series of dogmatic precepts, and particularly those of the first table. It's easy enough to show that those precepts are identical to those of natural law. And once you've done that, you have established the condition whereby you can develop a system of philosophy that gives meaning to those commandments. But until you have done that, you have only a series of dogmatic utterances, no ethics.

2. Socrates presupposed ethical values, but you cannot understand him unless you accept that his theory of knowledge, which is very important, proceeds from a moral postulate. We must know things. Did Protagoras say we must know things? No. We must know things because moral values, virtues, imply knowledge. Without moral values the world becomes a monstrosity. The almost divinely rich moral consciousness of Socrates, makes him want to reconstruct a whole moral system which he cannot construct unless he first postulates the necessity of knowledge. You must be good, but to be good you must know. Therefore you must reject any system that does not postulate the possibility of knowledge.

With Socrates there really begins what we might call an ethical system. The others were not. Why can't you call Thracymachus and the others ethical philosophers? They had a system and, what is more, they had a system that was naturalistic. They had a card they played: always establish what is natural as opposed to what is conventional. Put all values in the natural and reduce correspondingly the values of what is conventional. This philosophy of the natural makes room for human action.

In their language, as far as Protagoras expressed it, all we can do is grasp things with our senses. There is only sensory perception.

11. PLATO'S IDEAS;
THE FOUNDATION OF ETHICAL CONDUCT

The great contribution of Socrates was his answer to the challenge of Protagoras. He boldly affirmed that there had to be knowledge of the truth, of something existing over and above the things of the senses that are constantly changing. There is a *Logos* or Reason at work in man and with the help of that *Logos* or Reason we get at something beyond the particular things of the senses, something which is different from them all, and yet common to them all. Here is Tom, Harry, and Dick, all different from one another; but if you examine them closely you see that they have something in common: the concept of the human being. Here is a bird, a horse or a dog; you examine them not with the senses but with the mind, and you get at something which they share. They are all different and yet the mind reveals, in back of them, a concept: animal, which is not taken up by any one of these, and yet is the basis of them all. That becomes the basis of all later thinking, taken up by the scientists especially; and it has remained the basis of their thinking — although Socrates would have spurned all this because for him it was of value solely in the sphere of ethics.

This concept is in back of all our minds. It is there waiting to be tapped. What the professor does is very much what the midwife does, when she extracts a baby from the mother's womb. That is why Socrates called the dialectic process *maieutikós*, which is the Greek word for the midwife's art. Although he never bothered to tell us exactly how this concept of reality comes to be in the human mind, Socrates tells us it is a process firmly grounded in self-knowledge: know thyself. He went about it by pretending universal ignorance, by professing ignorance of everything. By gradually pressing his own ignorance forward against the Sophists, who professed to know things, he pretended to accept their affirmation. This *maieutik* process was always accompanied by something else: Socratic irony. He would start out pretending that he didn't know anything and they knew everything; after a while, a point is reached where he knew something and they didn't know anything. We know all this through Xenophon — Socrates never wrote anything — and what Plato has told us, and, most important, what Aristotle has told us. There is a difficulty with Plato. So much of what is expounded in his dialogues under the figure of Socrates is really Plato and not Socrates. The figure of Socrates develops as we pass from the earlier to the more mature dialogues, and develops in such a way that you cannot assume that the figure has any basic historicity.

The concept Socrates introduced is something purely psychological. You're certain of something, have the realization that you know something, just as two and two makes four; you can't prove it, but there it is. Proof for the Greeks, and for many others after them, meant that without that certainty, ethical conduct is impossible; and a human being unethically considered — this, of course, was subsequently rejected — is not even to be postulated. In other words, man devoid of ethicity is a contradiction in terms.

To understand what of Plato's ethics is fundamental to Aristotle and also to Dante, one must know something of his general philosophy, and, more especially, his metaphysics. What we see Plato doing as he passes from the *Protagoras* and the *Crito* and the *Phaedo* to the late dialogues — from the first book of the *Republic*, which is early, to the *Philebus* and other late dialogues — what we see him doing is hypostasizing the concept, taking an act of the mind and making it a reality. It is the first time in the history of the world that people are asked to accept a reality which is not present to the senses: something that seems impossible, a reality grasped without any aid from the senses. The question is, how did Plato get the courage to assert such a thing? He had, of course, the example of the Pythagorians: here are two men, four cows, a hundred cows, but the two or three or hundred do not owe their existence — do not depend upon — the existence of cows. Remove the cows, and the twoness and the threeness remain there forever. We speak of beauty, goodness, truth and so on; take man away, and beauty, goodness, and truth remain. Later on, the criticism grows, and the answer given was: No, this is not subjective to us; there is a person for whom beauty and goodness and mathematical truths is subjective, and that person is God. But we are a long way from that.

These are not easy notions to grasp, but one must make an effort. You don't have to be a believer to understand the argument. Professor Montague at Columbia used to get very mad when challenged by anyone saying that such realities or ideas could not be grasped by minds in the ordinary sense. These ideas, for Plato, were a world, a *kosmos,* a universe, a world of ideas entirely detached from the world of the senses. There is the world of feeling and the world or universe of comprehension — one, the latter, is made up of ideas; the other, of sensation. And between these two worlds, the bridge between them is man with his mind. Man is the horizon; not in the physical sense but in the astrological sense, as the line that divides a sphere, any sphere, into two hemispheres. The relationship of this *mundus intelligibilis* to the *mundus sensibilis* is, of course, that one is transient and the other abiding and eternal. But are they completely detached from one another? No: the one below owes its existence to the one above. There is a *concursus*, something like that in Christianity. Eliminate God — what happens to that pen, to your capacity to move that arm? They cease to be; that's the doctrine of Christian divine *concursus*. Same here. Eliminate the ideas and these things here below disappear. Nothing remains. You have chaos, because these things below, which we perceive, are related, are doubly related, to the ideas as copy is to reality or to the exemplar. The exemplars are above: here below we have the images, constantly varying, objective to our senses but existing only because of a certain relationship they have as copies to the exemplars.

They are also related by *participation*. The old example that was always given to explain *participation* is this: here is the sun, where light is *essential*, but if the sun's light were shining into a mirror, that mirrored light would not be shining *essentially* but through *participation*. Things here below in this *mundus sensibilis*, in this world of the senses, *participate* in the ideas. There is a hyper-uranium (*hyper-ouranos*), and up there is the idea of man. We are somewhat like that. For a while it looked as if Plato claimed that there was a hyper-uranium, original or exemplar for everything — even for artificial things. Gradually he qualified that notion, reduced it: there is man in itself, and beauty in itself, and, above all these, there is goodness in itself — the most important thing in connection with ethics. These ideas are not juxtaposed; they form an order. There is a multiplicity arrayed to form a scale; there is rank, and therefore there is a highest idea, and that idea, the highest that tops them is the idea of the good — of God. And that idea, the moment you speak of action in relation to God, immediately plunges us into the sphere of ethics.

What did Plato mean by the *good*? In the *Republic* he gives us an analogy, repeated over and over again — there is hardly any writer who doesn't have some trace of it in his writings — that has to do with the relation between this idea and the sun: that idea is, in the upper world, what the sun is here. Let me add that the world of things and the world of ideas are not in the same order, nor does one proceed out of the other. The severance is original and eternal; the only bridge between them is man. Man is the horizon. The analogy is this: we have the sun; without the light of the sun we would be unable to see the things that we see. We see because the sun shines on things. Here is the sense; there is the object. In order for the sense and the object, or something about the object — in this case, the color — to be connected, we need the light of the sun. Analogously: here is my mind and there are the ideas; but my mind cannot grasp the eternal verities unless light shines on them (as the light here below shines on the leaves of the trees). In this case, the light that shines upon the truth, so that it may be grasped by the intellect, is the light from the highest of ideas, the idea of the good — which, of course, is something indeed divine. Here begins, here is the root of what happens centuries later, 600 years later, with Neo-Platonism. For Neo-Platonism, the important thing is that this highest idea, this father of all, is beyond being. It is the thing that no one in the dialogue seems to be able to understand — perhaps it is unintelligible after all. Nevertheless it is there and has played a great role in the philosophy and religion of West and East. It is the metaphysics on which ethics is suspended.

We have reached a point where we can see the relation between this metaphysics and ethics, centering around the idea of the good. But before we can make sense of that, we have to go into the sphere of psychology. At this point we are no longer in the world of Socrates, where, to do right all you need to do is to think right, where evil is only a matter of error. Or: there is a speck in your eye that prevents you from seeing well; remove the speck, brush it away, and the condition is corrected. Here, there is something more. We have a soul that is made up of parts, so that it is not sufficient to say: here is a beautiful woman, to think properly about it, one has to jump over the body and get at the idea. There is something in me — a force — that does want to appropriate that body. It is the part (we can't call it a faculty, we haven't reached Aristotle yet), it is the part that he calls *epithemia* (the sensuous desire); and next to it is the other part which is the *themos* (the spirit of courage). Here is the ethical situation: the mind that is meant to see the ideas may be helped or hindered by those two other parts. We have to do something with these parts in order for them to do good and not evil. We have to introduce virtue (*arête*), so that the soul may do its work properly. In the process, we come up with something that is still with us: the articulation of the four cardinal virtues. They appear and reappear, transformed sometimes, broken up, in every subsequent system of philosophy: temperance, fortitude, wisdom — these are the first three — and the fourth is justice.

The mind reaches to the ideas. For its purpose it has a certain virtue, namely wisdom or *sophía*, which is the goodness of that part of the soul. Then there is fortitude (*andría*), which will direct *themos*, the desire in us to fight, to its proper end. Fortitude is the virtue by means of which the instinct to fight is made to function properly for the right cause. And there is the other part of the soul that has to do with lust; that too has to be

trained, adjusted; and the virtue that does that, that
brings self-control, is temperance (σωφροσύνη). Finally
we have to see to it that each one of these virtues does its
proper task and doesn't interfere with the perfect functioning of the others (this is purely Platonic and will have
to be dropped). The habituation that is brought about by
the proper functioning of the first three virtues is
justice. This is the moment when the cardinal virtues are
first introduced, the cardinal virtues which Aristotle
accepts after a fashion, but which the Stoics and Cicero
make so much of, and St. Ambrose accepts and makes
thereafter the backbone of Christian ethics.

 The important thing for Plato is not the individual, but the species; not the individual good, therefore, but the common good. We have to see what these
virtues mean as we pass from the individual to the
species; how the individuals are organized into classes;
how in the state, morality takes on a fixed aspect: three
classes, each one the embodiment of one of the virtues,
and each performing its proper function because of the
demands of justice. This time, justice is the legality that
makes it possible for human beings to live together in
human society.

---

1. What do you mean when you say: beyond being?

 That's where Christian thought and common sense
break away from Neo-Platonism. In the Old Testament, God
says of himself: I am — *Ego sum* — *Ego sum qui sum*. But the Neo-
Platonic God says: I am both being and non-being. In other
words, the good can be predicated of many things that are
not.

2. Then, this is the *via negativa*?

 Yes, it is the negative approach. But the question here
is — and it's a hard question to answer — is the concept of good
more embracing that the concept of being? Things that are

not, one may say, by the very fact that they are not, are good. According to this way of thinking, you have a trichotomy: you have a *soul* and then *being* and then beyond these two is *mind* — *oneness*. The desire to find unity is constant; philosophical thinking is never satisfied until it reaches unity. And unity is not to be found in thought, for in thought you always encounter the dichotomy of thought and the object of thought. How does one break away from that duality? You have to rise beyond thought. And when you do that, you rise also beyond *Being*. As you pass from the ontological to the logical and predicate these things, you pass from the individual man to the species man, and then from the species to the *genus*, animal, and then to a higher species of animate things and so on to the highest which is, say, substance. And as you rise higher and higher, the concept gets thinner and thinner. What you can say of the highest is very little compared with what you can say of the species or the individual thing. You are approaching zero. The difficulty with these people, particularly the Neo-Platonists, is that having established or postulated a logical series, they then pass on to an ontological series: I think such a thing, ergo, there must be such a thing. That's the constant trick of the Neo-Platonists: passing from a logical sequence to an ontological one.

3. Doesn't St. Thomas also say the same thing?

Well, yes; but in St. Thomas you have something else. He does say that the good is more comprehensive than being, but having said that, he goes on to say, and he makes it quite clear, that it is purely conceptual and not real. Of course, he has to face it in his commentary in *Dionysium de divinis nominibus* (divine names), which is neo-platonic; and also in his commentary on a work of Proclus. You can say, if you want to, that he is a Neo-Platonist. But, and this is very important: when he is commenting on Aristotle or on some neo-platonic writing, he does not feel it necessary to say at a certain point, however this is what he thinks. He leaves that for you to grasp. He has proved already that he is a Christian; now he goes on to explain the thought of Aristotle or Proclus.

4. How do you think this doctrine in Plato differs from Hinduism?

I don't know about Hinduism, but there is a strong resemblance. People whom I respect — not personally, for some of them wrote long before I was born — have said, though admitting that Greek science developed in complete independence from the Orient, that there is a strong resemblance between Neo-Platonism on the negative side and Hinduism. I am ready to accept their view, since they also make the first statement about the independent development of Greek science. (I should explain that I don't give final judgment on any subject in a language which I am not able to read. I don't rely on translations, and even less on works about the subject. Unless I can read the original text, I clam up.)

5. Is there a notion of evil in Plato's conception?

Yes. Eventually, there comes out of Plato — long before the Neo-Platonists and St. Augustine — a notion of evil, which, almost without modifications, the Catholic Church accepts, and that is the conception of evil as having no *essence*. Evil is the absence of good, the absence of good where you would expect it to be. The word we have for that is *privation*.

Here you have a mind that strives, not aimlessly, but toward the good, the highest idea. To get there it has to cross over a bridge, it has to go through the world of sensation, a world that in one case, pulls you up the ladder; in the other, it's the anchor that weighs you down. Or, put another way: how does man get to these ideas with his mind? We have our senses, but how does the mind get the ideas? By *anámêsis* — recollection. For the first time, we have a whole theory of immortality — which Aristotle will brush away completely. Long before I came into being as what I am now, my soul was, and my soul will be embodied later on, perhaps as a fish or a horse or a pig.

The way we approach the ideas is by recalling them. That means that we have known them before. How is that? We have known them before because we have lived another life.

We learn in the *Phaedrus* that at some moment we pass through the field of truth and see reality, only to be plunged back into this world of change. When that happens we forget everything we saw. How is the memory refreshed? What is the occasion by which the memory is vivified and helped along? Help is to be found in the things of the senses. They are the occasion without which the ideas cannot emerge. The ideas come to us by recollection, the possibility of which is conditioned by the world of the senses. In that way, of course, the goodness of the world of sense is very clear.

But this world of sense can operate in a different way. What is the phrase? *Sôma, sêma,* the body, is the sepulcher. This body which has afforded man the means to rise to the ideas, can also be a burial ground, or rather a coffin when sensation is made an end in itself, when we forget the beautiful ideas seen by the mind, which tells the brave element in our soul, the *themos,* to lash to pieces the *épithemia,* the lustful element. When the mind succeeds in doing that, it rises where it should rise. But what if it does not succeed? The search, the quest stops at the beautiful body; one of the two horses dominates. You have disconnected from the world of ideas that body which was meant to push you up from sensation to intellectual contemplation of reality. If it is thus disconnected, that body, which was so beautiful, becomes a coffin. The world of sensation becomes not a ladder to the ideas, but their coffin. Evil consists in using things contrary to the purpose for which they are intended.

6. What is the relation of the charioteer to the two horses?

The charioteer relies on that one of the horses, that is, in this trichotomy of soul, the *thémos* (θύμος), which is the part that has to do with bravery, that is very close to the *nous,* and serves it great-heartedly; without it, the mind could never subjugate the *epithemia,* lustfulness. You need the *themos* and the *epithemia.* You can't get along without them; but you have to subjugate the one. If you don't, then comes evil.

7. If man's mind reaches the ideas by recollection, how far back can that go? Is there any idea of creation?

There is an idea of creation, but not of ideas. You read in the *Timaeus* that the Demiurge creates the world; he shapes it like a sculptor; and while he is doing that he keeps his eyes on something, like an artist keeps his eye on the model before him: he keeps his eyes on the ideas. Somehow one, in a previous incarnation, as a bird, or a hog, or God knows what, one had a view of the meadow of Truth generations back, maybe a hundred generations back. The beautiful myth at the close of the *Republic*, the vision of *Er*, also answers the question. It's a myth, of course, and that is the trouble with reading Plato. The great joy you get out of reading Aristotle is that he speaks out clearly. In Plato we have a myth, a figure of speech, a beautiful piece of writing; but to extract any notion is quite a job. So: evil consists in misuse. It is connected with the double role of the things of the senses — which can serve as a ladder and as an anchor, or quicksand, weighing us down.

12. PLATO'S CONCEPT OF THE SOUL

Until now the soul was identified with some act of the individual or rather, the moving force in a person. The soul controls the movements of the body in a certain way; it is the force that controls the body. Some of the early philosophers said the moving principle was air, or fiery atoms; or blood, or number, or harmony and so on. With Plato, however, the soul has become substantive. It is no longer merely the moving force of the body.

When we come to Dante, we will be dealing with souls without a mortal body and not yet given an immortal body. This conception of the soul appears for the first time in Plato. How Plato came to have this view is not clear. Of course, the hypostasized soul — the substantive soul — plays a very important part in the Mysteries of Greece, where you find the idea of the soul imprisoned in the body (σώμα-σήμα) and the Pythagorean doctrine of the transmigration of souls. These all indicated clearly that the soul was substantive. The doctrine taught that the kind of body you occupy now — that your soul occupies now — is in relation to the kind of life you led in a previous existence. If in one life, when you are supposed to be living like a human being, you live like a pig instead, you will eventually inhabit the body of a pig. At the end of the *Republic*, Plato, in the form of a myth, works out the whole doctrine. You have the soul confronted by chance and freely choosing, then being bound by necessity to the choice made. These three — free-will, necessity, and chance — are all involved.

The soul is what it is; and the body is merely something it puts on, a kind of cover. All one has to do to carry this into Christianity is to drop the notion of transmigration — the rest is the same. Dante will take up and develop this Pythagorean or Platonic theory of the substantive soul; instead of the doctrine of transmigration, of previous existences of the immortal soul, we have God, the Creator. That explains why, for such a long time, people insisted on the doctrine of innate ideas, a doctrine which St. Thomas had great trouble killing.

What Plato tries to do is to give unity to this soul which is made up of three parts. The greatest question, the bitterest controversy of the thirteenth century and of Dante's day was about the plurality of forms; the question of unity against plurality. The human soul has three parts: the vegetative, the animal and the rational. Are these separate souls or are they one? Or are the vegetative and animal parts merely a vibration of the rational soul? In the *Purgatorio*, Dante gives us the effective and beautiful presentation of the matter at the beginning of the fourth canto.

This hypostasized soul is quite a novelty. At one time it was in contact with ideas, with reality (for only the ideas are real; the things here below are not real, they are merely shadows of reality). The soul comes from the realm of ideas — and thus the doctrine of recollection (ἀνάμτησις). The soul comes, not in complete forgetfulness; it remembers vaguely. This recollection is strong enough to arouse in us a nostalgia, a longing (Dante has a beautiful description of the operation of this longing) for the reality the soul was once in contact with; and that longing arouses a love, and that love is called *Eros* — philosophical or Platonic *Eros*. We all have heard of Platonic love. It's the love for the hyper-uranium, the love for the ideas in general; more particularly, for the idea of ideas, the highest of them all, the idea of the

Good. All this immediately suggests a system of ethics — if by ethics we mean, as Cicero put it, the search *de finibus*, the search for ends. Reaching these ends we find happiness. Morality means nothing, unless it takes into consideration these two facts: one, a good to be striven after; and two, the consequent or resultant beatific condition. A great modern philosopher, Kant, has tried to show that all the philosophies of the past, even the Stoics, and everybody else, were not able to consider ethics except in a eudaemonistic way. Kant may have been very wrong in criticizing this, but certainly there is a nobility in his own ethical system that we find nowhere else.

Such is the nature of the quest for the beautiful, eternal unchanging world: a moral system that tells us — and the Stoics worked it out — there is a good, and there is a bad. The search for inferior things in themselves, the departure or deviation from the way of reason, making your goal anything that is not rational, is bad. The good is the opposite; it is the quest for the highest things. And the highest quest, the highest virtue, is love of wisdom.

Of course, eventually the Stoics will say that you get nowhere with these two poles; and so they introduced something in between. There's "good," "bad," and "indifferent." Such things as wealth, health, physical beauty, are neither good nor bad; they are indifferent.

Does Plato go along with this? Does he tell us that yearning for terrestrial things is bad and yearning for ideas is good? Fortunately not. If he did, we wouldn't be talking about him. Plato does not make that sharp dichotomy. He loved the artistically beautiful too much, he was too much of a poet, truly Greek, and therefore disinclined to shut out the beautiful. He brings before the eyes of the people a doctrine showing that the world of change is not evil, not bad. This world is an avenue, a bridge. It has certain advantages. Of course, if you make a mistake, if you use this bridge as your palace, or if you use any means as if it were an end, then it becomes bad. The world is what it is — a world of change. We see it, we recreate it with our art; it is what it is not because it denies the ideas, but because it embodies them. If we want to rise up to the ideas, we have to take advantage of this world. And since we're in the sphere of ethics, the transition has its effect on theology and on morals — in theology not in Plato himself, but in his immediate successors.

Those ideas eventually become deities. And, of course, the highest idea — becomes το άγαθοτ, THE Deity. In the twelfth century, when little of Plato was known, they spoke with awe of this tremendous idea, this wonderful, beautiful deity. The phrase Plato coined had quite a success in later centuries. But between the supreme good and us, there are a lot of intermediary things, low things; but not only things, beautiful things in matter, but all sorts of intermediary superhuman powers also, like Demiurges — Demigods — high, but not high enough to be ranked with the highest idea. This, again, is a very beautiful notion. Christianity found it useful when it inherited angels and archangels from its Hebraic ancestral tradition — there was a ready place for them. That is not to say that the scriptural account of these matters are false; but whenever there were difficulties encountered in the scriptures, any rough spots, one of the functions of Greek philosophy was to provide a way of smoothing them over, gilding, sugar-coating a pill that people at first were inclined to reject.

These intermediary deities of the Platonic writers had the essential characteristics of the angels. There is a great book in which all this is fully illustrated. Dante knew it; it was a book very dear to him. It was a work of

Dionysius, who has left us many books: the "divine names," so popular in the thirteenth century, which is a regular tract on the Platonic doctrine; "celestial hierarchy" and "terrestrial hierarchy" on the relation of the priesthood to the superhuman world. That whole structure is carried down to Christianity and Dante. When you're told that the thirteenth century, and Dante, repudiated Plato, that's true enough — provided you apply certain restrictions and don't overlook something in the great system of Christian theology, put there by St. Augustine, that couldn't be shaken out. That is why, if Dante is treated as an Aristotelian poet, that serves to explain only the surface.

The virtues that Plato has described are: Bravery, Self-control, and Prudence. Justice, Prudence, Fortitude, the cardinal virtues. Did they exist before? Probably. Certainly there must have been a word to describe someone fighting boldly. Why focus on Plato? The virtues were there, but they were scattered things. Plato put them in a system, an organic whole. We see this again and again in all the systems of the philosophers. Even the Epicureans. How do the cardinal virtues fit in with the Epicurean system? Let's say you want to have a good time. Well, you have to have foresight, surely, and you have to have courage to take your pleasure, and above all σωφροσύνη — you have to be sure you don't have such a good time tonight that you'll never be able to have a good time again. You have to exert temperance, self-restraint.

You have in Plato this continuum from material things to spiritual things. The philosopher, in his wisdom, is going to rise to God. But he has a soul made up of parts. The rational is only one part of the soul; and he must not only train that, but he must also train the other parts in virtue — train them not only in themselves but also into one another. For he wouldn't be able to do his work well, no matter how well he uses his mind, if all the time his heart is bent on eating and drinking. So, in connection with this view, the ladder is built, with the other virtues scaled to help the highest, wisdom, to do its job.

What Plato and Aristotle and the others mean by preparing the soul in virtue, is this: you have a man who drinks excessively; he becomes virtuous. Does that mean that he wants to restrain himself when he is tempted to drink? Would restraining himself be considered a virtue? No; it becomes a virtue when it becomes *habitual*, yes, but something else too. There must be pleasure in the doing. One is virtuous when he does with pleasure what before he had to do by restraining himself. You begin by restraining yourself, by kicking aside the bottle; but if you continue doing that, you soon find what a joy it is *not* to drink. That's what ethical education means. You reverse Dante's *licitum* to *libitum*. Virtue is making something that you begin by doing as a *duty* into something you do with *pleasure*.

The two virtues I mentioned are means to enable the highest wisdom to walk through the world and walk well — to reach the enjoyment of things you should enjoy. Justice comes in when each part of the soul does what it should. Justice is the proper harmony of the parts. When you have that harmony you have justice. This is something peculiar to Plato, unique with him; this αιοσύτη, which must have sounded very strange to his contemporaries used in that sense.

All created things have to be measured by reality. They respond to the highest reality; and that response has to be measured. In Dante, of course, you measure that response in terms of beauty, in various gradations. The important thing in this: the individual as such —

Tom, Dick and Harry — isn't much from Plato's point of view. Back of the individual there is mankind. We all mean something, if we can manage to become a part of a whole; as scattered individuals we are nothing. This is a very old view. We have on one side the people who stress the totality and make of the individual very little. On the other hand you have political atomism, which makes of the common good, of the state, a crutch which you make use of only when you can't get along without it. In theory, you can have anything you want, but in reality, historically, you have something that belies both. It's an in-between affair. We say that the state is only an instrument for the individual's happiness. Then you are sent to Korea to die for that instrument. It ceases to be an instrument, surely, under those circumstances. Some try to keep up the fiction; they only create other problems.

This is an old position. Plato, is, of course, famous for being completely on the other side. Not he, but some of his disciples spoke very eloquently on the subject and they cited as examples birds, swallows, etc. How wonderful they are when they are bunched together in the flock. They can cross oceans, etc. Release them, let them go alone, and they are lost. Of course, the answer to that is that man is not a swallow. But they have a rich collection of very impressive examples. And, of course, the atomistic theory makes no sense at all (I mean, of course, the political atoms and not the Democritean atoms which make a great deal of sense).

But this is Plato's position; what counts is the group, the *ordo*. And by order, I mean a multiplicity which has been reduced to unity because of a certain relation between the parts, which relationship is called *ordo*. Therefore, for Plato, the important thing is not the individual but Mankind. The *Republic* is a social structure, created with the materials of his psychology. There is a soul made up of three parts: one part that craves to perpetuate itself as individual and as species. Therefore you have in you this ἐπιθυμία, this desire for all the things necessary for perpetuating the individual and the species: wealth, food, etc. Then you have another part, θύμος: bravery, the inclination to fight, to defend, to fight for things and die for them. There is that in the soul; men do willingly fight; Roman history, surely, proves it. And the third part — we haven't gotten very far from the animal species, the rabbit and the lion — the third part is reason. These, as we noted earlier, are the three parts of the soul: the part that wants to reason, to know; the part that wants to fight; and the part that wants to live and have a good time of it.

Mankind is really a projection on a large screen of the soul of the individual man. In other words, in the state you still have three parts, you still have this trichotomy in the three classes of society: you have those who love to fight, and these are not priests by nature, but soldiers; then there are the people who love wisdom, and they are called Philosophers, lovers of wisdom. And then there are those who work, the laborers, the mechanics, and they are a class of people who are not expected to fight, who are not given to courage, or to love of knowledge, not θύμος, not philosophy, but ἐπιθυμία. They love wealth, money, to satisfy their material needs (the third part of the soul is also called φιλοχρήματοϒ). This may seem superficial to some of us, but it has had enormous influence.

So much for unity. As for philosophical eros: how does the poor farmer share in it? As part of a body that becomes one and, as a whole, acts philosophically. By doing his job well in his particular class, he participates in the act for which the state exists as a whole, namely, participation in the highest idea.

---

1. You spoke of the things of this world being embodiments of the ideas. Don't you think the word takes one somewhat beyond Plato's position into Aristotle and the later Platonists?

Well, perhaps embodiment isn't the right word. Call them reflections instead. Something that bears some stamp or trace of the paradigm and exemplar. There is something in the exemplar that is shared with the copy. When Plato says this, he is coming very rapidly to that subsequent Platonic development you speak of. Once you have a situation such as I have described, where you don't have merely two extremes but a middle ground also, some kind of rapport has to be introduced, some kind of causality. Can you have efficient causality between an idea objective to the mind and material things objective only to the senses? Obviously not; not in the way we mean causality. We have now developed or introduced a new kind of causality. Not efficient causality, finalistic causality. Some ice falls into water; the water splashes; the splashing water wets someone; and so on. You have a series of contacts, a series of efficiencies that produce effects. But you may have a different situation: a magnet, for example, and some iron ore. The magnet pulls the ore to itself. Or you have a beautiful woman and a benighted knight; the knight is drawn by this lure, or, if you don't like to speak of the beautiful woman as a lure, take the hawk as an example. In this pulling by the magnet or the woman, or the lure, you no longer have efficiencies; you have not effects, but *affects*. You no longer have *efficere*, but *afficere* (I use the Latin terms not to go to the Greek words which are the source of the distinction). This affection is Love, is an inclination. That, of course, provides the two kinds of causality; you are moved by either one or the other. We're in the world of love, again. Love is the cause. Love for the highest good. But you have to have in these things a change of some sort to make them rise, to make them respond to this pulling. And so we come to Aristotle and Dante. This magnet, this lure moves the young man to the beautiful woman. She, in turn, has to do something to move him. And something moves *her* to do what she does; and so on. You move in this way from one level to another, rising to God, the highest point. How does Aristotle define the highest? God. He is the mover who moves, himself not moved. In the beginning of the *Paradiso*, Dante sends a thrill through our hearts, through our religious hearts, when he takes this up as he begins to rise — *Quando la rota che tu sempiterni desiderato* (he is talking to God here) — when that sphere that you make eternal (or move eternally) by being desired. In that phrase Dante is translating literally the κενεῖ δε ὡδ ερώμεοτ of Aristotle. All the stars move because there is this desired mover; and by their motion, they manifest their love of God. Things here below partake of that desire that was so clearly and perfectly manifested in the revolution of the sphere of the stars and becomes fainter and fainter as you come down into the world. We all know the phrase: "love makes the world go round." In other words, this unmoved mover moves, not as an efficient cause, but finalistically. He is not an efficient cause producing effects, but an efficient cause, if we may use such a word here, producing affects.

2. I don't understand in Plato why the world of sense exists at all.

Well, I suppose that question might be raised in connection with any system. The Stoics, Cicero and the rest tell you that the only real beauty is harmony. Unison is very dull and monotonous. St. Thomas asks, what about a universe made up entirely of angels? It would be a pretty dreary place (not his phrase). Beauty implies harmony; and harmony requires diversity, more and less. Therefore you have the infinitely great beauty of the highest ideas, and less and less of it as you move down and further down. What you're really asking for is a thorough Platonic theodicy. Without going into it we can say this much about the things of the senses, in Plato: they're there, and he tries to explain them.

3. What about the musical spheres that Cicero talks about in Scipio?

Of course, the music of the spheres is a Pythagorean doctrine, a doctrine in many ways ingenious, and very provocative; it provokes mathematical studies of great value. Aristotle rejected it completely, of course, and it was not accepted by the Middle Ages except poetically. Dante loves to think of the music of the spheres. Particularly when Neo-Platonizing or Neo-Pythagoreanizing, they say, the music of the spheres is a great hymn of love to him who moves them.

13. THE STRUCTURE AND PURPOSE
OF THE STATE IN PLATO

We have been trying to work our way towards the moral system of Dante — what he's driving at in his *Inferno* and *Purgatorio*, and how that is connected with what happens there and what happens in the *Paradiso*. *The Divine Comedy*, we said earlier, is a moral poem. What moral data have we now to support that contention? What have we seen so far? What do we think is ethics? When is an act ethical? What does an ethical act aim at?

Let's go back to morality. You can take a dogmatic attitude and say: this is good, and that's bad. But that's for Sunday school teachers. An act is moral when it strives toward some good, in which good it finds happiness. But is any act along any path toward good moral? If you drink and get pleasure out of it, is that good, is that moral? No. Because it's not rational. A moral act is a conscious choice of a spiritual good. A moral act is one directed toward a good that is rationally constituted and subsists rationally. What that means is that the happiness you get out of that good is not the happiness of a part of the body — the stomach or some other organ — but of the mind; not sensuous excitement or exhilaration, that won't do; it's got to be reason. Why is intoxication not moral? The answer is, it would be moral if there were any morality in animals. When a man yields to the life of the senses, when he acts like a beast he is not a beast, but a monster (to use the word St. Augustine used). A monster is something that acts contrary to the ways of nature.

We found in Plato that the good you strive for consists not exactly in avoidance of the things the senses grasp, but in a utilization of those things to attain a spiritual good, to find the ideas — the highest of which is the idea of Good. What exactly that is, Plato didn't tell us, because he couldn't, because that idea is God, and God is described negatively. God is immortal — that is, not mortal; he is infinite — that is, not finite; he is omnipotent — even in that, if you study it closely, you will find it is essentially negative. St. Thomas touches on this in his *de divinis nominibus.*

What is virtue in this context? Why should we be virtuous? Why be temperate? Because Granpa says so? What's wrong with excessive drinking? Obviously, it disturbs the operation of reason. There's nothing wrong with drinking too much, except this. In a way, you can call this moral build-up naturalistic, because it is based on a concept of nature: the nature of man is rational, his good must be rational. Of course, when you come to Christianity, this aberration, this deviation from nature, becomes a sin. At that point we have to add something else to make it a sin. First it has to be made an offense against God. It has to be made a transgression of a command, an act of disobedience contrary to an order of God.

This brings up the question: Does God command against something because it is bad, or is it bad because God commands against it? For example, the commands not to fornicate, not to kill. Are these bad in themselves or are they bad because God forbids them? Of course, to common sense, this question makes no sense at all. To kill is bad, and that's that. But what was it that stimulated men like Ockham and Duns Scotus to say the latter? Well, suppose God condemns something because it is bad, that limits him, doesn't it? It makes of God a sort of bookkeeper of good and evil acts. If you add up good you're rewarded; if you add up bad, you're punished. God becomes the rewarder of the good — a pretty humble role for God. He becomes a kind of general administrator. To keep God from being merely this, we add the concept of Grace. Do what the child does — grace is when, grace is if. If I go to heaven because I have acted well, is that Grace? When does Grace come in? Grace comes in when you get a reward you don't deserve, something for which you have done nothing. The moment you have done something worthy, there can be no Grace. Therefore, with the help of this concept of Grace you are able to build up a divinity who is something different from that queer God people like to push forward; that bookkeeper or policeman that blows the whistle and sends you to heaven or hell.

Such is the psychological and moral structure of the individual and the three parts in the soul, which require three virtues to act well. There is the rational and the fighting part, and the sensuous, voluptuous part; but in order to control these, you have to develop certain virtues. To reason well you have wisdom; to use your courage well you have bravery or fortitude; and to control your libido you have temperance. And in order that the soul may not be split up, in order that the unity be maintained, a certain harmony has to be established among the parts, and that is the fourth virtue, justice.

Still a man by himself, so treated, would be like an arm detached from the body. Would you call a detached limb an arm? It still looks like an arm, but in that condition it is only a piece of matter, no longer able to function like an arm. Man, by himself, is like an arm or a leg or some other member cut off from the body; cut off from the large social unit, the state, to which he belongs, he has no real function. The state is a larger screen on which the individual is projected — it is man writ large — to translate Plato's phrase. Those three virtues mentioned must reside in the state, also.

Plato identifies or places them, connects them with social groups or classes. There is the class which is not brave, cannot think (I'm not disparaging them, but this is what Plato says); they are the farmers and the craftsmen and mechanics. They have to do the kind of work in which the only virtue they need is temperance. Then there is the class that has to fight against enemies of the common good, interior and exterior, and who are the warriors, whose virtue is fortitude, bravery. But if you have only people who feed and fight, you don't have a state yet; you need another group (despite what some of the economic materialists may say), the rulers. In Plato's world, the rulers are such not because they are brave or temperate, but because of an intellectual capacity. But in the state too there must be unity, harmony of the parts. Each class must do its task, and not something else. The craftsmen must be craftsmen and not soldiers, the soldiers must not be rulers. And so, when you have a state that has harmony as a result of these three classes doing what they are supposed to do, you have a state with justice. So constituted, that state is able to move forward to the acquisition of knowledge, reach the ideas. In other words, the state of justice is the vehicle by which the individual ascends to the ideas. We're outside the world of the *Phaedrus* now, where the individual climbs up the ladder of beauty to the ideas. We have something more here, a much more complicated situation, not just an individual but a whole society — the workers and the rulers — rising. The analogy of the army is relevant here. An army has its general and, of course, the poor private. But there is a moment, the moment of victory, when they are all — private and general alike — exultant, when they are all carried up, as one, together.

The state exists, therefore, for knowledge. Therefore philosophers must be kings, and kings must be philosophers. That, I suppose, is the one phrase of Plato everyone knows. Was it known in the Middle Ages? Dante ends his *Monarchia* on that note. Plato thought it possible to have such a state; history has shown that perhaps it is not possible. But the conditions he sets for it have had more success in history than the state itself. For example: if this is the end for which the state exists, then the rulers must see to it that whatever is necessary for the attainment of that end is done. And it is man's duty to do what the rulers command him to do along that line. In other words, to use that phrase which so many despise: the end justifies the means. Doesn't the end always justify the means? Take the war against Germany. Humanity is turned upside down, thousands die, cities are destroyed. How do we justify that? There is an end that justifies it. Or, if the maintenance of peace at any cost is the end, then you can justify cowardice. What may horrify us is a combination of two things. First: take an end, any end, and fix it as final; then take any means and call them necessary. For example: I have to steal in order to give alms. What's wrong with that? Well, in the first place, giving alms is not an absolute end, and, moreover, there are other means, besides stealing, to get money for alms. The two have no necessary connection in this case. The ends and means are one and the same thing, a block, if the means are necessary for the attainment of the end. The means are always justified by the end, if the end is acceptable to us.

In Plato, the end is fixed; there is nothing higher. And he provides certain norms. In the upper classes, marriage doesn't exist. Of course, generation has to go on, but the process is regulated in such a way that the children won't know who their parents are. The other class can marry and have families. Why? To maintain where it is most needed the sense of the public good. When you have a family, you develop a sense of private good. This probably led to the institution of the monastic orders, with their vows, including celibacy. The necessities of the common good demand the abolition of the family.

How about property? You must have heard it said that Plato was the first communist. He tells us: there must be in the first two classes no private property; the other class can have property — for reasons given already. St. Thomas both approves and condemns this. If we were good enough, yes, we should and could do it. When you have an elect group, such as the Dominican Order, or the Franciscan Order, of any of the other great orders, then you can have communism. For communism is a very aristocratic regime. It is only possible for those who are really concerned for the common good and not for their own.

There is more to this question. Can you lie, cheat, deceive in the state we've described? Yes. When the philosophers who are the rulers feel that something must be concealed for the common good, then deception is justified. Or you can sum it up in another way. Plato did not have the phrase *raison d'ètat*, but surely he had the idea. *Raison d'etat* refers to a transgression of norms that apply to the individual human being — a transgression that is justified by the higher interest of the state. Thou shalt not kill, the Bible says; but the state says that under certain conditions you must kill. Eventually you realize that everything that happens in a state involves, explicitly or implicitly, *raison d'ètat*, the violation of norms that apply to the individual, when doing so is for the common good.

Some may wonder if this argument applies to Plato's banishing of the poets. He doesn't really banish them. He says some very harsh things about them in the *Republic*; but if they write the proper kind of hymns, they can stay. The condemnation is not a political one but a philosophical one. Poets are the imitators of a copy. It is bad enough to be imitators of reality, but poets are imitators of a copy. They copy copies of the ideas. The ideas reflect themselves in nature, nature being a copy of the ideas, and the poet depicts nature. That puts the poet in a pretty low position. But in the *Phaedrus*, the poet is put on the same level as the lover. He goes to the highest ideas, with or without the help of reason. And that's exactly what Dante claims for himself. Out of the two, he makes one: love creates, produces poetry. The two are one. In the *Republic*, even the poets exult when the state, in harmony, and moved by justice, rises to the ideas or makes it possible for its members to achieve their natural goal. Even the poor devils in the army share in the collective ecstasy. There is a common joy; they don't all get to know the same thing, but there is participation in the common joy.

Plato was writing all this with the example of Athens before him. For Athens, the lowest had gained the top. There was also the question of slavery, challenged by the Sophists but defended by Aristotle. Still, Plato maintains his philosophical position: the individual must give way to the higher end of the state.

There is, however, a larger unit beyond the state: the universe. Throughout, there is an order, from the lowest elements up to the highest ideas. There is order in the state and in the universe too. The state is only a link in the chain of order of the universe, in this order from the stone to the highest idea. And that means, there is something in this huge mass that regulates it —

regulates the motion of the body, makes one act in a certain fashion: the soul. The universe too has a soul. Here you meet what was first suggested by the Pythagoreans, the *anima mundi*, the soul of the universe. This *anima mundi* is taken up and developed by the Neo-Platonists, and is eventually utilized by the Christians to explain the trinity — what the Platonists supposedly first flashed before the mind. You have a father, son, and holy ghost. Clement of Alexandria and all the others said frankly that Plato, so many years before Christ, had seen clearly into the trinity; and they quoted the second epistle and the sixth epistle and took parts from the dialogues here and there to trace and make up the trinity. When you come to the twelfth century you have a whole group of thinkers — Abelard, and most of the school at Chartres — who get into trouble because they say that the Holy Spirit is the *Anima Mundi*. Of course, they never said it so bluntly in the second century A.D., but now it had become impossible to say it at all.

Of course, it was not from Clement, not from Plato, that those who follow — St. Augustine and the rest — got this conception. It came to them from the Neo-Platonists, who elaborated this idea. Neo-Platonism gave much to the Christians, and the Christians gave much to it, in return. The whole system of the Neo-Platonists is built upon the Trinity. There is the highest good, which is the Father; the *Logos*, which is the Son; and the *anima mundi* which is the third person of the Trinity, the Holy Spirit.

Through the concept of the state that Plato gives us in the *Republic*, we have a new approach to the ideas, a new relation between the hyper-uranium and the world of man. We see philosophy creating again, coming again to a recognition of God. The Sophists, the Democriteans had wiped out the gods. According to Democritus, nothing could be immortal except the atoms. The gods themselves were made up of atoms. The Sophists destroyed the gods in the most effective way, by explaining them away: they were reduced to natural forces. Some wise legislator made them up, as beings that could force people to be good in their private conduct as well as out where the law can get at them. θέος όέος was their pun. God is generated by fear. Worst of all was the huemeristic way of explaining the gods as men of the past who were deified because of our great admiration for certain qualities in them.

---

1. Is the doctrine of innate ideas the one that Plato held?

It is one of the many forms of innate ideas repudiated by Aristotle, brought back into circulation again by St. Augustine and others, and then finally thrown out completely for the Church by St. Thomas. You hear so much about what the philosophers did in the eighteenth century. It is very amusing. You pick up a modern text book on the history of philosophy and you find high praise given to those men of the eighteenth century for their great discovery, and then the author quotes in Latin (for some of those philosophers did know Latin): *Nihil in intellectu quod prius non fuerit in sensibus* — there is nothing in the intellect which has not previously been in the senses. (Leibnitz will add: *praeter ipse intellectus*.) But it wasn't a discovery of the eighteenth century; St. Thomas said that at least a thousand times. He makes it rather embarrassing, that extreme dependence on the senses. Except for a miracle — anything can happen miraculously — short of a miracle, nothing gets into your mind except through your senses. To many people this was very disturbing. Dante too was disturbed by it.

2. Are there any bases in their philosophy — any philosophical reasons — why the Greeks never managed to unite themselves?

Nothing in their philosophy, but a great deal in their intellectual make-up: extreme individualism. This comes up again even in our own times, particularly with Italy. It is the same thing with the Italians. Unification for extreme individualists like the Italians is an almost hopeless task. You unify and then break up. Of course, in the case of Italy, the elements are so far apart historically that any kind of unity, of real unity on a national level, is practically impossible. The Greeks were the same way. Their only unity, the only thing that really held them together, was their love of Homer.

3. But what about the idea of the state that you find in Plato?

Oh, the idea is there. So, in Italy, from the ninth century on, the Italians talk about the barbarians and the non-barbarians. The Italians are the non-barbarians and the barbarians are everybody else. But it stays there, doesn't move on. Or you might say: the Greeks, like the Italians, exhausted themselves in the proclamation of the idea, until they got to feel that the extolment of the act and the performance of the act were the same thing. It is what must be called the rhetorical frame of mind. You keep proclaiming a thing and eventually you begin to think that you have actualized it.

14. THE ARISTOTELIAN SOLUTION: POTENCY INTO ACT

One can do very little justice to what is a recurring act of the history of mankind: the destruction and resurrection of religion — for example, the war that goes on between the men of the period of the enlightenment and the romantics, or what happened in the Greek world. We have very little material to guide us in pre-Homeric Greece, when back of everything, back of that particular fountain, back of that brook, or that tree or that mountain, there was a power. Those early Greeks thought of this power not as a whole — not yet — but as an individual power, that moved that particular thing. We see it described most beautifully in the poets.

That power appeared to them at the same time (and this is very important) as something to be feared and revered. We know what the Epicureans had said about it: man's fear had generated the gods; their pun in connection with it. But there is also a sense of holiness in their attitude. Man doesn't want to be the artifex of his own existence and destiny; he is afraid to take responsibility, he wants a higher power to depend on. And this sentiment is operative even where we don't see it. Man put this *daemon*, this power, not only in back of the brook, the fountain, etc., but also in himself. In man this lasts as the individual independence of reason, of rationality. The one who we remember most in this connection, who followed the voice of this power in him, the voice of the *daemon*, contrary to public opinion, is, of course, Socrates.

As man liberated, detached himself from this

world of *daemons*, and acquired personality, he liberated his surroundings too, the things of the outer world. There is not a particular power for this fountain, not for this river that flows from the mountain; there is not a particular *daemon* for this mountain, or a *daemon* of the sea that surrounds this continent, and so on. What happens as the process continues is that man creates a personality for himself and for the deities. Instead of the obscure powers back of individual things, you now have Jupiter for the sky, Neptune for the sea, Venus for love, and so on. It's the world of Homer, the world of the *Odyssey* and the *Iliad*. Those strong individuals, those gods of Homer are big men. It's the most anthropomorphic religion ever conceived. Not only were they more powerful than men, but much more vicious and immoral. It was a religious conception that could not last very long among people like the Greeks. Religion, for them, was always the result of, was always controlled by, their need for an absolute.

The trouble with the Homeric gods is they have no independent power, they can't so much as budge except as fate, *heimarmene*, directs them. What's more, they have no real power because they are a multiplicity, and the power of one checks the power of another. The power of an absolute is absent in them. They are represented as controlling, or disturbing, our lives, disturbing our morals, and fighting among themselves. What they do immorally, of course, you all know. And they have a power to disturb mankind. That's how they appear in Homer.

Among lovers of poetry, this provoked a feeling of disgust, as in Plato. Throw them in the wastepaper basket. It leads the philosophical mind to a complete condemnation of poetry, which is looked upon as a source of immorality. As a result, there immediately arises something that has been a shroud over the whole history of literary culture — the allegorical interpretation of poetry. To save the gods in Homer one must say: he didn't really mean this when he represented such and such. All that fighting and deceiving, those acts of adultery, they're all really representations of natural phenomena, and so on. From this first defense of poetry down to the sixteenth century and afterward, literature is weighed down by that esthetic criterion: that you must be able to read into poetry several senses, two or three or four senses. Torquato Tasso was still writing that way, and that's pretty late. Dante, of course, wrote that way too. We know how, for centuries, great poetry was allegorically defended; we know the great works of the Neo-Platonists to save poetry. The great problem is that, after the first attacks comes the systematic practice of the defense of poetry. It begins with allegorical interpretation, but then, like all things, it proceeds for its own sake. And it lasts from about 400 B.C., to the sixteenth century — a couple of millennia.

This dreary situation of the Homeric gods, this helplessness among themselves, their cruel dominion (for that's what it was) over men, perhaps deserves a little more respect than we have given it. That there might be something else in it is shown by the way they are treated by the Greek tragedians. When your read Aeschylus — *Agamemnon* or the *Choephori* or the *Prometheus* — you don't get the feeling that they are saying: look at those gods, what skunks and scoundrels they are! Agamemnon has to sacrifice his daughter. Orestes has to kill his mother. Why? Because one of those gods tells him to, and he has to do this terrible thing. Or Prometheus: here is a god who is oppressed by another god for having done things beneficial for mankind. But where is the condemnation? Some harsh words are said; but at the same time

you realize that Aeschylus has not make up his mind
about how to treat these gods. He is perhaps aware of an
antinomy, a difficulty that can't be solved. Sophocles
takes the side of the gods — if the gods say so, it must be
right. The next one, Euripides, takes man's side. As you
look at these tragedians and the problems they depict,
you realize that their significance is not only for that
moment but persists for the entire history of religion
and the relation of that to man. Against the harshness of
the philosophers, the tragedians show a more profound
thinking about the gods.

The first philosopher who raises these charges
against the gods is Xenophon. They are not really
supreme beings; they can't do anything, they can't get
real immortality except through *ambrosia*. But then,
ambrosia — the nectar of the gods — should be the real
god. Without it, the gods are not immortal, he chastises.
His words have been quoted and have been repeated
perhaps a hundred thousand times in the history of
human culture. If the oxen had arms to draw, he explains, we would have a nice set of deities, all of them like
oxen. They are adulterous and they fight among themselves. Obviously these gods of Homer have got to be
overthrown because they do not correspond to the
conception of the true deity. The criticism goes on and
culminates in the period of the Sophists, which we call
the enlightenment, properly, where the biggest attack
against these gods, served to explain them away. The
explanation, of course, that the Sophists gave is something that people later on have always somehow managed to discover as their own. How often have people
palmed off as theirs something they got, directly or
indirectly from the *Critias*? I was reading some proofs on
Machiavelli recently, with a friend, who was saying that
Machiavelli had taken quite a step forward with his

account of the nature of religion as something necessary
to control mankind in the secrecy of their lives. I had to
pull down my fragments to show him that what Machiavelli
was saying, Critias had said two thousand years before.
There are others like Brunetière who came out with a
staunch defense of Catholicism, of Christianity. It may
be all false, he said, but still it makes people behave, it
keeps them in order. The law can control many things,
but where the law can't see, there must be something else
present to exert control; and God, for those who hold to
the belief, is always present. That's exactly what the
Sophists said. Some wise statesman found a way to use
the power, directing natural phenomena, like thunder,
earthquakes, etc; making of them tools of invisible
deities, unseen by us, but which at all times can see us.

Olympus had to go. Did it go? It went, as far as the
Sophists were concerned; and a hundred years later
Huemerous elaborated the theory that the gods resulted
from the deification of great men who were called
deities by the people as a sign of gratitude and admiration. But did they succeed in explaining them away?
Obviously not, because the great mass of people continued to hold to it; and even the great philosophers, even
the monotheistic philosophers, had to make conces-
sions, had to condescend. They had to force the issue
and utilize those gods as links in their system. Why?
Because Greek civilization is made up not only of philosophy, but of art too. How could you reject the gods
with Greek art before you — the sculpture of Phidias,
Myron, Polycletus, Praxiteles, and so much else? Having
seen the Mercury of Praxiteles, you feel it is almost
blasphemous to say that he is there only because the
Greeks cheated and had to have a deity for cheating, and
so they have Mercury. Art is a great force, perhaps a
greater force than anything else. But fortunately, or

perhaps unfortunately, the dethronement of the gods of Olympus was the occasion for a development along another line. If you want an absolute, you have to look for something else, something other than a magnified man. It is Xenophanes, again, who leads the way. He is the first real monotheist in the Greek world. Though his resources are poor, his vision of God is very much like that of St. Augustine in his early days, when he was still a materialist: an entirely materialistic concept. God is a great sponge; he wants to touch it, communicate with it. It was Plato who liberated St. Augustine from that crude conception.

St. Augustine paid great homage to the Platonists for liberating him and preparing him for the Christian conception of God. Eventually he had to tone down his praise. The liberation, the rejection of the Olympus of Homer, brings about a crude form of pantheism as the first response. Many people today call themselves religious but reject Christianity and the scriptures of the Old Testament — like my dear old friend, Giovanni Gentile, who begins a chapter in one of his books with the words: "the fool has said in his heart, there is not God"; and yet his books are on the index because he says that Christianity has been *sufgehoben*, has been superated by the new philosophy. Gentile's religion was idealistic pantheism, Croce's too. Spinoza's is materialistic pantheism. God realizes himself in the world and in man.

Here, then, is the first appearance of pantheism. It did not stop there. The one God, the ἑν καί παν of Xenophanes, by which he was able to dethrone all the deities of Olympus, had to be made more acceptable; with the help of the Pythagorians, a forward step was taken. What counts, they said, is not the one mass, but the laws that operate in it, the numbers in back of things, and particularly the order that comes out from the

numbers. God is order. Here below there is no order
(take the weather, for example, and other phenomena);
but there is a place where there is no delay, where
nothing untoward happens: the quintessence, the fifth
essence of the Pythagoreans, the ether, as Aristotle calls
it. It is the realm of the celestial bodies: the planets, the
sun and the fixed stars. The two worlds of Plato come to
mind; but what counts in this fifth essence is that there
is a complete compliance, without exception, to laws.
After 365 days, the sun returns to the same place; after
so many days the moon completes its cycle west to east.
You know how clever the Pythagoreans were with their
astronomy. And where is God? God is the sky; not the
matter, but the *order* in the sky, the root of all things that
happen below. The sources of all these motions, say the
Pythagoreans, is up in the sky. Dante adheres to this also.

   This new Olympus proves very influential. Unfortunately at this moment the theory of the two motions is
introduced, which Aristotle accepts in large part. You
see them every day. The sun rises in the east and moves
west. On the other hand, when you look at the moon two
of three nights in succession, you see it moving from east
to west but also, with each successive night, from west to
east, completing that cycle in twenty-eight or twenty-
nine days. That's the origin of the month. The sun moves
that same way. It creeps along from day to day, all the
way around in 365 days. There is a poem by Giacomo
Leopardi about the little shepherd in Asia Minor who
watches the sun rise in a certain constellation, the
constellation that is there on the horizon just before
dawn, and a month later sees it rise in a different
constellation. In other words, he noticed the revolution
of the sun from west to east. Shepherds and hunters,
people who get up early are aware of this motion of the
sun. The planets were observed to move in a similar way,

the fixed stars too (but that was long after Aristotle).

These are the two motions. From the east, from Syria, unfortunately, comes the practice of astrology, and the two are fused. From now on you have the belief that a divinity guides our lives, regulates life, plants and animals — controls all things — not only the motions of the waters, but our own existence. The gods now are the skies, or the movers of the skies. From the Pythagoreans and from the East we now get that strange, untenable and yet immortal belief in astrology. From now on, even those imbued with a sense of Christianity, who know that when you draw up a horoscope you are practically denying free-will — even those try to patch the two together. Dante himself comes very close to doing this.

The answer is: yes, these stars *do* control human life, as much as they control everything else here below; but they control the matter only. The spirit that proceeds from God has dominion over itself. Here is a man, who is by nature a brawler, because he is under the influence of the planet Mars; but he has a free will and can overcome that influence. Virtue triumphs by conquering the impulses that come to us from the sky. How many legends there are of women sanctified or not sanctified, but exalted because, although they were given over to an almost irresistible influence, succeeded, by their own free will, in crushing the demon in them. It is almost impossible to resist the impulses that come down from Venus, but free will can triumph over them no matter how strong they are.

The new deity is a deity of law that operates in the heavens and determines things here below. Beyond that, we have the process that begins with Anaxagoras and lasts with the Panlogists, with the idealistic Pantheists. There is this mind, and it is a mind that produces, creates, and shapes, and yet is *outside*. The criticism of

Aristotle is that Anaxogoras never used this *nous* of his much; he had it, but he let it drop. It was used by later men who looked at deity as being the creator of order, not the creator absolutely. For the concept of God creating everything, we must go to the Jews. The Greeks could never accept, or conceive, or swallow the notion of a God that creates matter. Matter is there; the demiurge doesn't create it, he just shapes it. Where does one look for a God that creates in the Old Testament phrase: *Deus creavit caelum et terram?*

This God represents order or is the creator of order. We have seen it in Plato as the idea of the good, the power of the secret deity spread throughout the universe, namely the *anima mundi* that enables everything to direct itself toward God. The polarization of man toward God is nothing else than religion, and a religious basis for ethics. We are now approaching a century where you could not conceive of an ethical system without a religious basis. Even today, there are many people who believe that ethics, if there is to be any ethics, must rest on a religious foundation. There were those, among the Greeks, who didn't accept this. For the Epicureans, the gods may be there, but they are not concerned about us. If we have an ethics, it is only by human consent.

This is as far as Plato goes. One step more and this *anima mundi*, this polarization of the entire universe toward God, is transformed by Aristotle. Of course, Aristotle, like everyone else, tries to answer that eternal question raised by Greek philosophy: what is the abiding thing, the οὐσία that is the background or basis against which or on which all things move and change? The Eleatics, Parmenides, we saw, had a rigid conception of being that completely ignored the world of change: genesis. No attempt was made to reconcile genesis with being. Genesis is an illusion; nature is that which is not. That was one view. The other view was that of Heraclitus: the one thing that is real is change, motion. You must look for reality in the abiding laws of change. Aristotle fuses these two views. The abiding thing is that something which from a *potential* status acquires an *actual* status. Everything, individual things, the whole universe, is constantly passing from potency to act. The universe is a ladder in which this passage from potency to actuality is visible. One rung is the potentiality for the actuality of the rung above; which, in turn, is potential as it looks up, actual as it looks below, and so on, up the rungs of the ladder, until at last you reach a point where there is no more potentiality, only actuality. The plant, which is in potency an animal, is actualized in the animal; the animal or beast in turn is potentially a human being. The plant is the actuality of what organic compounds are potentially; and the organic compound is the actuality of compounds not organic; and those are the actuality of something not compounded: elements. And elements are the actualization of primal matter, which has no form. You find this primal matter, matter not formed, in Dante and many other books. In the Old Testament, God created *terra* from primal matter.

Primal matter has no form. We can't understand it; it isn't intelligible to us because intelligibility depends on form. Primal matter, or pure potentiality, is actualized in the elements, and these elements are actualized in compounds, which, in turn are potentially what the next higher rung is actually; and so on, until you reach a point where there is no longer a way to proceed beyond, where there is no longer anything potential, and you have pure act. And that pure act is God.

As human beings, we are always potentially intelligent, but our intelligence is actualized by examining external reality. That's how we understand. We have the capacity, the potentiality, but it becomes actuality only as we communicate with the reality of external nature. The God of Aristotle cannot possible debase himself to that level. He does not think of something external. What he thinks about is *νόησς νοήσεως* — the thought of thought, thought thinking itself. We wouldn't get very far if we thought about ourselves only. The Christians took up this magnificent concept: God thinks himself, and his thinking is the reality of things as they are. We understand things as they are, but things are what they are because God thinks them. God's thought is the origin of all thought.

We have reached the God of Aristotle, the Mover that moves, himself not moved, as well as Thought thinking itself. These two — the mover that thinks himself — now come together. God does not create matter; he creates motion in all things, every variety of motion — quantitative motion, qualitative motion, and, above all, substantive motion, which is the passage from life to death.

15. THE RECEPTION OF ARISTOTLE IN THE THIRTEENTH CENTURY

The importance of Aristotle in the thirteenth century, the century in which Dante was born, cannot be stressed too much. European culture was remade by Aristotle in all its spheres: ethics, politics, metaphysics. Everything was transformed, not in details merely, but radically. He gave a new language to the culture of Europe. To this day, the vocabulary of European culture shows the stamp of Aristotle. The French, Germans, Italians, English have all adopted that language. Whether you take one group, the Germanic, or the other, the Romanic, you find there the imprint of Aristotle's thought. We adopted his political, metaphysical, and ethical terminology; we speak of form and matter, finality, and the rest. Those who opposed Aristotle, who were antagonistic to his views — Galileo, Descartes, Spinoza — were still carried away by his language. It is only recently that translators of Aristotle have begun to use a language which is completely incomprehensible to everyone but themselves, repudiating seven centuries of culture, one that alone enables us to understand Aristotle — for it is only as he comes to us through that culture that he is intelligible to us.

Before the thirteenth century, Aristotle was known as the logician, as the man who had given the rules for constructing sentences, prepositions (judgments, as they called them) and for building up syllogisms. In the schools you studied the *Categories*, and the *De Interpretatione*, which shows the construction of a judgment; and résumés of the doctrine of syllogistic reason-

ing coming down to the Middle Ages from the work
Boethius had done on Aristotle. He was known as the
logician, the logical master; not the master, as Dante
calls him, of all those who know — the universal master.
But by the end of the twelfth century, the rest of
Aristotle's logical work was needed. The *Organon* came
first (frequently mispronounced as orgànum). Bacon's
Novum Organum could be named the *novum* because you
had an old one. The *Organum* is nothing more than an
instrument, a tool for scientific investigation. In it,
Aristotle provides mankind with a great gift: a complete
system of logic. Many have attempted to modify it,
oppose it, reject it; but it has continued to do service for
2000 odd years.

Until this point, therefore, there was the work on
Catagories and the *De Interpretatione,* and also the famous introduction to the *Categories* of Aristotle by
Porphory. It was that introduction that unchained the
great war in the Middle Ages (and later in the modern
world), the conflict between the nominalists and the
realists. As thinking matured in the twelfth century, it
was felt that much more had to be known about logic —
science as they knew it had obvious gaps in it. And so
those other works had to be translated. With the realization of the need, in a flash, everything was translated —
the *Ethics,* the *Politics,* the *History of Animals,* the *Aesthet-
ics* or *Poetics.* There was not a thing that wasn't known of
Aristotle by the year 1270. Some works had come down
by very devious ways, some from translations from the
Arabic, which in turn were translations from the Syriac,
which, in turn, were translations from the Greek. From
the Arabic, these passed into Latin, into vulgar Latin;
and then, finally, through the help of the Dominican
order, that had kept great scholars in Greece expressly
for the purpose of studying Greek, all of Aristotle came

forth — and when I say *all*, I mean all. You hear from time to time that the *Poetics* wasn't translated at that time; it was, and in its fullness. These works were not simply translated, but became also the subject matter of instruction, and, as such, shaped a way of life.

Of course, with the *Physics* and *Metaphysics*, trouble appeared. Here is a man who says lots of things that are closer to Christianity than what Plato says; but there are certain things he says that cannot be accepted by Christianity. One of these is the complete rejection of the doctrine of creation. For Aristotle, there is no creation. Things have been so forever. Eventually this doctrine of Aristotle was tuned down, but so great was the power of this man that many great Christian thinkers said — and St. Thomas was one of them — that you cannot prove by reason the doctrine of creation; faith compels us to accept it. Because this and other doctrines of Aristotle couldn't be accepted by the Church, the teaching of Aristotle was suspended, through the voice of Paris, until the unacceptable parts of his writings were corrected or rejected. It was decided to correct him.

Committees — as they say today — were appointed. The work dragged on. The Dominicans and the Franciscans handled the matter with a certain amount of tolerance. The fact was that before the middle of the thirteenth century, Aristotle had gained control of higher education. The Church relied upon his wisdom: St. Bonaventure the Franciscan; St. Thomas, a Dominican; Egidius Romanus, an Augustinian. It is well known that the thirteenth century is distinguished not only because of the return of Aristotle, but also because there were groups like the religious orders who were interested in the reform of education, moral education as well as religious education; who encouraged scholarship as well as the administration of religious instruction on the part of the regular rather than the secular clergy. In other words, one of the most important events in the history of the Church was the formation or re-formation of the mendicant orders: the Dominicans, the Franciscans, the Carmelites, the Augustinians. The supreme importance of all this was that the great orders left the monasteries — they weren't satisfied with copying manuscripts, studying in their cells — and came out into the open, into the universities, into private homes and families, everywhere. Dante reminds us that in his own time, the Dominicans of Santa Maria Novella were educating the uneducated, the ordinary people; and in Santa Croce things were being discussed by preachers of the Franciscan order.

This great exodus of the monastic orders into the world is especially interesting in the role they took as educators. They became teachers of Aristotle. The Dominicans encountered the greatest opposition, not because they repudiated anything fundamental to Christian faith, but because they had a different interest. They leaned too heavily upon the non-Christian Averroists. St. Thomas himself was accused and almost condemned for leaning too far in that direction. They were opposed either because of that or because they should not have given up so much of St. Augustine, as they seemed to have done in adopting Aristotle. The split was by Orders; and the champions were, on one side, the Order of St. Francis, and on the other side the Order of St. Domenic.

Here then is a fresh body of educators, with a fresh body of science: the teachings of Aristotle. Eventually, one is bound to ask: why was the transformation so radical? One or two things are worth mentioning at this point: the first is the big change that took place in the sphere of psychology. Until now it had been taught that the intellect was on two planes. Perception led us to one kind of intelligence, knowledge of things that comes through the senses; the other intelligence, on a higher plane, required direct information from a higher source, not from the senses but from a divine source. More important still was the issue concerning the doctrine by which the process of understanding was explained. On the one side you had the Aristotelian doctrine of *abstraction* and on the other the Augustinian doctrine of *illumination*. The doctrine of abstraction is briefly summarized in that often repeated teaching of St. Thomas, for which he is rarely given credit by those who quote it: there is nothing in the intellect that was not previously in the senses. You don't *understand* unless you *see* first. If you kill sense perception, you kill knowledge. You start with sense perception and proceed by a series of abstractions, stripping away a certain number of things, until finally the process of stripping and abstraction reaches a point where light comes, not from the outside, but from a faculty of the mind, the active intellect, which strips away all materiality and releases the notion from the possible intellect.

Dante wavers in this matter. Some people consider him or say he was an Aristotelian; but, of course, he was never really a philosopher. He was a dilettante obviously, and took what material he wanted wherever he found it. At the end of the *Purgatorio* he gives us the complete doctrine of abstraction. Yet, elsewhere you find that he apparently does not give up that beautiful doctrine of St. Augustine: that, at a certain moment, we surely don't see God, but realize that all intellectual activity is the result of a light that comes, not from any faculty of our mind, but from God.

This Aristotelianizing lasts a long time. After the development of moderate Aristotelianism at Paris comes the movement terminism or nominalism from England, which claims to be a more authoritative and more orthodox interpretation of Aristotle than that of St. Thomas. The nominalism at Paris was perhaps of no great importance in philosophy: it had a destructive effect on ethics, but it gave those men the opportunity for engaging in scientific work in metaphysics and physics that started the wheels of scientific investigation rolling at a new pace and in an entirely different direction. This goes on until those rather mediocre masters of the Renaissance. The Greeks who had come in before and after the fall of Constantinople; and the Italians, engaged in a fruitless war about who was greater, Aristotle or Plato, caused almost as much bad blood as the Reformation itself, in its struggles against Catholicism. Aristotle was, in turn, dethroned and re-enthroned, dethroned again, and so on, until a certain moment when a Jew, a Frenchman and an Italian — Spinoza, Descartes, and Galileo — thought they could dethrone him once and for all. They succeeded, by showing what the Greeks themselves had shown before them, that the physics of Aristotle had great holes in it. Because the Physics had holes in it, they thought they could dethrone Aristotle in everything else. But Aristotle remains the master in metaphysics, in ethics, and, if you will, in politics. There is perhaps no one book today so significant, so powerfully thought out as the Politics of Aristotle. The fight still goes on in a somewhat childish way between those who call themselves Platonists and Aristotelians.

In all of this, St. Augustine could not be repudiated. Later thinkers couldn't accept the doctrine of *gratia irresistibilis*; they didn't like the idea that God sends the light to Peter, an irresistible light, and doesn't send it to Judas. Of course, they didn't dare make changes and never have changed those terms. The same thing in ethics. For St. Augustine, for one to have virtue, real virtue, he has to have grace; the idea of having virtue without grace is impossible. You can't begin to do anything virtuously, you can't even begin to *will* to do so without direct grace. That again is a very hard doctrine, just as hard as the one that says that you cannot have a just state because, by its very nature, by the very conditions that have brought it about, the state is an immoral institution, potentially or actually; tolerated only for the little good it does do. What do the critics do with this doctrine? Well, they do what so many of the commentators on his political theories have done: they take the arguments of his opponents and they pass them on to St. Augustine — I don't know exactly for what motive, whether malice or fraud or what. Even St. Thomas does it. So perhaps they really didn't see what St. Augustine was after.

The doctrine that St. Thomas teaches is, of course, that of Aristotle. He does bring in original sin in the beginning, but he never works it out; he never once talks about the state as if the men engaged in building it were operating always under the handicap of original sin. Reason does function properly; when it's not disturbed, reason becomes right reason. When it is that, it can dictate the proper course of conduct. Ordinarily, however, reason is not right reason. It is attacked by passions in one way or another. Even if reason does dictate what it should, the passions interfere with the capacity to follow its dictates. But if you follow the conclusions reason reaches in its right state, you get conduct that is as right and ethical as it can be. Back of it is the doctrine of habituation. You have to do these things not with difficulty but *habitually* and with pleasure. Take a child trying to walk, or take dancing; you know how painful it is at first, what an awful job it is to move, and then finally a moment comes when you do everything gracefully, as if by nature, and then you find pleasure in it. The same thing is true in the ethical world.

Generations and generations of men for centuries have believed that if you take a child at a certain age, when he is still young, and teach him and train him, he will eventually learn to do spontaneously things he would otherwise not like to do, and do them habitually and with pleasure, as in dancing. If he is made to perform acts of temperance, for instance, under the direction of a master, those acts of temperance will eventually become, or result in, habits. That is the theory of habit that is the basis of this ethical system.

Of course, to speak of it from a theological point of view means to bring in Grace. But for the time, a satisfactory theory of ethics is possible without reference to Grace — admitting, of course, that no act can really be called virtuous unless there is Grace.

Dante gradually comes to grasp St. Augustine, particularly in the *Paradiso*. He comes to that point of view where you have a moral condition, a moral condition that aims at joining God to man, that repudiates as evil any goal or act which you engage in without taking into consideration its relation to the final goal, which is God. Therefore, no matter how brave, how noble your action may be, whether it be an act of courage or charity, if you do it without relating it to God, instead of being a virtue it becomes a vice. How fine of us to be so chaste, how wonderful I am, because I'm chaste, says the nun. St. Augustine answers: you're worse than the worst prostitute. Why? Because you suffer from pride which is the worst of sins. You ascribe to yourself what should be ascribed to God.

St. Augustine calls this striving toward ends,

without relating them to God, *cupiditas*. The opposite —
striving toward God in everything you do, whether it be
eating, traveling, or anything else, doing it always in the
light of the connection it has with God — is called *caritas*.
The good man acts charitably, always striving toward
God. The moment he deflects from *caritas* and thinks of
himself not in relation to God, *cupiditas* begins, he
deflects more and more, until he is aiming almost in the
opposite direction. He may have moved 180 degrees in
the opposite direction, but not quite, because in all
Christian teaching, in Dante and the whole Church, you
cannot have absolute evil. What happens in the configu-
ration of Hell, as Dante presents it; what he does accords
with the ordinary teachings. What would happen if evil
could be made the absolute? What would happen if the
line of *cupiditas* could be brought all the way around?
Existence is reduced to zero, in the doctrine of privation. Dante articulates this in the construction of Hell.
He maps it as a cone, but a cone that doesn't come to a
point. In other words, even at the very bottom of Hell,
where we find Brutus, Judas and Cassius — a new trinity
of the diabolical principle — even there, evil is not
absolute. At a certain point, the cone is truncated and
becomes a cylinder.

The first thing we find of Aristotle in *The Divine
Comedy* and in Dante's other works is the *Logic*. That is
the one thing Aristotle finished, the work that for a long
time was not challenged, or, if challenged, never effectively. What he wants to do in making affirmations in the
process of knowledge is to find some way to judge a
proposition that might not be dependent upon the
content of it. That's what mathematics does. Two and
two are four; it doesn't matter whether the two are pears,
or oranges or what have you. Abstract from individual-
ized things and construct principles that still work no

matter what you make A or B or C stand for. There is
predication; there is equality; there is such a thing as
equation; and there is similarity.

What is predication? Fido is a dog; the human
species is part of the animal genus. In other words, the
truth of the particular is in its subsumption to the
universal. The particular may be an individual or a
species in relation to a genus, or a genus which is a
species in relation to a higher genus. That is predication.
How do we proceed in order to be sure that our predication is sound? I say, man is mortal; in the big sphere of
mortality, man is subordinated to it, as a particular to a
universal. The matter is solved by finding the so-called
middle term — the hunt for the middle term, as it was
called — something operative which you can be sure will
place subject and predicate in proper relation. In this
case, man is mortal. The middle term you need is
corporeality. Then you can say: all corporeal things are
perishable, man is a corporeal thing, therefore man is
mortal. Through the middle term you have proved the
statement you set out to prove. Of course, you may
challenge the middle term; you might say: not all corporeal things are perishable. In that case, you have to hunt
for a new middle term, construct a new series, and
another, and so on — but not to infinity.

In Aristotle, in the thirteenth century, in this
whole sphere, the one thing that must be taken as dogma
is that in none of the causes — whether the material
cause, or the formal cause, or the efficient cause, or the
final cause — in no causal series can you go to infinity.
There must be an end. But how are you going to prove
the ultimate statement reached in the process of
syllogizing? You cannot. There are two things you have
to say. In your hunt for the αμεσον, you have reached the
immediate. Of that there is no longer any knowledge

possible, but we have a special faculty for apprehending
it. This goes back to Plato and distinguishes two parts in
the intellectual faculty, the *diámoéá* and the νόημα, the
diagnostic and the *noetic*. You have them in English: the
discoursive and the intuitive. In other words, to grasp
ultimate principles, you have to rely on νόησις, intuition. Νόησις is the grasping of principles. And to fortify
your grasp of a principle, you proceed on an inverse
process — that of induction — that leads in a direction
contrary to the one aimed at, to demonstrate something
that you have grasped intuitively. Are there any such
principles? Ordinarily we call them axioms. In logic
there is the crowning axiom, the axiom of axioms, which
applies to all the sciences, whereas each science has its
peculiar axiom. This one is above them all — the principle of contradiction. Euclid built up two propositions
that are contradictory. If one is proved false, the other
may, or *must* be true. This is simple enough in the case
of some propositions. But suppose I say someone is
blind, and someone is not blind; both are true, are they
not? And if I say that everyone is blind and everyone is
not blind, both are false.

There is another approach, a pragmatic one.
Protagoras used it but refused to accept it. Aristotle
wrote two books on the deductive procedure: the *Prior*
and *Posterior Analytics*. The *Posterior Analytics* is a very
important book for the examination of the scientific
approach to knowledge. For individual judgments that
are not *apodeictic* — above doubt — for judgments that are
probable, there was what was the most used of his other
works: the *Topics*, which has to do with the probable
syllogism, what the Middle Ages called the dialectical
syllogism. That word, *dialectical* has more meanings than
the letters in the word. It has one meaning in Plato, in
Aristotle, in vulgar parlance; and now, we have another

(besides the rhetorical meaning). Here *dialectical* is used in the sense of *probable*. The dialectical syllogism is the syllogism of probability. It is the third work of the *Organum*. Aristotle adds a treatise on the way to refute a false syllogism, which is perhaps a continuation of the preceding and it is called σοφιστιχοί έλεγχοι. But in order to have a syllogism, you must be able to construct it right; the science that teaches you that is found in *De Interpretatione*. Still, you cannot construct a judgment unless you have a subject and predicate, substance in relation to objective reality. And so you have the part of the *Organum* — the first part — which discusses the ten categories.

---

1. Isn't there a great difference of opinion between the Franciscans and the Dominicans about free will?

Not a great difference. Of course, the Franciscans are a little more Augustinian, but that wasn't a great issue between them. The issue becomes much greater later, when we come to the Nominalists. The great phases are: St. Augustine, the moderate St. Thomas, and the position of Molinism, which is the opposite of St. Augustine as far as opposition can go. Of course, the Church has taken a position that in a way cuts the Gordian knot. It orders the affirmation that the will is free, that man has free will, and also orders the affirmation that God is omnipotent. The problem is, how do you reconcile the two? The Church is fully aware of the problem. It says: don't reconcile them, just accept them. The See of Peter will tell you what to do.

16. ARISTOTLE'S FORM, MATTER, AND THE DOCTRINE OF PLACES

In the *Paradiso,* Dante tells us the angels say "we are substances." What is a substance? Here is Mr. John Smith. He was once smooth; now he's wrinkled. He was once big, but as he grows old, he gets smaller, he shrinks. But no matter how he changes, he is always Mr. John Smith. A substance, *οὐσία in* Aristotelian language, is just that: the individual thing. Aristotle mentions also a second kind of substances (δεύτερ οὐσία), but let's focus on the individual substance. Here we have John and James and Harry, individual substances; and we classify them as men. But is it the same as classifying books in a bookcase? The big ones here, or those that begin with a certain letter here, or the red ones here and the white ones there? In other words, is there or is there not something common to them all, not originating with your classification, but objectively present? And, secondly, this objective thing, if it operates in man, is it separate or immanent? The possibilities are three.

If it is separate, if that something that makes me a man, and makes this other a man, is separate from me and him, we are in the world of Plato. But if we say: that thing looks like a monkey, and that is some sort of woman, and that is a child of some kind, and I call all of them together by some name, then we are in the world of the Nominalists. Or, the third possibility: there is something objective, like Plato mentions, but it cannot exist separated from the individual in which it operates. It is like light in a mirror; not like the light of the sun above, separate. It is in every mirror that the sun shines on, but only in the mirrors. It can't exist separately. That is the world of Aristotle.

Those are the three possibilities, the three formulas that were fought out with bitterness, which we today give vent to only in more serious matters, like politics. First is the universal, *ante rem*, that is, before the individual Tom, Dick and Harry (the individuals as such). If I were talking to an eighteenth century audience, I would probably use the name of Socrates. Or, to indicate other species, they had special names: Prunella, for horse, another for donkey, one for the dog, and so on. Now, if this universal dog is *ante rem*, you have Plato, and that is called realism. If you say the universals are not *ante rem*, but in re, then you are a moderate realist like St. Thomas and Dante. But if you say that those universals are simply names that come after — *post rem* — then you are a nominalist The great school of Nominalism flourishes in the fourteenth century. There was also a development of Nominalism in the twelfth century, but in the fourteenth century it was well-rounded scientifically, robust and potent. If it had not been for that little book which was so influential down to the thirteenth century, the *Introduction* of Porphory, this question or controversy over the universals (already raised in Boethius) would not have persisted.

You can say the same for all things — men, animals, and so on. I am a substance, and in spite of all that happens to me physically in the course of my life, I remain what I am. And, according to Aristotle, there is a universal in me, but that universal can only be found in me and in others like me. That is the individual substance. But how can we nail technically that substance in a proposition or judgment? Suppose I put this substance in the predicate position, what can I put in the position of the subject? In other words, can I find anything of which a substance can be predicated? No. That's what Aristotle means when he says that a substance is that which can be predicated of no thing, except itself. All we can have is the equation: John is John. Those things which can be predicated, the things that can vary in relation to the substance of which they are predicated are called *accidents*. Aristotle enumerates nine of them, three of which have been of great value to us. Of the remaining six, two have been used, the others have been dropped. Those that have proved valuable are: *quantity* (ποσόν), *quality* (ποιόν), and *relativity* (πρός τι). In other words, the *numerical*, the *qualitative*, which is the internal capacity, and *relation*.

What is relativity?. What is this accident of relativity which changes all the time? It is a predicate that establishes a tie between two substances. Some common correlatives are father and son, sovereign and subject, husband and wife. There is a list of at least five hundred in any ordinary textbook. As a substance, I am what I am; but I am also a husband, I'm also a son. We call these family ties, relations. Why? Because of that initial distinction of Aristotle. So this something is one thing now, but it will change with the vicissitudes of time and become something else. The sovereign of today may be the abject slave of tomorrow.

In addition to these three, you have *position*, and *habit*. Habit of course in one of the three senses, that of *condition* (εχειν), as when you say: habit does not make the monk. There you have *agree*, or *acting*. I am an active person, I do this or that. Then there is the opposite, the passive, which is subjected to another person's action. You can count nine of them. Three, as I said, have been of great use: *quantitas*, or quantity; *qualitas*, and *ad aliquid*, which is *relation* (πρός τι). The central thing, the *quid est*, takes you to the substance. The word is *quidditas*, quiddity — but it has been dropped in all languages except scholastic Latin.

Of course, none of these accidents that are predicated of a substance, is self-subsisting; in order to exist they all demand a substance in the Aristotelian sense of the word. There can be no brother if there is not the man; there can be no sovereign if there is not the man. Here is John Smith. If you put John in the predicate position, all you can say is John is John. But in the Aristotelian context: here is John Smith. Something happens and John Smith is dead. The body is the same, but is he still the same John Smith? He is the ex-John Smith. Externally the body is there. But he is a corpse, a *corpus*, a body without a soul. Or take a tree. It is struck by lightning. The body, the trunk is there, the soul is gone. Same thing with animals.

In Aristotle, that something that makes a thing what it is, that makes of this something that particular man, is called the *form* of the thing The rational soul is the form of man; the sensitive soul is the form of animals; the vegetative soul is the form of the different plants. And all these, as they change in the course of time, as they lose the rational soul, or the sensitive soul, are still beings. They are still real, and therefore must still have a form of some kind, another form: the bodily form, corporeality. (We're working our way toward the four causes.) Here is a substance. If the soul is the form, then the body has that part of the combination that makes up the individual substance: *matter*. Form makes matter what it is; it is also the source of action. That is, all action depends on form, and all potentiality depends on matter. The entire system of Aristotle can be described by saying that it is an attempt to show how the whole world is built up by the interplay of these two: actuality and potentiality.

The seed is potentiality. That little bean, that seed is a tree — potentially, not actually. For the being of anything is not only the actual being it has, but also what being it has potentially. The table of every school boy in the Middle Ages would have at the top, the transcendentals. The trancendentals are *being*. A thing is only insofar as it is *one*; and insofar as a thing *is*, it is *good*. Then there is the true, the *verum*. The Latin words are *Verum, Bonum, Unum, Ens* (they also add *Res* and *Aliquid*). These are the transcendentals, Here is substance, and here are the accidents. And these four transcendentals, therefore — *being*, and *good*, and *true*, and *one* — can be predicated of both substance and accidents, as the basis of the relations of substances and accidents.

Being and the other transcendentals can be predicated of both substance and accidents. The word "accidents" has been used in all the various languages. In the last twenty-five years or so, people have tried or wanted to find new words for it. And so, the poor devil who tries to read one of these histories of philosophy, begins to think that some whole new set of Aristotelian theories have been discovered somewhere in South Dakota.

So, here is a compound of elements which already has form. At a certain moment, in the process of generation, it receives a form and *ipso facto* it is in reality transformed; and this something that developed in the womb is again to be considered matter, this plant organism is again considered matter, and receives a form from its animal generator, and you have passed from plant to animal. This, of course, is the famous recapitulation, which is not anything new. It's very ancient; it is illustrated fully by Dante in the twenty-fifth canto of *Purgatorio*.

Here, then, you have this animal organism, another species, which has absorbed the previous vegeta-

tive form, and the form of the original compound. The
Christians will say (Aristotle says something else) the
form that next comes upon it comes from God, and is,
of course, the rational soul. So that this animal organism, this fetus, has become, in relation to the form that
comes from God, matter. The fetus, having an animal
form, having previously had a plant form, is now a
human being. The form is the rational soul, the matter
is the previous fetus, which actually was a fetus, but
potentially was a human being.

This relation is to be well kept in mind: matter is
the basis of potentiality, and form is the basis of actuality. Is that seed a plant? What you are really asking is,
does it have the matter that can receive the vegetative
form? You can't tell now, but six months from now you
will be able to tell. You will see by the actuality — if there
is a sprouting of leaves, if the tree begins to blossom six
months from now — that it is a plant.

How do we know when the plant has reached its
final form? Well, if it is that vegetative soul, its activities
will correspond to the acts of the vegetative form. If
there is that form, it will be made visible by leaves, and
so on. It's a pragmatic test.

Consider the corpse again. It has a certain form
and a certain matter. If it has a form, it is the tendency
to sink; that is its activity. Therefore, it has as its form
gravitas, which is the tendency to sink. If instead, when
you placed it in water it didn't sink; if it rose when you
placed it on a table, then it would have the form of *levitas*.
In other words, from its various acts you derive the form.
I suppose the idea of a corpse is a little too complicated.
It sinks, and then what happens? Something further, but
it still has a form. There are bones — I don't know what
form they have, whether they sink or not — but supposing they do, they have an act.

Or, take water which is moist and cold; it has its own matter and its own form. You apply heat to it and it becomes air — we call it steam. And that has its own matter and its own form. Well, steam rises, and it is struck by cold (Aristotle's example). What happens? It freezes, becomes ice. Compress this and you have crystals. This may not be true, but it was a favorite thought.

Water. cold and wet, is one element. The others are fire, dry and hot; air, wet and hot; earth, cold and dry. As you change these qualities, you go from one element to another. You can pass in reverse of what we said before — you can pass from the stone or crystal to water. Or take another example: a statue. What is it made of? Statuary marble. What is statuary marble made of? It is made of the element earth. But what is earth made of? What is that something you pass into, going from one of the four elements to another? It is primal matter, matter without form, and therefore capable of being worked on. What is this primal matter? You postulate it because, first of all, you have a logical construction; you pass from the statue, to the stone, to the element earth. We can't go further. The earth is something, but that something is an X, and in there you have primal matter.

Of course it is quite different from the primal matter of Plato, which was space; and quite different from the primal matter of the thirteenth century or Dante, which was just a huge chaotic mass out of which everything else is shaped. In Aristotle, primal matter is simply an energetic moment, that's all — necessary to account for the passing from one element to another. When you pass from one element to another, you pass through primal matter, which has no form. You have here a piece of earth, a dry twig that is dry and cold. You apply heat to it, and the cold becomes hot, and the twig itself becomes fire. When you have taken the cold out of it, it has changed its form. What primal matter simply means is that in this process — which is the very basis of Aristotelian teaching — not only is every individual thing the actualization of a form, but in each case you have something which is actual from one point of view and potential from another. The fetus is actuality to the plant, but potentiality to man. And this double role is true all along the line, except where you reach that point where you have no form — that is, primal matter.

Form has a double role. In any given individual substance, it actualizes itself into something perfect; but it does so with a double power, a double relationship. You have form that is fixed in so far as it is a goal: the form of reason in you will actualize itself in your life, but it operates also as something removable. In the first role, it sees to it that you are what you are; and in the second role, it sees to it that you take or occupy a certain place in that array that extends from primal matter up through the celestial intelligences.

In primal matter, however, and in all matter in the Aristotelian universe, there is an irresistible desire for form: matter desires form. This desire interpenetrates the whole Aristotelian system. Why is there this craving for form? What is actual, looked at from below, becomes potential looked at from above. Why? Because this whole Aristotelian universe is constructed in such a way that there is a God that operates in such a way as to move everything, not by actual contact, but by being desired.

All this is far removed from Dante's universe and the Christian universe generally. God did not create this primal matter of Aristotle, or the forms. These have always been there. Nothing comes into existence that wasn't in existence before, or except as a result of something like it which was in existence before — and so on to infinity. To the question: which comes first, the chicken or the egg, Aristotle's answer would have been: neither. There is no first. Why? Because it is an eternal process.

In this picture, nature is a power and a sum total. For Aristotle, nature is both. Nature in Aristotle acts finalistically. The things and processes of this world have to be looked at from two different points of view: our own and that of nature. What does Aristotle mean by saying that God, or nature, conceives the universe as a whole and keeps it going? In order to be a universe there have to be many things related, linked together, all the links from primal matter up to the angelic intelligences, closely fitted together. Nature aims at the making of the animal kingdom, it aims at the making of the vegetable kingdom and at the making of the elements and at the making of man. In the making of man, man has to be not only a rational being, but also an animal. If he is to be an animal, he has to have arms, legs, and other bodily members; he has to eat a certain kind of food. Therefore, nature will see to it that he has these arms and legs and this food.

The first thing nature aims at is the universe; but to have that, nature has to have these other things. So, if someone asks: why do you have teeth? You answer teleologically, from the point of view of nature: you have to have teeth because you have to be an animal, you have to be an animal because you have to fill a certain post, and you have to fill that certain post because there has to be a universe — you have to occupy a post between the animal without reason and the angel without a body. That's how nature looks at it. Man looks at it in the reverse way — the opposite of teleological. You have teeth because you have a head, and teeth are part of a head, and you have a head because you have the body of an animal, and a head is part of such a body and so on. In other words, it is the very reverse of the other explanation. When we speak of teleology in Aristotle, we have to recall this example and that what he says is the very opposite of what happens in Democritus. If you are going to explain anything — if you are going to tell what teeth are, to resume that example — you are not going to give merely the chemistry, the composition, the elements; you have to begin at the other end and explain the purpose. And that's the origin of the opposition we are all familiar with, between understanding and reason, *Vernunft*, although Aristotle doesn't press the distinction very much.

And so this problem, this appetite in matter for form, still remains. There is nothing in Aristotle, as there had been in Empedocles, like the passing from one species to another. There is nothing Darwinian in this. The species are fixed. But nature, or God, prospecting the universe, putting it in order, has put in matter a desire, and that desire takes different forms, or, rather, differentiates itself according as the forms are different — plant, animal, and the rest — passing from species to species.

Dante will say there is a desire in all things to assimilate, to conform to God; a desire somehow to become similar to God, to conform to God's wishes. Heavy bodies, the element earth, have a form — this earth, this sphere, surrounded by air, with a globe of fire above it, and beyond that the celestial spheres — all of these are material things, all have a desire to rejoin God, to comply with the will of God. And so the act that will comply with the form of a heavy body is to go to the center of the earth. The act of fire, since you are going to have this magnificent order, fire too has a form that enables it to satisfy its desire to join God. And that form will lead fire to the highest physical surface of the sublunary world, to the concave side of the sky of the moon. You have a series of motions in correspondence with which you have a series of places.

And here comes the Aristotelian doctrine of places, against which the Renaissance, Galileo and the rest fought so hard. Where does the heavy body go? To the center of the earth — but not by physical attraction of a mass. Supposing this sphere of the earth — Aristotle of course knew that it was a sphere, had to be a sphere — if this sphere were destroyed, the heavy body would still go there, because that is its τόπος; the natural appetite of the heavy body will bring it to that place. There is a series of such places: the heaviest bodies go to the center of the earth, the lightest to the sphere of the moon, and the others to intermediary spheres. And, corresponding to these places, you have upward motion, downward action, and intermediary, horizontal motion. All this applies to the four elements. But there is another, a fifth element, not like the rest, and therefore it has a different motion, a circular motion. We can conclude, therefore, that there are certain possible actions in relation to certain places, to complete the design of God, who keeps these things moving by means of a desire in them, which desire is satisfied by motion, which motion in turn is the result of a power exerted by the form on the matter.

17. ARISTOTLE'S FOUR CAUSES. CHANCE AND FORTUNE. GOD AS PURE ACT

In the context we are discussing, there cannot be substance without accidents and there cannot be accidents without substance. Substance is related to the accidents as the substratum. For Aristotle, substance is that which is not predicated of a subject and which is not in a subject. It has two different meanings: in one case it signifies the subject (or first category) in relation to the predicates; and in the other, it is substance as the substratum of the accidents. In other words, Aristotle distinguishes substance in this primary sense from accidents and universals, which can be predicated of a subject as the *genus*, and which are called by Aristotle secondary substances. Substance and accidents are related to the so-called transcendentals, the good, the one, and so on. School boys, young men in the Middle Ages learned the catchword "Reubau" — the letters of which word are the initial letters of the transcendentals: R for *res*, E for *ens*, U or V for *verum*, B for *bonum*, A for *aliquid*, and U for *unum*.

Then there is the metaphysical scaffolding for the so-called causes, which are not really causes, but which are indispensable to our thought about reality. We cannot think, you cannot relate your thought to reality, you cannot proceed to operate in your mind unless you have these four principles or causes. The first is matter, the material cause, which changes or differs at any given moment: it is form if regarded from one side and matter is regarded from the other. To matter we added form. In the case of a human being, the form is the rational soul;

in the case of the animal, it is the sensitive soul; in the case of the plant, it is the vegetative soul; in the case of fire it is that something which makes it rise. All these things, as we know, were made much fun of later, in the Renaissance, still later by Molière and others; nevertheless they persisted, and the fun that was made of them was, for the most part, the result of their not being understood. Then there is the agent. If there were just form and matter, things might remain static; but there is nothing static in the Aristotelian system. Therefore, there must be something that sets things in motion, something in consequence of which the form moves toward something. And that brings us to the last, the final, the teleological; that is, the crowning of the causes, the cause of all causes.

For Dante, for St. Thomas, as for Aristotle, it was inconceivable that there could be human activity not directed toward an end, except when you are scratching your head or something like that. You have, therefore, the inevitability of finality in man; and, likewise, we have it in nature. For Aristotle, nature acts teleologically; and the end is the cause of causes. The first thing that comes to our consciousness is that, no matter how you look upon reality — that is, reality in this world of becoming — it has a purpose, a final end. Here's a man who doesn't feel well; from now on he aims at a certain goal. Call it recovery, or anything you want. That starts a whole machinery going. He sees the doctor who sends him to the surgeon; the surgeon sends him to the hospital, and all the rest. In the series, of course, what started the whole system of causation is the last thing attained. What is first in causation is last in actualization. Of course, we posit an end; but one might ask, why should I want to get well? We are now in St. Thomas' universe, but it is Aristotelian also. Have I a right to make getting well an end in itself? If to get well, I have to do something that is monstrous — for example, devastate my soul — then I may not want to get well. Getting well, therefore, cannot be the ultimate cause. But whatever the ultimate cause may be, when you reach it, it's the one that starts the whole motion and the last to be actualized, the last to receive fruition.

All this is related to the four causes, all of which are found in Dante. Normally in nature things are not so detached. The goal is in the thing, *in re*; it is in the form in me; it is in the rational soul in me, in all of us. What is our purpose? Our goal in acting rationally is to perfect, to magnify and bring to perfection the form in us, the rational soul itself. In other words, the soul is at once the form and the end. And the soul too is the moving thing, it is the efficient cause, the agent as well as the form and end. A thing can be the same in many forms of oneness. The form of the father is not the same as the form of the son *numerically*, but *specifically*. The first of the four kinds of unity is numeric; the second is specific: things are one when their species is the same; the third is generic unity; and, finally, most important, there is unity in order, such as you have when out of a multiplicity of human beings you make a group that has to work toward some end. You can't just take three hundred infantry-men, fifty cannons, a squadron of airplanes, throw them out and say: fight the battle. First you have to have unity, not numeric unity — the men and cannons cannot be made one numerically; not generic unity — but unity by order.

This takes care of the world of natural things, but we have also the world that man makes. Man does not make this world of nature. He gives it *form*. The word is τεχνη in Greek, *ars* in Latin — which, when you find it in Dante, does not mean fine arts, or university degrees in the arts, Bachelor of Arts, Master of Arts, and so on. It doesn't mean fine arts, nor what it meant in the Middle Ages — guilds, corporations of workers. In this context it means something very precise: the realm of man's free activity. Here is a man. He is a sculptor; he takes a piece of marble and shapes it. If he is a real artist, he has an internal end, an internal world which he must make external. What are the causes? The marble is one: the material cause. What is the formal cause? The shape of the statue. And what is the agent, the efficient cause? The sculptor. It is the free action of the individual, who is the sculptor. The difference between the things of nature and the things produced by art (using the word freely, now) in the Aristotelian world is in the principle of motion. The principle of change in a natural thing is different from that of art. How do we account for the change from an acorn into an oak tree? Where is the power of change? In the acorn. The change that makes a statue out of rough-hewn marble is not the same. It is outside the marble. Nature is the principle — and by principle we mean the fountainhead — of motion, including such motion as the transformation of an acorn into an oak, or the rest. A stone falls naturally, and if unimpeded, says Aristotle, it goes to the center of the earth which is also the center of the universe. And when it gets there, it stops, it comes to rest. Not artificially — as when I stop something and hold it still, keep it from moving; it comes to rest there naturally. Why? Because that is its place, that is its ὄὐδϊὸ.

Nature, therefore, is not only the principle of motion, but of rest. That principle is in the thing itself, not accidentally but *per se*. In other words if you have a piece of marble that is a beautifully modeled Praxiteles, the fact that it is a statue isn't going to make it act, naturally, any different from any other piece of marble.

If you dropped it in water, it would simply sink. The principle of that motion is not in the statue as such at any given moment, but in the marble itself, a heavy substance, that falls by nature.

That's the difference between nature and art. The principle of motion and rest in art is not in the thing itself. It is outside the object. It is in the sculptor, or builder, and so forth. The change that takes place is not produced internally.

Aristotle very often says Nature is of God; Dante says Nature is the art of God, the power that makes all things part of divine ordainment. Can we speak in Aristotle of providence, of πρόνοια, as the Stoics understood it? Is there providence in all this? Yes, or at least the fact that there is order indicates very clearly that we are not in a chaos, such as we encounter in the world of the Democriteans. Or, put another way: do we account for reality by the operation of Nature and the human will? No. There is something else we must take into consideration: Chance. Of course the difficulty is — there is that terrible phrase of Aristotle, that puts chance not in the mind of the creator, where St. Thomas puts it, and where it obviously becomes a part of divine providence but not really an element of causation — that Aristotle says with great wisdom, but also with great obscurity, that chance is a cause, an efficient cause, and it is, like all efficient causes, directed toward an end, except that the immediate agents, the human agents, are not aware of that end.

A farmer, to use his example, plows the field or wants to locate a spring to irrigate. That's his purpose. While digging he stumbles upon a pot of gold. He wasn't trying to find it, but he found it. There was cause, an efficient cause, working toward an end; but an end which is not before the eyes of the immediate agent and yet is such that had it been before his eyes it would have constituted an object for finalistic action. What is that intended to explain? The farmer, as he plows, may find stones, sticks, a dead dog, leaves. Do we speak of chance or fortune in those instances? Do we call that chance? Of course not, because those things are not good for anything, and would not have constituted an object of desire, would not have made the farmer act finalistically, had he known they were there. That operates in nature as well as in the sphere of volition. And we have two words, two different words, in most languages, one for each. As we said before, nature too is finalistic; yet, in nature too, things happen that are apparently not intended by nature: these are monstrosities.

Aristotle would explain: here is nature operating in a bird, as the bird builds a nest on a branch of a tree. The tree branch extending outward behaves naturally, and the wind also operates naturally. As a result of a complex interrelation of natural operations, the branch falls and the birds are killed. Was that intended by nature? Obviously not. Nature does not aim at destruction but at generation. Does a bird build a nest to kill its offspring? The destruction comes, but nature does not intend it. You account for it by introducing a new cause: chance. Not fortune, for that applies to the realm of free will. We have the branching out of a tree, which is the natural act of a tree; and another natural act, the building of a nest; and another, the wind, which in itself is useful. As a result of these three lines meeting, something happens unintentionally. Nature wanted those birds, those nestlings to live. Of course, someone will say: they would have to die eventually anyway. That's right; but then you can say what the Roman philosopher said: since life is such a dreary thing and since I couldn't kill myself when I was a few months old, why didn't my father kill me?

In nature you have the passing on of life from generation to generation. Life is life, not destruction. Of course, the individual does die, but individual corruption is remedied by generation, the procreation of the species. This is efficient causality — fortune in man, chance in nature. It was finally looked upon as a series of lines of action which met in an unintended way; and that power which brought them together, the power behind it all, which is not in the lines, not in God, or elsewhere, we call chance.

Or take the example of the volitional act of a man crossing a street; another volitional act of a man driving a car. They have no intention of meeting. But the lines cross, causing death for the man crossing the street. Who brought the two lines together? Where is the motivation? We don't know, says St. Thomas; the angels don't know; but God knows. In other words, what seems casual to us, is perfectly clear and intended in the mind of God, but in a way we cannot fathom. Aristotle's answer is: chance has a realm of its own, but the more the realm of knowledge expands, the more our knowledge increases, the more the realm of chance is forced to retreat. Complete knowledge means chance disappears.

The two realms of nature and volition are both finalistically oriented, but they are not sufficient to account for everything that happens until we bring in chance, which is a realm of causation where man has no control. The typical example is wealth, certainly the most uncontrollable sphere of human activity. That's why in many languages wealth is synonymous with *fortuna* — fortune. What goes on in the atmosphere, weather, that too is typically uncontrollable and part of the realm of chance. But in all cases, the power of indeterminism springs out of matter. It is matter that makes it possible for things to happen as it was not intended they should. Therefore, you have the various grades in Aristotle of more and less chance.

You have a sphere, a realm,where there is no chance, where matter is not such as to resist or obstruct the application of form, namely, that part of the universe where matter is in complete accord, where it corresponds exactly to its form: the heavens. There you have nothing casual, nothing unexpected. There foresight is possible. We know for a million years from now what the stars will be doing, where the sun will rise, where it will set. I'm speaking in Aristotelian terms, where there is no end of time. In that world, you have a realm without chance, because the matter there is not one of the four elements, but a fifth element: the quintessence. We still talk about quintessence; certain perfumes are referred to by that name. It is simply an echo of a being that was perfect and therefore allowed its form to operate without exception. From this sphere there is a descending scale, until finally you come down to the sublunary world. In the sphere of chemistry, chance is rare; it is less rare in physics; and in biology it is more and more common. The more developed matter is organically, the more you see the power of chance increase. The fact that someone is born with six fingers instead of five, or that this other is ambidextrous, or that still another is left-handed, that your left hand is better developed than your right, is due to the interference of matter, to the introduction of something that doesn't correspond to nature — what we have called chance.

This divinity, this nature that moves the skies, that makes the waters flow, the tides swell and recede, turns man from a heavy body to a compound body, an organic compound that grows, nourishes itself, reproduces, and gets rid of what it takes in and doesn't use.

Then there is something that man does as an animal, and
finally there is something — unless you don't want to
distinguish man from all the other animals — there is
something for which all these are only the potentiality.
And that is reason, the capacity to think. Therefore
nature, which makes the heavy body fall, fire rise, gives
man a place too. We refered earlier to the doctrine of
places, that terrible doctrine, that chain that Aristotle
put on man's foot, on his capacity for scientific thinking.
Man's place is not the center of the earth, not the surface
of the sublunary sphere. It is mentality, reason, knowledge; not knowledge that two and two is four, or that if
I cut off one finger I have four left, but high knowledge,
the highest truth. In a word: man's place is heaven, the
place of absolute knowledge. So man too has a place, a
spiritual place, where he finds himself when properly
reconstituted, when he has actualized — completed his
form. Nature then shoots him to his proper place. Dante
describes this in the first canto of the *Paradiso*.

   This divine principle, nature, is also the principle
or source of motion. Things are not static; we don't have
a museum of statues, forms and matter. They are all
moving. We, and everything else in the world, move.
And we have seen that things move with a certain
proportion of parts; a force moves them, in order,
toward certain ends; and those ends constitute a scale,
an order, a cosmos. Every force has a goal, and every goal
has a relation to a higher end, and that to a higher, and
so on. This enables us to establish a scale of values in
Aristotle's world. Which is higher, a stone or an organic
compound? The organic compound with sense and
reason or the organic compound without reason? And
so you have a scale or system of values, arranged, so that
at any given level, looking up we have something which
is potential, and which is, looking down, actual in rela-

tion to something below it, and so on down the scale until at the very bottom we reach something which doesn't have this double role: primal matter.

What is the cause of this kinetic or qualitative motion? What is it throughout, from the stone all the way up? Why do we change, why does the stone move, change its position and come to rest when it reaches the center? Why does matter want to be formed? Because everything wants to reach God, or, if you will, to conform to the will of God. Later, people said "Love." The stone moves toward the center of the earth because it loves that place; fire loves the place to which it rises; and surely man loves the acquisition of knowledge. You don't have a museum of statues; all these things are kept in motion. Why? Because in one way or another they want to actualize, to bring to fruition, an impulse toward God. That's what Dante describes at the beginning of the *Paradiso*: this bow that shoots everything to its proper place, in accordance with the will of God. Therefore all this scheme of nature is kept alive, is kept going because of its love for God. Therefore, God can never be potential, for if He were, the world would stop. And if He can never be potential, He must be pure act. But He can only be that if He is not determined by any external thing. Therefore His only activity is *thinking*. What does he think? He thinks Himself, the thought of thought. He, being truth, thinks truth, and is forever actual, corresponding at one extreme, to the other extreme, which is primal matter.

Out of this scale of natural ends emerges. the Aristotelian ethics; and from his ethics, his politics.

18. ARISTOTLE'S DOCTRINE OF THE "GOLDEN MEAN." THE TRANSCENDENT LOGOS MADE FLESH IN CHRISTIANITY

We come now to a problem, which is very much more important for Dante than it is for Aristotle: the norms for an ethical system. What are the norms in Aristotle? There is, you recall, a method and a system. All things in this universe, from the lowest to the highest, actually move toward a certain end, as the result of an impulse that is not of their own making, that comes not from within but from Nature, which is the first emanation of divinity. So, all things move toward their ends as the result of an impulse, and that impulse — we saw — is a kind of love, a love that directs the different things to their appointed places, the famous places of Dante and St. Thomas and Aristotle, the natural places. All things move by love to their appointed ends or places. Some things, like the elements earth and fire move, as the result of a physical quality which is their form. Others, animals, as a result of perception about which they have no choice. Animals spontaneously follow their perceptions when the object suits their needs, and run away equally spontaneously when the opposite is the case.

Men respond the same way, like animals; but they have something else: choice. Man too is shot to his place by Nature, but if he doesn't want to go there, he needn't. The first canto of the *Paradiso* reminds us of all this. Aristotle operates on this scheme. Form is what sends the stone to the center of the earth, fire up; what sends the mind of man, to its place or plane of eternal truth. All these things proceed to their appointed ends in consequence of their forms. Form is something given to each individual in a given species, to a number of individuals of the same form. Man is no exception. His form too determines his motion, his goal, and the happiness he is to get from his motion toward that goal. When we come to Aristotle, we have to drop the notions of a fixed state of happiness. There is nothing static here; happiness is life, nothing else. And life is activity. If you cease to act you cease to be.

Man's form is the soul, the rational soul. His obligation — what he has to do — like that of every other being, comes from his form, the German *sollen*. This is very important because the whole system derives from it. What do we have to do as a result of the fact that our form is the rational soul? That's the beginning of the problem. There is an obligation entailed in having a rational soul.

It means, first of all, that man cannot go to that place where the plant goes, or where the lower animals go. His form is different. The sphere where he must go is that of rationality. In order words, we are not very far from the Platonic system, or those teachings deriving from that system. The Platonists will tell us that, because of that nostalgia we have for things once seen, there is a constant impulse in us, a power that comes to us from that ideal world, which is only a memory to us now, through beauty; and that impulse is not satisfied until man reaches that ideal world. Virtue, therefore, is anything that will help you to reach those ideas. From that some great exaggerations emerge about ethics. The worst is the opposite of what we ordinarily meet. Ordinarily, many people think it's perfectly natural to want to eat and drink and sleep — if he has money enough — why not? Or if he has to work, then he will do it, curse the day he was born, then rest, and then go back to eating and sleeping some more. Why not? Because man's form is different from that of an animal; if he acts like one, he doesn't become an animal. What happens is, he loses his own form without acquiring a new one. The opposite exaggeration is that a man may think and act as though he were an angel. It is the exaggeration that proposes to crush all the feelings, all the impulses, all the things that man has in common with the animals, and exalts the others that distinguish him. The Stoics said that. I hate to say anything against it, for there is hardly anything nobler than the Stoic idea. As Christians, of course, we can't say too many good things in its favor, we can't support pride. I crush all the lower impulses in me to deify myself, or that terrible statement of theirs: Jupiter owes to mankind as much as mankind owes to Jupiter. What that means is that the divinity is a growing affair. If you take the materialism out of it, you have the position developed early in the nineteenth century. In other words, mankind is in a constant process of deification. Man then forgets what he has in common with the lower animals — it's a magnificent ideal — but the Stoics themselves soon realized that it's a remote idea, a far-off ideal. Their poor world is made up of a very few people who try hard to live up to that ideal, a very few who reject it entirely, and the great mass of the people. You have the good, the bad, and, in the middle, the great mass of the indifferent. There are doctrines of this sort in the Christian world. Realizing that it is exceptional, we can admire it.

Aristotle is for neither one nor the other. He doesn't sanction your making a pig of yourself, but he doesn't encourage you to try to be an angel either. You are a rational being, with a soul imbedded in matter, organized with a system of sensation which puts you in with the other animals. They used to say (this is very un-

Thomistic): man has four forms, his own specific form which is the rational form, the animal form, the vegetative form, and finally, the corporeal form, which a man has even when he is dead. So Aristotle reminds us that we are not angelic intelligences; we are human beings in the flesh — and we cannot destroy that flesh and its impulses. And yet you have to reach your goal as a result of what comes to you from your specific form; your action must be rational, and your beatitude must be found in rational activity.

How do we move along from there? It should be perfectly obvious. We may have the instincts of a wolf or of a rabbit; we may be like the lion or like the pig: aggressive, cowardly, or lustful. We may be all sorts of things. What we must do is see to it that our reason affirms itself, and that in the activity of reason we find happiness. And to do that we have to have reason regulate those impulses; the impulses have to obey reason, they have to be regulated rationally. We have to see to it that the cowardly impulse to run away, or the contrary impulse to go ahead rashly are brought under the control of reason.

We are now at the central point of the whole system. How do we gain such control? By virtuous habituation. The whole system hinges on the development of those virtues by means of which reason is able to control the passions without killing them. By passions they mean, not what we mean when we use the word in the romantic sense — not those passions, but passions in the scholastic sense: all those things we have in common with the lower animals. This doesn't mean that reason must always interfere and say: now, look here, you are making a pig of yourself and tomorrow you won't be able to do your work well, you won't be able to give that lecture. That's not an ethical solution. Reason must be protected from the onslaught of passions by something that operates habitually. Virtues are habits. You do a thing well, not when you have to think about it every minute. You do it well when it comes almost automatically, spontaneously. Virtues are habitual. It means that when we are born, and when we are very young, the animal in us is very strong, much stronger than the rational, obviously. Then we want things very like what the little animal near us wants. If we let it have its way, we will gradually become very like that little animal. So we have to see to it that, by compulsion if need be, that little creature is made to begin very early to do what he is supposed to do. He may not like it at first, but in the course of time it will become habitual with him and he will grow to like it.

All this is far removed from what we are taught today. Today, we are apt to say: let the sweet little thing do whatever it wants to do. It is worth recalling in this context that terrible line of St. Augustine, about the twins, one of whom is fed at one breast until he is satisfied, and then he is moved and the other is fed. The first, looking on, apparently forgetting that he has already been fed, turns purple with rage, and tries to scratch the eyes out of the other. St. Augustine used that example to indicate that there is the devil in us. Don't trust the dear little thing too much, either here or abroad. Of course, you don't have to go back to St. Augustine for that truth, but his words are such that nobody who reads them ever forgets them.

It is this habituation that must take place. In our so-called western civilization, which is so rapidly degenerating that it hardly seems worth fighting for, we are inclined to reject it. But, if you turn to other people of the world, people with some fresh stock in them, it is not so senseless to them. Of course, you must kill in you that extreme individualism which is the beginning, the source of the death of personality, and realize that there are other things just as real; that there are things higher than the individual — country, religion — which are not here for our comfort, but which exist in their own right on a higher level. In order to do that you have to break away from the enlightenment, all enlightenment, including that of the Sophists. War, yes, sure, I'll fight for my country, if it suits me; if it doesn't, I won't fight. That's what we make laws for; not for some end in itself, but to satisfy ourselves. You have to break away from all enlightenments. Enlightenment is constantly with us. It keeps rising up in the course of history. The characteristic thing about it is it says the state is my instrument, it is there to serve me; if I don't like it, I change it. It's a pretty hard position to hold historically. But we don't have to justify this or any other doctrine, or apologize for anything; we simply have to explain it and support it so far as this argument is concerned.

How do we go about it? What are we going to do to habituate the individual that has those impulses of the lower animals and yet wants to rise to the plane of reason? How can you make these impulses serve reason, make them instruments of rational activity? And here we come to the famous Aristotelian doctrine of the middle path. You shouldn't try to make yourself an angel, and you shouldn't try to make yourself a pig. Reason, eventually, will not only build up its own realm, but will guide man in controlling his impulses, so that he will not stop, in his progressive action toward that realm. This doctrine of the middle path, the golden mean, tells us that for every extreme of vice there is an opposite vice, and somewhere in between is virtue.

Take temperance, for example. One extreme is excess. The word is gluttony. Still, Aristotle tells us, our animal impulses are not in themselves vices; they are very necessary. The impulse to eat is necessary for the preservation of the individual, as well as the species. The second impulse is procreation. The third (some of the ancients tried to find it in the animals too) is the impulse to store up, to save, to accumulate. The extremes in the case of temperance are, on one side, eat, drink and be merry, and so on; and on the other, what Aristotle calls frigidity. He considers it mostly in connection with sex. All those extremes — frigidity in sex, fasting, and so on — are all considered vices. What the hermit in the desert, what Christians admire so much — monastic life and all the vows that accompany it — Aristotle would condemn. That is the reason why his system could not be taken over wholly into Christianity. The animal cited by the ancients, by the Middle Ages, as the example of the impulse to store up, is the mole. You meet in Dante people who wanted nothing else but to accumulate land, real estate, which meant wealth then, like stocks and bonds are wealth today. Dante's punishment is transparently clear: they want the earth; so let them eat the earth; and there they are, like moles. We should save, we should accumulate. But not to excess; nor should we seek the other extreme. Pope John XXII warned the *fraticelli*, the poor Franciscans who didn't want to own property — who said that every penny you touch and don't use for basic needs or for others is of the devil — that man is a gregarious animal; he needs society; and society couldn't exist without the accumulation of wealth. Therefore it is perfectly natural to want to save. (Still, it was no reason for condemning the *fraticelli* who didn't want to live that way.)

On the one hand the miser; and on the other, the prodigal. That's the only example Dante uses to illustrate this conception of vice and virtue. You find it in the

Inferno, the theory of the middle path, the golden mean. Of course, some people have said this isn't a very noble conception of morals; but that's because they haven't read those beautiful lines of Aristotle, where he reminds us that the doctrine of the golden middle operates only where there are natural impulses at play. It doesn't mean that if you have on one side the sin of adultery, you have on the other side, if you restrain yourself, an opposite sin. Adultery is a sin, but the opposite, which is the repudiation of adultery, is surely not a sin. Aristotle, it has been said, is the humble little man who is content with the middle course; he has no vision of the great. That sort of criticism is like saying: look at that archer — he doesn't shoot way up high, he doesn't shoot way down, he shoots in between and hits the target, poor man. There have been many serious men who have written interesting commentaries on the poor little deer that tried to buck the train. The man who does not take into consideration his powers in relation to the force he wants to oppose is not a brave man. He is a fool; his action is foolhardy.

This doctrine of the mean tells us we must domesticate those impulses we have in common with the lower animals. When man has so domesticated them, he can proceed to the realm of truth; and does so as a result of his form, which is not separate but imbedded in matter, of which the immediate potentiality is the animal soul, of which, in turn, the immediate potentiality is the vegetative soul — to recap — and so on down to the form which is corporeality, the bodily form. This doctrine doesn't seem to accord with that of the Stoics and the Christians, that the attainment of moral conduct, or the carrying out of the purpose of our form, is always accompanied by happiness. Man's happiness consists in the continuous exercise of the mind in quest of truth. Of course, you

might say, we don't do that. Aristotle was more convinced of that than we are. But there is no doubt that if
we accept this postulate, and also if we listen to what is
deep in our hearts — our conscience — then we have to
grant that if we really are human beings and our action
is our being, we have to differentiate ourselves by our
actions, and in that action that differentiates us, find our
happiness. There is no other kind of happiness for us as
human beings.

So far so good. But there is something more in
Aristotle. Man doesn't simply live to let his reason
operate freely and regulate the passions. There is something else in man. In the concluding pages of book ten
of the *Ethics* — where he talks of man, as man — he also
talks about the divinity in man. The tenth book is very
important. This divineness, this part of our intellect
which is divine is separate, immortal and unchanging.
Of course, this is the beginning of that famous heresy
that Dante seems to have accepted at one point, but later
rejected. It is the doctrine of the separate intellect. Why
are we all united at this moment? We are united in the
same way that that ray of sunshine is united with the
other rays — because they all come from a common
source, and that source in the case of man is the separate
intellect. The separate intellect is the sun that shines on
our souls. We receive the rays, but the source is immortal.

The Christians repudiated the idea because it
denies the immortality of the individual soul. Whether
Averroes is right in this, or St. Thomas, might be worth
pursuing at some point. Aristotle is clear enough: there
is this intellect in us which can grasp the divine, which is
separate. Why should we be virtuous? Why should we
liberate our reason? Simply to be virtuous for its own
sake? Not at all. We must be virtuous, we must try to

eliminate all complications, because reason may enable the separate intellect to reveal whatever it is capable of revealing of the divine. In other words, a moral system cannot possibly fit in a divine world. Can gods be moral? Can a god be temperate? Of course not, because to be temperate you have to have impulses. Well, the gods of Homer had impulses, but they were relegated to the background eventually, except in the minds of the populace. They were not gods, but big men — or rather, big animals. Gods have no appetites of that sort; gods, in other words, do not have to conquer temptation or passions, because they are not in the flesh, and therefore they have no occasion to exercise virtue.

There is something else after our impulses have been brought under control and reason has been freed, a new act that gives us real beatitude, real bliss — the act of contemplation, continuous, dispassionate. What this means is that man has ceased to be a human being for a while and comes to realize that he has something in him that enables him to enjoy — as if all of a sudden the cataract has been removed — the vision of the highest truth. That is the *theoria,* that is the keystone to that magnificent arch of Aristotle, which is taken over by Dante, at the culmination of his journey where thought becomes sight.

How many get to enjoy this contemplation? Very few. But all these things operate not on an individual basis, but on the basis of an order; and, by participation, all the individual constituents of that order profit. Still we have a situation — as we had in Plato, and in many other philosophers that followed — where the human soul is striving for something that is very high, transcendent, inaccessible, striving for a bridge, for something to mediate, to connect that soul with its goal: which is eternal truth. Aristotle finds it in a structure that embodies a rigorous moral system that itself will contain a political system. Eventually man will want everyone to have this connection. You will find this voice not only in the Greek world but also in the Hebrew world, where it is echoed by the great Jewish philosopher, Philo.

The mediator or mediation must be such that it will reach all, not only the top of the heap. Therefore, the question of knowledge must be changed to another question. The mediator is not knowledge but Faith. And this system of love that is behind this entire discussion, that is in Plato and in Aristotle, this love by which the world is kept moving, will have to change its nature. It will be a love that proceeds from the mediator to us, and to the mediator from the father of all. From this moment on, the situation will develop both within Greek, Hellenic culture and the Hebrew world. This situation prepares us for *Caritas*, a love that connects in two directions, a love that does not have a cosmic quality, a love that operates through our fellow being to bring us to God. This new love, this mediator is Christ, the Logos — it is Christianity.

The contemplation of Aristotle is such that, sooner or later, man who has transcended the moral, will find an impasse — like the Stoics found — and will try to find a solution. Looking ahead: how was Christianity able to triumph — these poor illiterate fishermen, coming into a world which was culturally so advanced (not technically so advanced, but in every other way, literarily, artistically) so much superior to them? How did Christianity triumph in an Aristotlelian world, in a system of thought like the one described? Through the *Mediator*, through the transcendent *Logos*, which has taken flesh.

From this moment, historically, the situation matures in the direction of Christianity.

1. There are any number of subjects one can still explore in this context: for example, Dante's view of the two beatitudes — you can see what Gilson has to say and expand it from there — the whole political system of Dante is based on that; or you can examine Dante's moral system in the *Inferno*, how he starts off with the seven mortal sins, and then — sensing that it's going to be heavy and that duplication will come in when he gets to purgatory — changes it, and changes it in a way that gives it a unified scheme of morality. He finds this possible by identifying moral conduct with love. But he waits until the middle of *The Divine Comedy* to indicate — and in this he follows St. Augustine — how moral conduct takes on its full significance when it is part of universal love.

Or, one can explore the topic of Dante and astrology. People tell me that crazy pseudo-science is popular again. Italians seemed to have had a special weakness for it; some of them even got burned for it, and I mean physically burned. Outside of Italy they used to speak of the Italians as particularly addicted to it. Not astrology in the broad sense; this was particularized. They measured it, or yes, with a horoscope. Of course, how that can be reconciled with free will remains to be seen. To operate with astrology you have to be able to arrive at a precision in measuring angles of displacement, which is 10,000 times more difficult than what is possible. To account astrologically for the differences in the destiny of identical twins, for instance, the measurements have to be infinitesimally accurate — the tenth part of a hundredth of a second — and you know how accurate their instruments for measuring were! In spite of all that, here is Dante who takes it up; but it must be said that he realizes its limits; he doesn't stress the capacity to measure, he looks on man as free. It's an interesting subject, anyway.

Or astrology in Italy. Look at some of those poor fellows who took it so earnestly, who stubbornly refused to retract, and paid the terrible price.

19. ARISTOTLE'S IDEA OF THE STATE. ETHICS AS A FUNCTION OF POLITICS

For Aristotle, as we saw, conduct is immoral when it is not rational. Man has a nature that obligates him — this is a completely naturalistic system — to normalize his conduct according to the dictates of reason, in order that reason may have a clear sphere, an unobstructed plane on which to operate for its own sake. Reason controls the passions — not simply to control them, but so that it may proceed to build for itself a world of its own. Exercise of control is necessary, for we are not pure reason but animals with reason. The end to be attained from this rational control is the emergence of a power that is more than human: a power that is divine.

This is different from what follows later, in Dante and in Christianity in general. What you need if you want to take this into a Christian sphere, what is lacking in Aristotle that is not lacking in Dante is the idea of sin. To put it in moral terms: a transgression of those rational norms that should guide us is something immoral for Aristotle, and for the others — immoral because it is irrational; for Dante it becomes a sin. What has happened in between? Why is it that a violation of a rational rule, a fault for Aristotle, becomes a sin for Dante? Because God has ordered it. It isn't simply that you break the law of reason, but also that you violate the will of God. When you violate reason in the Christian world, you go against God, you disobey His order. All of this applies fully to Dante, who also reminds us that we are in a world where sin has acquired a profound new meaning. The *Inferno*, with its conception of sin, as

Dante describes it, would be impossible in the Aristotelian system.

Of course, there is a great deal more to say about the Aristotelian concept. The only other thing to keep in mind is that you have here not a rigoristic ethical system, such as we have with the Stoics and even with Plato, and some Christians also, but, a very reasonable moral scheme. It is a scheme that has taken into account the fact that we control our body with a tyrannical rule, but the control of our reason over our passions is not a tyrannical, but a democratic rule. I can kick the table before me according to my will, but I can't turn around and in a similar way kick out of my consciousness the appetites, the impulses and passions that arise there. What Aristotle does is to reshape, re-substantiate rationally those appetites. He shows how these appetites, which we have in common with the lower animals – this appetite of reproduction, for instance – becomes a beautiful thing in the institution of marriage; or how the acquisitive impulse can be a source of culture.

He has given to the concept of beatitude the exalted impression the Stoics gave it, but one that finds satisfaction in little things. You can't be starving – as the Cynics said you could – and still be happy. Or, and this was something which irritated St. Augustine, if you lose all your children, you can't be happy. You need all sorts of things, and if those things are forthcoming, they help to make life happy and beautiful. In other words, he shows and emphasizes the connection between the individual and society, the fact that man is not an isolated atom, but a social and gregarious being.

Even fortune comes into it – that's important in Aristotle. A man who has had bad fortune, who has fortune against him all the way, can't be very happy; he needs to straighten out his moral life. Fortune for

Aristotle is an event resulting from the act of a person other than yourself, which is not designed by that person, or by you, and yet has great importance for your life.

This is where Aristotle is different from everybody else. You are led up to God, to a world that is beyond you, by reason and contemplation, and yet you are made up of other impulses also. Those blessed by the gods satisfy those appetites that we have in common with the lower animals and they become beautiful things. Some of Aristotle's followers have written fine pages on the subject, but who reads the commentators of Aristotle these days? *Graecum e st ergo non legitur.* It's Greek, therefore it isn't read. Of course, it's been translated into Latin, but that's just as bad. It's in German! Why read German? Who wants to read the language of the enemy? French? It's a decaying language; why bother to read that? So much for the commentators. Fortune enters into it, as we explained. A man is happy when at the end of his life — *laudo finem*, I praise the end — he is not too much troubled by the blows of fortune, by the loss of dear ones, and with the loss of proper functioning of his physical body, and dies serenely.

This is a very beautiful ethical system, but it is all built in air, because man never is quite so ethical and moral in isolation. He is always part of the state. He is always a particle in the state. Therefore, ethics is really a function of politics. We speak of one thing as a function of another when it varies with the variation of that other thing. Ethics is intimately bound up with politics, or, if you will, an ethical structure has to build upon a political foundation. This is done through those laws, those norms by which man is able to fit into a state, into the political organization. We need to examine, therefore, the relation between the laws of the land and the laws that we call ethical or moral. We must also understand what we mean when we say that moral man has to fit himself into the higher unit, which we call the political — which differs from any other association by the fact that it is held together by laws which, if necessary, can be enforced by coercion.

St. Augustine says man needs coercion as the consequence of original sin. Aristotle tells us that it is because in early life men are apt to go off, that they have to be brought back with a certain amount of violence. More important still, since this organization, the state, is natural and therefore of necessity must be kept up — there is nothing optional about it, the state has to be, it's a must in the absolute sense — therefore man, man in general that is, feels that he has to crush at all costs anything that threatens its existence, and that's what coercion is. In other words, you can have all sorts of organizations: family, club, university, all of these function because they are protected by a higher association, the state, which operates in such a way that anyone who transgresses the laws and rights of those inferior organizations, can be corrected by coercion — coercion that can go all the way up to capital punishment. All these inferior organizations have their norms, their rules, but those of the state are norms the respect for which can be made coercive.

What is the difference between these laws — this legality — and morality? There are people, no doubt, who don't think there is any difference. How often have you yourself or others said: if a thing is immoral, the state ought to pass laws that make it obligatory to refrain from doing it. There have been attempts to do exactly that. They are often called noble experiments but are doomed to fail, being violations of the fundamental principle upon which the distinction between legality and morality is based. Morality is internal, and the laws (legality) are external. As St. Paul says, a man who covets another man's wife has already committed adultery. The law does not care about the coveting. The law punishes only when the act of adultery has been committed. The fundamental difference is that one punishes acts and the other considers intentions. Can you say that a person is moral or ethical when all his instincts, all his desires, his whole internal life are turned against — Aristotle would say — "against reason"? Christians would say "against God"? Would the acts of such a man be called moral? Obviously not. What counts from the moral point of view is the intention, the disposition. What legality requires is the external act. What about murder, someone may ask. When a man is tried for murder, his motives are taken into consideration, as well as the act itself. The murder has actually been committed. If the person had just wished it, wished to murder, the law wouldn't come into it. But morally, if I have spent night and day hoping to kill that man, am I to be considered a flower of blossoming ethics?

The point is: virtue is a disposition. The law, the state, doesn't ask you about your disposition. You might have to pay a debt, and you might hope and curse that the man who loaned it to you may die. If you pay the debt, the state is satisfied, although you certainly did not possess the disposition of justice. In one case, all that is required is the performance of the act; in the other, it is required that you also have the corresponding disposition, which, among other things, implies that, when you perform that act, that act is accompanied by pleasure. If you curse every time you refrain from getting drunk, you're not virtuous, you're not temperate, even though you do refrain.

But, most important of all, the state, as Aristotle

has pointed out, has created the kind of justice that is called legal justice. What that means simply is the enforcement of virtues other than justice, because of an obligation you have toward the state. For example: you violate legal justice when you run away from a battlefield. The state can command you, in the name of legal justice, to die on the battlefield. Morally no one ever goes so far as to say that if you don't have the virtue of fortitude you are a coward, you have to die; but politically, the moral sanction in time of war, for cowardice, becomes a legal obligation. On the other hand, conversely, there are violations of morals which the state ignores. St. Thomas gives the example — following Aristotle — that the state punishes adultery but does not punish fornication; and yet fornication, according to the teachings of the ancients as well as of the Church, is a sin. But it does have laws to punish adultery. From these examples you can draw the conclusion that the state proceeds against acts which endanger its existence. Legalized prostitution may shock some of you, yet it has been usual in most European countries at all times. Why such legislation to protect what is morally ugly? Because adultery interferes with family relations, and the family is a necessary constituent of the state. Fornication does not interfere in that way. The important thing is that the state has to take care that nothing is tolerated that endangers social relations in any realm of life.

I have forestalled any possible objection by saying there have been states that have passed laws that forbid moral transgressions. Even in antiquity there were such attempts. What word can we use to describe such a polity? Ordinarily we call it a puritanical state. In ancient times, or rather in St. Augustine's time, they called it a Donatist state, that is, a state that excludes the immoral man, that throws him out of the bounds of the political order — exterminates him.

The first thing to note about Aristotle's conception of the state is that contrary to what the Sophists taught, for Aristotle the state is natural. Man has a natural tendency that leads him toward a social life, that leads him to participation in social and in political life. Some have tried to say that Aristotle did not call it "political life," but they're wrong. The social group and political group characterized by coercion, which is the inevitable resolution of any transgression against the state, is not reached, according to Aristotle, until the social order is such as can proceed to guarantee its own existence. In his *Politics*, Aristotle discusses the process of ratiocination needed to build up a social organization. In building up a family you are guided by nature. We don't sit around and decide whether there will be families or not. If mankind didn't have families there would soon cease to be beings that are animal and rational. The same natural impulse that leads to the formation of the family leads to the formation of the state. However, at the very beginning of that magnificent book, Aristotle speaks of a break in continuity; although the whole process is a development, at a certain moment there is something like the breaking of the shell of an egg. At a certain moment, certain men appeared and took charge of this natural gregariousness and laid down the foundations of the state.

So, the state is natural; and that means two things for Aristotle, both fundamental to his thought. One is that nature is never found lacking in necessaries, and the second is that nature does nothing in vain. These are the two poles of the axis on which the whole thought of Aristotle turns, and not only of Aristotle, but also of the thirteenth century. I don't think one can read two pages of any work of the Middle Ages without encountering these two fundamental thoughts. If nature gives you an impulse toward the state, that means that nature will see to it that that impulse is satisfied, because nature never does anything in vain. It will see to it that all those practical tendencies are satisfied, including coercion to the extreme, to enable the social impulse to reach its goal.

Nature is never wanting in necessaries. A state made up of people all alike — a unison — is not a state. There has to be a harmony. Everything is built on harmony. Not diversity simply, but unified diversity. St. Thomas, following a line of Aristotle, said something for which he was called to task soon after his death: that a world made up entirely of angels would be a very dreary world. You have to have men of all sorts. Infinite repetition of the same element adds nothing to it. Unison is a quantitative matter, nothing more. To use the example or the language of musicians, the violin may be a better instrument that the trombone or the kettle-drum — or whatever instrument you want; yet an orchestra made up only of violins would give worse results than one made up of violins and drums and wind instruments and all the rest. The orchestra — like the state — is diversity unified by order; diversity that carries within itself its own norms that make it function as a unity.

Law and order early come to mean the same thing in medieval language — though they hadn't meant the same in the classical languages. You need to have different kinds of people, people with physical prowess, people to teach, people to defend and carry on the order. And since this order is natural, nature will see to it that you have the various kinds of people to fill the different posts that are necessary for the unified diversity, without which the state cannot exist. In discussing these naturalities, as we may call them, Aristotle said something which is not very sound, and that has brought him much criticism. Among the different kinds of people you have not only brave men, priestly men, and so on, but also slaves. To show that slavery is a natural thing, all he has to do is prove that there are men who are very dull and gullible, and very strong, who are unwilling and unable to improve themselves, and so must stay where they are. We cannot take such people and make them presidents or generals (although sometimes we do).

A slave means property. A slave is a tool, and, therefore, can become owned. As I said, that is something that doesn't flow at all from the Aristotelian doctrine. Moreover, and this is the weakest point of all, he has to take into account the fact that there have been slaves who were far superior to their masters — slaves taken in war, for example. One of the consequences of defeat in war was to become a slave. The old Romans found a very pleasant etymology for the word *servis*. They interpreted it differently. The *servi* were those of the enemy who should have been killed but were spared or saved. It is a play on the word *servere*. Aristotle has a great deal of difficulty in explaining the presence of these slaves. He tries to fit them into his scheme by saying something which is very poor: such people become slaves for lack of fortitude. It is so superficial, we need say nothing about it.

So: Aristotle's state exists by nature, and nature sees to it that it is furnished with whatever is needed for its existence. If this were all, and if it were followed through, we would have a perfect system of totalitarianism. But there is another natural tendency in man connected with all this: all men by nature desire to know. Those are the first words, repeated several millions of times, the opening line of Aristotle's *Metaphysics*. Can a single individual, or a single generation satisfy that desire? Obviously not. You need communication in space and communication in time. And such communication requires a safe order, a safe vehicle: the state. The state is natural because there is that natural goal toward which it is striving, one which gives us culture. Aristotle conceives the state as a vehicle of culture. The thirteenth century gives us a similar situation. The state is there to satisfy our material needs, and to guide us morally. But when our economic and moral needs are satisfied, when we have satisfied our economic needs and built a basis for moral education, a new goal sets in so that on top of it, for St. Thomas, St. Bonaventure, and the rest, you can build a spiritual structure that can take you to God, to fruition of the desire to know. The state can command all sorts of things. It can compel you to kill or be killed on the battlefield. There we are the instruments of the state; but here the process is reversed: the state is an instrument to serve us. In other words, the state plays a double role. Those who say that Aristotle regards the state as an end in itself, may have read those first ten pages of his *Politics*, but they surely haven't gone beyond them. For Aristotle, man is a medium for the enactment of the idea of the state, up to the point of moral education; then the state becomes an instrument and the individual man becomes dominant.

How strong is this conviction of Aristotle that the state is natural? Some are shocked by what he says: that the state is anterior to the individual. Obviously, that doesn't mean that the state would exist without men; that, if all men were killed, there would still be a state. There are two kinds of precedence. There is precedence according to our point of view — *quo ad nos* — and precedence according to nature. Nature operates not in view of the substance, but in view of the acts that proceed from it. Nature looks out for the knowing act, and in order that that act may be performed, it looks out also for the political act which is instrumental to it. In that way it can be said that the state is anterior to the individual, from the point of view of the final cause.

If an individual is not incorporated in this system, if he is not a citizen, he is either a God or a beast — a God, because only a God can dispense with the political institution because he doesn't have impulses of the body to control; otherwise he is a beast. The Church will have to find a way to accept that view. It will have to deal with such men as St. Anthony of Egypt. You can't call him a God, and yet you certainly can't call him a beast. The answer given is that such men are miraculously able to live apart.

But that's an exception. The individual, apart from a miracle, cannot live apart. Aristotle must have had in mind the existence of the poor devil that has been excluded from the state and cannot gain admittance into any other state, who has to wander helplessly, who can be beaten and robbed and killed at pleasure. You have to realize how much more complete was the dependence of the individual on the state in Aristotle's day than it is now.

The next subject to consider is how the state is constituted, what its parts are; and to see how all this has come down to our day. As to Bertram Russell's criticism of Aristotle's ethics: the man interests me when it comes to mathematics; otherwise, elsewhere, I ignore him. There are monumental voids in his arguments; he doesn't know nearly everything he thinks he knows. Or perhaps I should say: he thinks he doesn't have to reach out for knowledge but can get it through inner feelings of some sort. He is the most unhistorical person that ever lived.

20. THE FORMS OF GOVERNMENT

What are the alternatives, if the state is not by nature — as Aristotle, St. Thomas, and Dante tell us it is? One is, by position, or (that word that has come all the way down to us) by contract. The other alternative, on the other end, is something you find in the Hebrews, but also in Homer, and that is that the king is appointed by God, by Jupiter. So, *natural* excludes not only the conventional, but also the divine. It is human; but it is a humanity which is beyond our control. Somehow, there is this *a priori* instinct, by which men are made to gather together; and they make their gathering together a succession, to reach the end which is the conquest of the realm of knowledge. The view of posterity, of St. Augustine, hardly comes close. For them the state is a remedial institution. The state of St. Augustine can be compared to a hospital. If you're healthy you wouldn't need a hospital. The hospital is necessary because man is sick. According to St. Augustine, the state is natural because God permits it; but what kind of natural? It is natural enough, but fallen nature — a far cry from Aristotle's conception.

What prevails in the Middle Ages is the contract theory of the state. When the king grows strong and wants to assert himself — or when the fight was on between the emperor and the pope, between Henry IV and Pope Gregory VII — it was in the interest of the Church to debase the power of the political order, and what better way to debase it than to make it derive from a contract? This was the argument of the publicists. All the political orders, from the lowest up to the highest, are bound as the result of a contract. If the ruler breaks his part of the contract, the subjects are released from their part. They can renounce their loyalty. When a pope excommunicates a king, the subjects can go on and act as if the king doesn't exist.

The alternative for Aristotle's position is there long before. It is found in the Epicureans, of course. The state, as the Epicureans conceived it, is conventional. It is very much like the state of Hobbes, in a general way. You go ahead and do anything you want — it doesn't matter what you do. Get whatever it is you want — it doesn't matter how many people you grind underfoot. The trouble is that the others do the same thing; and it is doubtful if any amount of good you can enjoy by crushing others offsets the amount of evil you suffer by being crushed. Therefore an agreement is reached. This is a very old doctrine, criticized with contempt by Plato but resuscitated by the Epicureans. The state is a contract. If you won't hurt me, I won't hurt you. It is not so good, but it is not so bad. Of course, the earliest conception of a state by contract is to be found in Socrates — or rather, in Plato's Socratic dialogue, *Crito*, where there is that magnificent address of Socrates to the laws, in which the whole contract theory is worked out. Something comes out there that was very agreeable to the people of the seventeenth and eighteenth centuries. It can hardly be taken seriously now — it's a joke.

Let's suppose the ancients did make a contract. How do we become bound by it? The answer given by Socrates was very acceptable to the seventeenth century, but not today. Socrates says that after you're born and as you reach adult age, the fact that you didn't leave, that you remained here, worked here, got married here, constitutes a tacit, implicit signing of that contract. If you didn't like it you could have left. And that's what many of them did. In the seventeenth century they said: we'll go to America, or we'll go to Sicily. Try to carry it out today and see where you can go.

Against this general background, we can trace other theories of the state. We are familiar, of course, with the contract theory as it appears in Hobbes and in Locke. Locke presupposes a state of nature in which man, not yet joined to a state by contract, has certain rights. How you can have rights as such before a state is formed Locke never explains. But there they are, these rights antecedent to the state; and the state is formed in order to guarantee them. Of course, this is a doctrine very dear to the souls of Anglo-Saxons, in spite of the major difficulties connected with it. The doctrine of Hobbes, simply put is *bellum omnium contra omnis* — the war of all people against everybody — a general fight. To put an end to that terrible condition, a contract was made and the state was formed. Of course, for Hobbes, as well as for Locke, it was a way to safeguard your rights and impoverish the ruler. In Hobbes, it turned out to be a great support for monarchy.

Then there's Rousseau. Was there a contract theory before Rousseau? Yes, hundreds of them. In Rousseau there is also a surrender, not to a monarch, as in Hobbes, not to one man but to everybody, to ourselves. You are at once one of those who command, and one of those who obey. First we have to get together, and for once, at least, be unanimous to create the law of the majority. From then on, we can get along as long as we have a majority — and the devil take the minority. Of course that is the great idea behind the *contract-social*, which we saw worked out in the Convention of 1793. These are all part of the history, of the opposition to Aristotle's doctrine. Aristotle does not in any way admit that there was ever a period in history when people roamed around without laws, without a state, an age that was considered bestial by some — Protagoras, and Democritus, and Lucretius, and even Cicero himself. You couldn't fit the contract theory into the picture unless you posited this Domocritean age, as it is called. The other was the theory of the golden age. That theory recalls the name of Hesiod. But, of course, the poet in the Roman world who gave it its most popular form, the form in which it was echoed through the Middle Ages was Ovid. It was Ovid who put the finishing touches on it as far as posterity was concerned.

Against the setting of the golden age, our ancestors created the beautiful, non-existent character of the Noble Savage. It was an imaginary character, but people believed in it. They described the life of such men: how they lived, what rights they had, and how they surrendered those rights. Of course, for Rousseau, every surrender of rights was bestial except a surrender to oneself in the name of mankind.

What are the alternatives to natural rights? When we speak of a state existing by nature, we are jumping to the very opposite extreme of what we mean by natural rights today. The word nature is there but with a very different meaning. Aristotle's approach to all things is through nature. As far back as you can go, there was never a beautiful period of roaming about alone; all men by nature — as they search for food to eat, as they propagate themselves — gather together. At first, this gathering may not be quite what it should be, but, eventually, as Cicero says, someone comes — an unusual man, superior to the rest — who shapes this instinct, gives it greater meaning. For some it is the philosopher; for Cicero it is the orator, who first sees what is best and then succeeds in convincing the rest. However it is done, it is purely a matter of extracting the ultimate act of a potency, carried to its utmost.

The next step in developing this political doctrine of Aristotle has to do with the variety of the several forms this state can take. Or we can use the word that translators used, when faced with the word πολιτεία, which simply means state-form: they awkwardly render it as constitution. Well, whenever we say there is an order — and this bears truth on the face of it, whether natural in an Aristotelian sense or otherwise — there must be someone who guides this order to its end. The minute you say there is an order, a multiplicity of different individuals in different parts, there has to be a guide. The hierarchy is there so that a certain end can be reached. So there must be one that guides. By one we mean an individual or a group; but, if a group, then it, again, must be united by order to act purposefully. There are many natural orders, orders of all sorts; but what distinguishes this natural order from other orders, its norms from other norms, are the laws. Whenever you have an order, whether it's a club, or a university, or anything you want, you always have order, and you have norms.

What is the difference, then, between the state and other groups? Force! There is coercion, all the way up. The man who leads, who guides the order toward its end, must be able to use force. He must be able to enforce the principles and norms that bind the state together. Therefore, says Aristotle, those of my predecessors who said there was only a quantitative difference between the various social orders, who said there was no difference between a very large estate and a small state, made a mistake. There is a qualitative difference, and this is shown by the fact that in the one case you can exert coercion. Why are we able to maintain our clubs, insurance associations and all the rest? Why are their norms respected? Suppose a member of a club wants to use the club exclusively for his own benefit; how can you stop him? You have no direct force. You appeal to the thing under which they all stand, to which they all must answer: the state. The state will exert coercion. All the other orders function only on condition that there be above them an organization which is capable of using force.

That is the fundamental distinction. There is another, just as basic. In order to do all that it must do, the state must be self-sufficient. The famous word — familiar in the days when totalitarianism was still popular — is autarchic, ἀντάρκεια. The "archy" in ἀντάρκεια has nothing to do with the "archy" in monarchy. It is just a blundering on the part of the Italians and the English (not the French and Germans, who retain the distinction), who in translating the two words obliterated the distinction by spelling both the same way. So the state can exert coercion; or, as Aristotle says, the state exists, its norms respected by those that rule and those that are ruled over — norms which exist in view of the end to be attained and which can be enforced by coercion. And all the several forms of government, all the varieties of states or constitutions (although that's a bad word) can proceed from it. I object to the word constitution because in our day the word has been so brilliantly colored in connection with the idea of constitutional monarchy that it doesn't give the meaning it should give to the word it was supposed to translate, which means, simply, form of government.

What are the possible relations that can exist between a body that rules and a body ruled? The governing body can be one, or some, or all. In one case you have a monarchy, in the second an aristocracy, and in the third case a popular government. He doesn't call this last *democracy*; he reserves that word for the corrupted form of popular government. The good form is not called democracy. Of course, the distinction was not kept and democracy came to acquire the good meaning and it has kept that good meaning coming down to our day.

Usually these forms are found mixed. But these are the three Aristotle distinguished — you find them in Plato before him, and elsewhere — and they have at their side, in each case, degenerations of each: the corruption of monarchy, the corruption of aristocracy, and the corruption of popular government. The corruption of monarchy is *tyranny*. The deterioration of aristocracy is *oligarchy*. And finally you have the corruption of popular government: ὁημοκρατια. The word for the opposite, for the good form of popular government is completely dead now. It's a word that had to die because it was too much used in another sense, for state in general, πολιτεια. Aristotle used it on one side to refer to all governments in general, and on the other side to refer to that particular form which is the good form: popular government. It died and remained dead for centuries but the thirteenth century resurrected it. The *politia* (you find it in St. Thomas) meant democracy in the good sense. But most of the translators have gone astray, for the meaning of the word in the narrow sense was not understood.

But the question is: what is the criterion? What distinguishes the good form of government from the bad? It is good when the ruler does not consider his own good but the common good. When the king considers only his own welfare, no matter how kind he may be, he becomes a tyrant. Or when the several people that rule consider only their own welfare and ignore the rest of us, you have oligarchy. And, finally, when the majority acts in its own interest, and turns out legislation that does no justice to the demands and claims of the rest, then you

have democracy, the corrupt form of popular government.

What does the "public good" mean? If the union,
for example, gets all it wants for its members, what
happens? Or, if we have a commercial situation, and we
think only of those who export? Somebody's being
sacrificed. We have to think of those who produce and
market their goods here, but also those who import
goods. Suppose we consider in our legislation only the
interest of those who import, then those who export are
excluded. So we make laws to include them also. But
there are others left out: those who teach, people in the
professions, who may be very badly hit, and often are, by
an effort to push to the extreme the interests of some
individuals. You get to a point where you must try to
define the common good so that no one is left out. That
is what the state always aims at — theoretically, at least.

And that is why about forty years ago the argument surfaced in France about the medieval estates —
the clergy, the nobility, and the third estate, the com-
mons. Just as the estates disintegrate the state by pursuing their own interests, so is it with syndicates and the
unions: they too are on the way toward destroying the
state by pushing their claims to the extreme. But is this
enough to make clear the idea of the common good?
When you have made a lot of people happy with a lot of
wealth, have you reached the common good? No! Because the common good goes beyond economic justice;
there must be social and political justice also. You can
only define the common good when you have decided
on the end, when you have established what the state
exists for. There, of course, we may well differ, so we'll
let it rest at that.

Of course, Aristotle, who in doing this was simply
resuming teachings that had gone before, realizes that

this is purely quantitative and there has to be introduced something qualitative. So he goes back over the ground. Here is a popular government. What is the assumption behind it? How did it get there? The assumption is that all the people are equal. If you start out by saying that thirty percent of the people are superior to the rest, you wouldn't have a popular government, but that thirty percent would rule. Every time you have a popular form of government, you have to have, openly or tacitly assumed, the notion of equality. You begin by establishing political equality, but then you go on — I don't say how — to establish equality in every way. Having established political equality, you go on to say that everyone is equal in bravery, in intelligence, and so on, and that is why republics deteriorate.

So you assume equality, and this equality becomes the condition for liberty, for a free regime which is such that everyone in turn is ruler and ruled. That's what freedom means. What else could it mean? Everybody is or can be ruler and ruled. Those who are ruled today will rule tomorrow. That was true then, and is still true today.

When do you have a good government of the few? Obviously, you can't assume equality; you have to assume some kind of superiority. You can't escape that. But what kind of superiority? Moral superiority, superior because some are braver and more self-sacrificing or something like that. There are but a few such, one might object. That's right. These few whom we suppose to have risen to power because of their superiority — these five percent (if that much of the population) having risen to power, proceed to exploit the situation by means of economic power. These few who govern become plutocrats, and then aristocracy degenerates into oligarchy.

Then Aristotle, with Plato who, in this, follows an

old tradition, assumes for a moment that θεός τύχη, divine providence (in reality, chance or fortune) puts out a superman whose virtues are so great that it is impossible for him to be a subject. When you have such a man in your midst you have two alternatives. You make him king or you drive him out, ostracize him. What does ostracism mean? Can anyone ostracize a person? No. It has to be someone who has the power or capacity to rule; not only those who actually do dominate, but also those so endowed that they could dominate. There aren't many such men. They are very rare. I haven't seen many, but democracies seem to like them by and large.

I've described the pure forms of government. Obviously they can be mixed up; you can have a little democracy, a little oligarchy, and a little tyranny all mixed up. Usually they are found running into one another until you have run through them all. This is the famous cyclical theory of Polybius, which we find for the first time in the political sphere in Plato (the last time I saw it was in connection with a little booklet that tried to justify the rise of Fascism). This is the επίκυκλος of Polybius — how one form of state degenerates into another. What happens when you have a good popular state that deteriorates? A popular majority, acting in its own interests, says: we have force in our hands, let's do what we want. Let's give the professional people, the professors what we want them to have and nothing more. What's wrong with that? Nothing, except that a state can't operate that way. A group gets control and then a tyrant steps in. There are several ways by which an oligarchy becomes a tyranny.

Ten or fifteen years ago, a theory emerged that was very popular, although nobody talks about it any more. It is a theory that said all this is nonsense, there is nothing to this idea of various forms of government. It is really all one. It was Pareto who put that idea forward.

What are all these states run by? Who runs them? An elite. And when you join Pareto and Sorel you get something that had an astounding development in Italy in the 1930s.

Well, how can you avoid it, this cycle, this deterioration from one form to another, which is so very destructive? Aristotle, Cicero, Polybius are the names to remember here. Polybius elaborates these ideas most fully. He is the biggest name in antiquity when it comes to political theory. Most of the wise things that Machiavelli cracks out now and then come from Polybius. Polybius says that to be stable a state should be a little of all three: part monarchy, part aristocracy, and part popular. Rome is eternal, he says — of course it wasn't eternal but it did last quite a long while — Rome is eternal because it embodies all three forms: the monarchic principle in the consuls, the popular assemblies for the democratic principle, and the aristocratic principle in the Senate. Rome has that mix.

What is the formula? *Senatus populusque*: the Senate and the people of Rome. The consuls represent the element of kingly rule, and this is true historically, as you can see in the transition of the monarchy to the republic. And you have therefore in the consuls, in the magistrates, *potestas*. In the senate you have not *potestas* but *auctoritas*, authority. And liberty is guaranteed by the pressure exercised on the state by the *popolus*. The first thing that comes to mind when you speak of this check the people have on the state is the tribunes, the power of the tribunes.

That, briefly, is the theory that emerges from the cyclical explanation of the changes of states, which in turn emerges from what Aristotle said about the different forms of states.

1. Can a state engage in trade and still remain a state?

All these states of antiquity are welfare states. The idea of everyone going his own way was alien to them. Not only Aristotle, but even St. Thomas, says that the ruler is not only expected to operate in the sphere of *lex*, but he must see after and suggest and carry out all those measures that have to do with the welfare of all. That is the common good. Of course, the notion of a socialist state as we see it today did not present itself. The means were few and —

2. I meant: if the state is dependent on products it gets from elsewhere, if it is dependent on trade, can it still be a state?

Oh yes. Aristotle treats that. There is trade. But he says, and St. Thomas repeats it, that a good state should try not to be dependent on imports. It should try to be self-sufficient, because if war comes it won't be able to carry on. But the answer to that had been given already. The Athenian fleet was an answer. What we don't have we'll get from elsewhere, wherever it happens to be; we have the means: the Athenian fleet. Thucydides tells us about it.

21. THE "ORGANISTIC" THEORY
OF THE STATE

A few words in connection with the theory which we today call "organistic." The organistic theory (a horrible word) has to do with the doctrine of sacrificing the parts for the whole. St. Thomas tells us that in case the need arises we have to sacrifice not only our wealth but our life, if necessary. He gives an example which was already fifteen hundred years old at the time. When an organism is sick because of an infection of the arm, you amputate the arm to save the body. The habit of mind that looks upon the individual members of a society as its limbs is justified therefore in sacrificing the individual for the whole, for if the body as a whole dies, no matter how sound any member may be, it too perishes. If the state perishes, if anarchy sets in, the individuals that constituted it either form a new state, or else they cease to operate as human beings.

It's a popular theory today. It sees in society the individual man writ large and sees in the various classes or castes of this big man, the various psychological faculties of the individual man. When you project the three psychological faculties upon a big screen, you get the state; and what previously were the individual faculties become the classes of the state. There is the faculty of desire, the faculty of θυμός — the spirit of daring — and the faculty for reasoning. Here we have the first systematic statement, demonstration, description of what we are calling today the organistic theory of the state. The famous example from Roman history records that when Menenius Agrippa was sent to the plebes, who had

decided to withdraw, he relates the fable of the body. If
the stomach refuses to function, the body suffers, but
the stomach suffers too. The story shows that this
organistic theory, as is the case with so many other of
these theories, is a spontaneous development, a spontaneous way of looking at things. But, this organistic way
of looking at the state — particularly in the Greek days —
differed from ours. There you start off with the state,
and you try to see to what extreme you can extend its
power. Today we start off with the individual and try to
keep the power of the state within as narrow limits as we
can.

Cicero had the organistic theory, the medieval-
ists had it, you find a full development of it in Seneca.
John of Salisbury has it, and so on through the ages. Of
course, what is behind it is a permanent body made up
of transient, changeable parts. Here you have the United
States. I die, you die, other people die, and others take
their place, yet the United States remain. Nobody living
here 50 years ago — better to say 150 years ago — is living
now, but the state is still there. It is an organization that
abides, but which, as time goes on, changes. As to what
the motives and directions of these changes are, the two
main lines of philosophy differ as black differs from
white. But there is a change, and it is a change that
preserves the past, and tries to experiment with it,
making it into a future that has been thought out with
certain needs in mind. And always this maintenance of
the past and experimenting of the future, tends toward
amelioration. We can affirm it or deny it as we see fit.
Most of us, most people, of course, think they see two
levels in all this: the level that history gives — the absolute
monarchies and the culture they produced, the period
of the enlightenment, the French Revolution, and the
Napoleonic period, all with their characteristic cultures

— and another level, which enables us to say this was good or this was bad about the enlightenment, the French Revolution was good up to a certain point and then it went bad, etc. You can take the position of Burke or the opposite, it doesn't matter very much which, and so on and so forth. There is the establishment of history, and the criticism of reason.

Some people deny that there are two levels and that there is a way to criticize history. It is not we who can judge or place values on history, but it is history that imposes values on us. What we think is an evaluation of our own is, in reality, imposed upon us by the actualization of history. When a thing is actual, historically, we look upon it as rational. Any number of things that have begun to happen in history have failed to actualize, and have been forgotten. But the French Revolution has not failed. We have a certain judgment about it. That judgment is not due to a subjective, interior conclusion of our own, but to the fact that certain things actually happened, that the French Revolution has actualized itself. The extent of its actualization determines our judgment of it. The objection to it which remains was simply a crutch to be cleared away. The person most responsible for this theory, that there is no criterion by which we can judge history, who presents this in its complete form is Hegel. This is the Hegelian doctrine. Everybody knows Hegel today, because of their interest in Marx.

Marx inverted Hegel. You always hear about Hegel now, but in my time, when I was a young man, if you talked about Hegel, about the dialectic process, you weren't understood by many people. Today even the barber talks about the dialectic — or, at least, about dialectic materialism. So it has gotten some currency in common parlance. It means there is no *raison raisonnant*

— mankind cannot judge what is historically good or bad. All we can ascertain is simply that it is good because it has established itself, that it is historically actualized.

The theory of Aristotle thus passes into the organic view of the state. In this context, we have to admit the great superiority of the Schoolmen over most modern thinkers, for they stressed that, above all other kinds of unity there is that particular one which establishes unity by order. It is very dangerous to carry the notion of individual unity into something unified, not as an individual is unified organically, but by order. What does it mean to say that something is unified by order? Where do we have unity by order? In the state, in the army, in the university, to name the most obvious. You can hardly think of anything that is not unified by order. What does it imply, this unity by order? It implies a multiplicity that is made into one; and that multiplicity must be a multiplicity that is very various. Would you have an army, for instance, if you had a million men all alike, the same clothes, the same capabilities? Order demands diversification. And what establishes unification? The fact that all the various elements of this multiplicity are working toward the same end. In this organism, this animal — the state — unity rests or depends on the fact that all the different elements in it are moving toward the same end.

And here we have to consider the distinction between what St. Thomas might think and what a Greek might think about this common end that gives unity by order. This end for a Greek might be an ultimate end. For St. Thomas, who is a Christian, it cannot be an ultimate end. The exigencies of Christianity require a movement toward a higher end: let's call it by a word that says everything and yet doesn't mean anything particularly — not God, but the fruition of God. You can pour into it anything you want, you can fill it with Aristotelian intellectualism or mysticism or whatever. But before you can accept as valid for you the end of the state, you have to ask yourself whether it does or does not contradict that higher end. If it contradicts it then you can't accept it. You build on that system, the kind of polity St. Thomas built on it. If you have this higher end, you must have an order higher than political — you must have a moral state. But we have been saying all along that a state by its very nature cannot be moral. The opinion of Machiavelli on it, as we have said, was merely the restatement of a commonplace.

Granting all that has been said, it would mean that the Pope in the days of St. Thomas, would have to give his assent to the emperor, to all rulers; he would have to say: you can do anything you want, but whatever you do must conform to higher rules. That is why it is a ridiculous mistake to use in connection with this system the word totalitarian. Surely you must do everything the state demands of you, providing it doesn't contradict the higher end. Of course, we may say today that the state wants to and can be moral. Some people do say it. But when they do, they are saying something that is a hundred percent wrong.

Well, is it right or wrong? Is St. Thomas right? Just as you sacrifice the arm for the sake of the body, so you sacrifice the individual citizen for the sake of the state. (I'm sure some German scholar could write a Ph.D. thesis on the number of times this was brought out up to 1600.) What do you say to that? Is it correct? If the state tells you to charge that hill for the sake of the whole, what do you say? Sacrifice the limb for the body? Have you a right to do that? Put yourself in that position. What would you do? What is the attitude today? You are drafted and you are sent out to be killed. What's the

answer? There are only two answers given to it, historically. One is, *necessitas non habet legem* — necessity knows
no laws. Here you can repeat that maxim, that principle
certified in its truth by all the activities of Rome and
adopted by all peoples in all times. *Salus republica supreme lex est*, which means: the safety of the state is the
supreme law; which the Roman jurists proceeded to
explain by the principle: necessity knows no laws. But, is
it necessary that the state should live? Or, one can turn
around and ask: is it necessary for me to live? Is life such
a thing that I am willing to pay any price for it? Remember those beautiful lines of the Roman Pompeius Magnus,
which Plutarch tells us he addressed to his sailors when
setting out with the fleet, headed for sure destruction.
The text is in Greek, but posterity has preserved it in the
Latin form. You find it written in a hundred different
places all over Europe: *Navigare necesse est, vivere non est
necesse* — it is not necessary to live, it is necessary to sail
out against the enemy. D'Annunzio, the Italian poet,
never seemed to tire of it. It was one of his favorite
themes. Well, you're not missing much if you don't know
D'Annunzio. Still, out of justice to him, it must be
admitted that he was a brave man. Most people respect
him today more for his bravery than for his poetry. You
find those words everywhere. They are written on the
gates of Lubeck, and in several — at least three or four —
Breton ports. The life of Brittany depended not on the
life of the individuals but on navigation.

    Some people have insisted that, if you let certain
things happen, life is not worth living. Non-existence is
better than tainted existence. It's a very good Stoic
doctrine — the doctrine of many people. I don't see how
you can really uphold a moral system without somehow
acquiescing to it. These people say: here are some
persons drowning. One gets hold of a board but he gives

that board to someone else. You say he is foolish? No, what he is doing is not foolish. To do otherwise would have been an act of cowardice, and who wants to live on forever, or until death overtakes him, as a coward? There are some who do, of course, but there are plenty who don't. It's not a question to be settled by argument.

---

1. This term, natural law, has come to mean many different things, hasn't it?

It shouldn't have. That's the trouble with this field. That's the advantage of mathematics. If you don't know, you're thrown out, and the same with physics. But in our world, in the humanities, the less you know the more you thrive.

2. Would you indicate some of the different meanings it has had?

Well, you have to take the term back to the distinction — for which the Sophists can never be sufficiently praised — which resulted from that habit of theirs of always inquiring, about any existing thing, whether it existed by convention or non-convention. If non-convention, then it is above our interference, it has a permanency conventional things don't have. People don't agree on the conventional, but if a thing arises without convention, then it has all those qualities of permanency that compel agreement. But in this period, if a thing is not by convention it is by nature. There are written laws; but over and above these laws, there are unwritten laws with which every man, if he wants to live up to his nature, must comply. You have the law: Do unto others what you would have them do unto you. The Christian will express it in a different way: always do good, and always avoid evil. Or you can descend to particulars. If you are attacked and you react violently to defend yourself, that isn't something Athens or Sparta decides, it is human nature that determines it. So far, so good. This is the way the Stoics present it and Aristotle. A natural law is, for the Stoics, a law the reason of which is not influenced by conditions of this or that kind, or this or that place. On the basis of this, if there is such a law, valid for all time and in all places, let's enforce it and thereby create a world state. In other words, the cosmopolitanism, the universalism, the internationalism, or anti-nationalism of the Stoics is due to their conception of natural law.

Then you come to people who believe in a state of nature — that state of nature which is so totally alien to Aristotle and which we have so often described: the Golden Age. Or, if you want to transfer it to the Christian world, in Christian terms, it is the Age of Innocence. (It didn't last very long, I'm afraid.) It is the period before the eating of the apple, before the fall, before the first disobedience. This was a very bad deterioration of the original thought; what was a moment of rationality becomes a period of world history. Therefore you begin to say that natural law is the law of the age before man was corrupted, the law of the Saturnian age, or the age of the Noble Savage — if you want to put it that way.

This law of nature was not a written law, except in the Hebrew religion. If you examine the history of the Hebrews, you find that they — who had the law like everyone else written in their hearts — at a certain moment ran away from it. And God, in his infinite mercy, gave them a written law so that they might be saved. What law was the mosaic law? We call it numerically: The Decalogue. Now some of the Roman jurists — not Cicero, but some of the others — took up the idea of a natural period. And they described the institutions, the habits, the goings on of that period. So there came forth this consideration: now there are laws and slavery and private property, but in that age, in that Saturnian age — and here the poets come into it — there was no property. People used and ate what they found, and all men were free. In other words, they said — these Roman jurists — that by natural law all men are free. And by natural law there can be no appropriation of things needed for the continuance of human life.

Here comes a hitch. The naturality or naturalness of a law is established on the basis of its universality. But now you find that slavery and private property are universal. What happens? You find certain adaptations made to this mythological story. They had a *jus gentium*, a law of nations, which served them in dealing with other peoples — with foreigners in their midst — and they worked it over into a new meaning. And then they said (and you find it in the *Institutes* of Justinian): this state of nature did not last long. After the state of nature wars came — they don't explain why, in this beautiful Saturnian age of theirs, wars should have arisen — but wars came, and you are thrown out into a Hobbesian system, with everyone fighting everyone else for personal aggrandizement and greed for power, and so on. (This is not in the *Institutes*). As a consequence of these wars things were appropriated as private property, and those defeated and captured in war were made slaves. Hence, from this time on you have a regime of private property.

The natural law that established the universality of freedom passes; and this new universality, which does not correspond to nature, is ascribed to the new principle, namely: the *jus gentium*. That is the distinction between these two kinds of law, between natural law and what is called (but should not be) international law.

By the side of these, there is a third kind of law — civil law. Every state has its own, with the understanding that nothing in it should violate the dictates of natural law. Hence the great difficulty: these men, including St. Thomas, have to show how, under a natural law by which all men are free, private property and slavery set in. They explain it by saying that it is a rational development from natural law that aims at social utility.

One more thing: this continuous confusion of the distinction between law and right, or, in legal parlance, between subjective and objective law. What is a right — or subjective *jus*? Remember, the Romans had two definitions of natural law, that of Ulpian and that of Gaius. That of Ulpian establishes the fact that natural law is law that governs all species of animals. Therefore, such law, as far as human beings are concerned, must be limited to what we have in common with the lower animals. That is one definition. The other definition is the one on which St. Thomas rests his argument in the Second Part (question 90 and after). Natural law is the law which is dictated spontaneously by natural reason, which is common to all men.

Now, whether you follow Ulpian or Gaius, it doesn't

make too much difference. Here is the law that commands all animals to do certain things having to do with self-preservation and procreation. That's the law. Now I, a slave, am made to starve, or am kept from marrying. Then I come out, and say: this may be civil law, but it cannot be maintained, because it violates natural law. For on the basis of natural law, I have a right to disobey that civil law. I have a right to support and to marriage. In other words, a natural right is a right an individual has and can claim by an appeal to an existing law — a *jus objectivum, recht, droit, diritto* — we have it in all languages except English. In English we do not have a common word, but must distinguish law and right. We cannot force the meaning of one into the other.

Confusion comes, you see, when you try to establish what these natural rights are. Some say that private property is a right by nature, others say that private property is not by nature. All you have to do is examine the jurisprudence of any country to see that all attempts at progress, or change in any direction, have always been resisted by invoking rights under natural law. You can't do it, whatever it is, because there is a natural law. The habit has been to erect a series of natural rights in order to protect vested interests. It is the business of lawyers to do that, and they do it very well. But the philosopher must do otherwise. St. Thomas asks explicitly: does the law in question do good or does it not? If it does good, it is good; if not, it is not. Of course, the good must be examined and determined from the point of view of the natural claims of the animal to sustenance and reproduction — but, above all, from the point of view of that natural claim, which is the good of man, to which the goods of all the other parts must be subordinated, namely the good of the mind, which is the promotion of knowledge and the investigation of truth both practically and theoretically. So, you have a series of goods that must be done, and the higher must not be sacrificed for the lower; but you cannot build up the higher by destroying the lower.

3. Does St. Thomas teach that private property is by natural law?

No, he cannot, for common law says that goods are common. Private property is by "derived" law.

4. Like slavery?

Yes. And St. Thomas adds: if men were different, if they were better developed — or better trained, I should say — it would still hold today. The naturality of communism, like the freedom of all men, is not denied. Social utility has forced private property upon us. If men improved noticeably, then we could have communism. We could have equality in the economic as well as in the social sphere. The differences would remain, of course, in the other spheres, according to St. Thomas. This private property is what the French call a *pis aller*; it's a remedy to avoid a worse situation. That is why he says in those cases where you have men who have been trained, who have learned to live like human beings — as in the great monastic orders — communism does prevail.

5. Do later theologians agree with St. Thomas?

They have to. Of course, as the saying goes, give a lawyer a stick and he'll make a battleship out of it. St. Thomas, by decree of Pope Leo XIII, is authoritative, is the law in matters of social organization and social problems especially.

6. After the Golden Age, which came first: slavery or private property?

War came first. The Roman jurists put it this way. First *bellum*, first war arose; then, as a result of it, conquest, property and the making of slaves. In other words, this pure fiction — it's a pity the structure of Aristotle was abandoned for this fiction — this Golden Age suddenly snaps. What broke the equilibrium was fighting. The jurists don't explain how, but war arose, and the rest followed: acquisition of wealth, slavery, and the rest.

So, we have the state of nature, then controversy — war, conquest, and slavery. That's according to Roman law. St. Thomas is obliged, because of the Holy Scriptures, to assume, to give a chronological aspect to all this. For now, the Church had accepted the idea of a decay of natural law among the Jews, and the Decalogue; and St. Thomas accepts it — what else could he do? — but he never uses it. He falls back completely on the Aristotolian system.

22. THE YEARNING FOR SALVATION: MEDIATION

Before we reach another person as capable of such philosophic rigor as Aristotle, we must come down to the thirteenth century; although, in between, there is the greatest thinker Christianity has ever produced, namely, St. Augustine (but his greatness is of a different order). After Aristotle — and the tendency is constant — philosophy becomes ethics. Or rather, as every teacher used to indicate, there are three parts to philosophy. The first two are propaedeutic — instruments, introductions to the third, which is the essential part. This threefold division of philosophy we find now and all through the middle ages, and it comes to an end only with the complete return of Aristotle in the thirteenth century.

Those three divisions are, of course, logic or dialectic first because without it you couldn't begin to reason. The second is some kind of ontology, whether metaphysical or physical, so as to have some notion of the universe; both of these so that you may live well. And this applies equally to the Stoics and the Epicureans; and, in a limited range, even to the Skeptics. Of course, the ideal of the Stoics was exalted, so exalted as to be practically unattainable — even for the most perfect men of their group. The Epicureans present a rationally respectable system. There is a hierarchy: pleasure is indeed the primary objective in life; and for the sake of the highest one, which is intellectual, we must be ready to sacrifice the lower. We must see to it that the lower doesn't interfere with the higher. The teachings, the lesson, the theory behind it, seems very satisfactory. But, in reality, actually, as we go on toward the first century B.C., morally the situation becomes increasingly worse. Everyone knows about the materialism of the period. People looked toward the satisfaction of their sensuous desires.

The best picture we have of it — although it comes many centuries after, and is gathered from scraps of information — is a picture of life lived for enjoyment, of a life lived entirely for the sake of man, a life from which God has vanished, except as an instrument. This account is given by St. Augustine near the end of the second book of the *City of God*. You know, of course, what was going on in the first century B.C. and what followed. It all happened, the Christians explained, because God had vanished from the earth. Or, what is a closer approximation, we now have a universe which is entirely man-centered, in which you believe the kingdom of man has come, wherein there is nothing but man. Of course, the aspirations of man were very high, but the pressure is inevitably downward.

What about the ancient religions? Long before, in the earlier period — in the Olympian days of Greece, when men thought of the soul as inseparably connected with divinity — there had been real piety and awe. But from the time of Homer down, unless you try to dispose of it by having recourse to silly allegorizing, you have deities that more and more became objectifications of malefactions. St. Augustine, again has some very beautiful pages on it. Why shouldn't humans be adulterers? Some of their deities were masters at adultery. Why shouldn't they be thieves? The deities were thieves. You don't have to multiply the examples; you know what Jupiter was like, and Leda and Venus. You know about the escapades of these Gods — some not quite so bad. There is Mercury, the patrol deity of thieves. We could pile up any number of illustrations.

The ethical system, then as always, served only the highest; the religiously minded did what we always do. We don't create gods anymore for our aberrations. We are too rational for that; but we do work up a little philosophy, don't we? There is a general philosophy to justify a life of indulgence, and then there is a particular development given to some novel aspect of pleasure; and there is always a very progressive soul who writes a book to justify it. Well, so it went. Then, after three or four centuries, things culminate in a direction which was the very opposite of what was aimed at. We have said that these philosophic systems – philosophic in theory – aimed at something quite respectable in theory, but which was in practice very unsatisfactory, to the critic and to the people. Those people who aimed at nothing but happiness, nothing but the life of pleasure, the life of joy, produced an economic situation in which on one side there were people who could hardly exist, and on the other side people that had too much – so much that nausea inevitably followed, so that there was irritation and disgust everywhere. Of course the picture is forced, but you find it everywhere – and it's fairly accurate. Windelband's description of the time supports what I have said.

So it is not astonishing that around the first century a reaction is felt, a reaction sets in that is both philosophic and religious. It is the time now when disgust with the present creates a theory of authority – the theory which the Christians will later work out. St. Augustine especially will show the great value of it, how important it is. These present days are rotten, and therefore *laudantur tempora antiqua*, the good old days are praised. Of course, the present times, at all times, are rotten; but it is much more than that now, and that it is much more is shown by the fact that everybody goes back to the ancient authors; and when they don't find the evidence they want in the ancient authors, they make it up, they falsify the evidence. Usually people work it the other way, they appropriate the works of others and put their own names on them. But these people, one after another, write works and ascribe them to antiquity. This was particularly true of the Neo-Pythagoreans. For a long time it was thought that Pythagoras had left a great deal of writing, because so much material was found bearing his name. But, in reality, he left very little, as Aristotle tells us. This mass of material bearing his name was a creation of the first century B.C., written by men who tried to give greater validity to their thought by fixing his name to it.

Now too, in connection with Pythagoras, comes the famous maxim for authority, first given in Doric Greek, because the falsifier was very smart and knew that the earliest sayings attributed to Pythagoras were in Doric Greek. Every journalist in the old days availed himself of it as least once a week: *ipse dixit*. He said it — he, of course, was Pythagoras. And, to indicate the temper of the period: philosophy being insufficient, deification presents itself. Falsification of authority is not enough; some of these men present themselves as men who are in contact with divine power. We have dozens of names of men who come with messages that were supposed to have been revealed to them. And with this we reach the second characteristic of the period. One was the recourse to revelation, the other was the recourse to authority.

Everywhere you turn, you sense — wherever you read, even in the humblest papyri — you find evidence to indicate that people were yearning for something. Again I refer you to Windelband for an account of the period, how the people were longing for a redeemer — not only the Jewish people, others as well. And that explains the popular recourse to oriental religions at this time, in the hope that somewhere, some of those people might teach mankind how to live. There were many, but, of course, the one that survived — all the oriental faiths passed away — the one that satisfied all these longings, and an infinitely greater one, was the one that came from the Hebrew people. Mankind, not only just Hebrews, felt that perhaps, not only in the words of the Old Testament that taught lessons for this life, but in the expectations of the Jews, there was something that might lead them to hope for a new life, something of this σωτηρία, of this redemption for the world, coming not simply for the Jews, but for all mankind.

The realization came and made itself felt everywhere, that the redemption would come only if men did something to deserve it. Among the Jews, and elsewhere, men came to feel two things. First of all, they came to feel that nature was such that it would inevitably produce some men that are strong and well and handsome, and some that are weak — the well-endowed and the not-so-well endowed. With all these disparities one could not find σωτηρία, salvation in this world, and therefore we should look somewhere else, where there are no differences of sex, of wealth, of looks; only the difference that distinguishes the good from the bad. And so, the thought surfaced that we have to do something to deserve this future, when the good shall be rewarded. In other words, mankind has to be liberated of its evil impulses.

Again, it is the religion of the Hebrews that provides the basis. In other words, the presence of original sin now makes itself felt. From the beginning, from Adam's day on, mankind, enhancing the influence that came from Adam's crime, multiplying the possibilities, had come at last to the horrible state, the deplorable condition described earlier. How could people improve themselves, when the whole of their nature was tainted?

How can you improve when you come into the world not with a weak spot merely, but with sin? In other words, what you inherit from Adam is that every act of your life is an act of sin: sin is everywhere. How can man again become just, so that he may again move justly, live a life that will be the very opposite of this life? How can man justify himself, so that he can again have a nature that will aspire to the good, which he doesn't have now, and a capacity to attain that good?

The answer is, of course, that man by himself could never do it, for it is an infinite task. The only way that man could change, or regain his nature would be by an act of justice. God could do anything, of course; for the God of the Jews is omnipotent. But, as we said, we are in a sphere of justice here. Man must do a just act; but man cannot do it, all the generations of man together cannot do it. That act of justice, from the very start, has to be an act of mercy, an act of God, in which God gives himself, becomes a man to atone for all sin, so that as the result of the expiration of the sins of the whole world, the nature of man will again be such that it can proceed to live, to some extent at least, as it lived before the original fall, deserving salvation (for that is the meaning of the Greek word we have been using all along).

In other words, what now emerges is the concept of mediation. This concept of mediation is very old; it first figures in the theoretic field. Now it arises in the moral field. In the theoretic field it arose from the efforts of philosophers, particularly the Platonists, to approach the idea of the Good. More and more, the idea of the good was thrown back. How far back it was thrown, how transcendent it became, we shall see when we come to talk, quickly, of the Neo-Platonists.

These people of the first century did not know the Neo-Platonists, but they knew Plato, who once, at least, presents us with a God that is beyond being, beyond thought. Beyond thought means beyond being, for the highest manifestation of being is thought. How can you get to it? How can you get to that divinity who is so far removed from you? Aristotle, you remember, transcended it, and at the same time brought it back, as a force: "love," which is attraction.

The idea of mediation came back through the Jews, and it came with Philo (unorthodox from their point of view, nevertheless it came). This great Platonizing Jew, Philo, gives us the philosophy of the *logos*, the idea of the trinity, of three persons. The first person is the God of the orthodox Jews, God the Creator of Genesis. The other is the *logos*, the word, the Son. The Father conceives Himself, and when you conceive you generate. This generation, this child, this son — for that is what you get out of the conception, is it not? — is the *logos*. In the beginning of the Gospel of St. John you have the *Verbum* — *et verbum caro factum est.* The word became flesh. This word does not figure in the Old Testament, but it does figure in Greek philosophy. It now appears as the mediator in Hebraic Platonism. This God, which the Platonizing Jews had hurled into infinity, now comes to have some connection with us, becomes the *logos* of the Christians, conceived as the Son of God, conceived by Him from eternity.

You always find Christ the mediator spoken of; but long before Christ, the Jews, Philo, had spoken of the *logos* as mediator, as something that comes between man and divinity.

At the time we are considering, this mediator takes on a new role. These people are not interested any longer in getting at the idea of ideas with their minds. The problem is not to use God as the light of our intellect. Let Him be that; God is, if you will, the light of our intellect. But above all, He is the power to regenerate our nature. We need this mediator to redeem us from sin, to make our nature become again something like what it was before original sin. And this implied, this required an act of atonement so great that no man could perform it. Therefore, the solution for the Christians lies with God, eternity passes over into time, the infinite becomes finite — or if you will — this eternal *Logos*, this child, this Son conceived by the Father, passed from His eternal state of ideas into flesh, assumed mortality to pay the debt owed to God — to God, mind you, not to the devil. For very often you hear that the reason Christ took on the flesh was indeed to make atonement, to pay our debt, but to Satan. Not at all. Some of the Greek fathers, it is true, did for a time hold this, but it was soon changed. We were indebted to God for our lapses, as a result of Adam's lapse, as a result of the workings of original sin. So that God, in this act, is both just and merciful. Man is made just again through the mercy of God. From now on these two, justice and mercy, are the chief aspects of divine power, and pass on to all power. You can hardly read ten lines in any treatise on government without coming on the statement that all power, because it must imitate God, Who is the source of all power, must be flanked by mercy — mercy, which is the twin sister of justice. Even those poor kings who have disappeared, used to claim a power characterized by *Gratia et Justitia*. In some nations, even the ministry of justice was known as the ministry of *Gratia et Justitia*.

That is the great event from which all that follows proceeds. You can look at it philosophically, rationally; or you can look at it religiously; or genetically, as I have been doing here, in connection with that deterioration of morals that finally called for remedial action, as part of the providential design. What was the result of this action of God, besides paying off the debt? The two things that count in the life of Christ, that must be taken into consideration, and depending upon which one you accept, you belong to the Oriental Church, or rather, Oriental Theology, or Occidental Theology — to the east or the west — are not the two natures, not the eternal passing into time, not the infinite becoming finite: God had to become man. The mercy of God consisted in the Son of God being man, so that by being punished though guiltless, the great debt of man might be paid. The two moments to be considered are: first, the humiliation of Christ, of the *Logos*, in taking on flesh, a humiliation that had an extraordinary result, that kept the Neo-Platonists away from Christianity, from the idea that the divine should take on matter. You know how the Platonists despised matter. It was a coffin. The second was the *resurrection carnis* — a resurrection of the flesh. The idea of a life, not eternal, but at least immortal, led in the flesh, was to the Platonists anathema. And, therefore, some of the finest minds in the pagan world were kept away from a religion which in every other way attracted them, a world in which they might otherwise have felt very much at home. They abhorred this resurrection of the flesh; the flesh which is so rotten here on earth. Why should we want it in eternity? That is what Porphyry tells them, and that is why St. Augustine scolds him so severely.

Besides the humiliation of the incarnation, there is the death on the cross. What is it that has saved mankind? The first act, or the second? Of course, when you come to the Western Church, when you come to the doctrine of ecclesiology, the second act, the death on the cross, becomes the dominating moment of Christ's action for mankind. The famous sentence, again from St. Augustine, that indicates what this moment means for the church is: From the wounds of our Savior as He lay on the cross, streamed forth the spirit which is embodied in the sacraments by which the Church exists and through which man is saved. This Church, shaped, formed by the sacraments, this institution, this association, this body (that's what St. Augustine calls it), is the mystical body, and we are but cells in that body. And — according to St. Augustine and some of his immediate predecessors, St. Cyprian and others — salvation is possible only if you become a cell in that body. Eventually, therefore, the whole thing hinges on the crucifixion. That is why western Christianity, Roman Catholic Christianity, is not satisfied simply with the cross as a symbol; you have to have the body of Christ on it. The criticism of this has been that it is in bad taste, very baroque. That may be true. But if it is, you have to carry your baroque back at least as far as St. Augustine, and you will have to show how your charges of bad taste apply to him, as well as to the others. Surely bad taste was not to be counted as one of his deficiencies.

But all of this is by way of anticipation, merely to indicate what the two moments are. One is the humiliation, the humiliation that glorifies the flesh so much that, as St. Augustine says, even the Platonists are bewildered. And the other is the crucifixion. What came of this for posterity? Those that saw it, saw it. But after that, what did Christ leave? What happened later? Who founded the Church, who shaped the Church out of Christ's death? To speak sober language, who founded the Church?

The Church has a birthday, the Pentecost. Who founded it? The Holy Spirit. And to return to the image of St. Augustine — which is more than an image — this body has a head, and that head is Christ. And what connects the head with the body (this much older than St. Augustine) is the Spirit. It makes the members of your body parts of a living organism. This is the third person of the Trinity, that proceed from the Father and from the Son, to those atoms, if we want to call them such, that constitute the body. Through the Holy Spirit, come three virtues. Of course, it doesn't mean that every cell in the body gets them — St. Augustine is very pessimistic about it; he says that very many, though they are members, do not get this emanation of virtues. They are, of course, Faith, Hope and Charity. Man becomes just through faith, but faith that is not only evidence of things unseen but something that blossoms forth into hope, and finally into love — *caritas* — which is love for God and love for mankind for God's sake. And this last virtue, *caritas*, is not simply a virtue, but God in us, for as you all know, God is love.

23. THE NEW RELIGION OF FAITH, HOPE, AND LOVE. ST. AUGUSTINE AND ST. THOMAS

What facilitated the passage to the new religion was the condition of the times and the constant repetition that the world is so bad, there is so much injustice and strife and misery in it, that there must be another one. From now on in the Western world, even with the Hebrews, this idea of a life that will do justice to all injustices, that will rectify all that there is bad in the world, makes itself felt more and more. Those who looked with forebodings upon the condition of the world could console themselves with this idea of salvation for which they were all yearning. We also stressed the fact that it was pretty hard to be religious in the proper sense of the word. Not that religion has to identify itself with ethics — when it does that it is the death, the end of religion — but from now on religion is such that it is not separable from ethics. How true were the words St. Augustine spoke: that the most immoral beings, the greatest criminals, were the Gods that appeared on the stages of the pagans. They were adulterers and thieves, and encouraged others to be so. The new God is the very opposite of these; he is the God of all virtues. You have only to look at the statement of the beatitudes, the Sermon on the Mount; compare the lessons you can learn from the utterances there, with what you can draw from the utterances of Jupiter and the other pagan gods.

This new religion is a religion that establishes and

sanctifies, in a way, morality. After all, most people who know very little about Christianity, as compared with what preceded it, accept the fact that it practically denied all values, except one: the sacredness or worth of the individual human soul. You know how they scoffed at all other values, at superiority of health, or beauty, or even of intellect. The pomp and pride of all these things were gone. The essential thing is to be good, as God proclaimed the good. But one might object: the god of Aristotle, or of Plato, or even the god of the Stoics surely is a lofty god of virtue. You can raise up the image as high as you want; but as you raise it in height, it becomes increasingly more difficult to reach that level and adapt yourself to his teachings.

And, of course, the god cannot be kept away in transcendence. You must see him, you must hear him; we must feel that he is taking care of us. Of course, the Greeks had a notion of providence, of πρόνοια, but this is not the general, cosmic providence, looking after the functioning of general laws. This is individual providence, looking after each one of us, for every individual must be taken care of. So it is the Father that must appear now, not the lodestone that moves all things by arousing in them a desire. It's the Father, and this is stressed now in opposition to the Hebrew religion — not one who rules with justice simply, but with justice tempered with mercy. That's the constant utterance we now find repeated everywhere: justice cannot function unless it is accompanied by and tempered by mercy.

All through this, religious people in pagan times had two ways of worship. One was the Saturnalia. Some of them have survived, like December 31st, St. Sylvester, the feast of Saturn. The Church opposed the Saturnalias but couldn't stop them, and finally tried to tame them, bring them under control. Every council of the Church condemned the feast of Janus, yet it survived. There were also the festivities of the solstice, which were incorporated from the practices of the Germanic peoples — what the Germans call the *Sommersonnenwende* — around the twenty-first of June. The only trait that has survived that is the bonfire. Now it is the great Roman Catholic feast of St. John.

That was one way you could be religious; by practicing certain rites, or, in other words, participating in these festivities. The other way was by rising to transcendencies; but for that you had to have knowledge, as we have seen. The question was, where is this knowledge to be gotten? It isn't easy to get that kind of knowledge. And now a teacher comes forth who says you don't need knowledge. All you need is faith. But there are two sides to faith; and, depending on which one you stress, you're either a Catholic or a Lutheran. St. Paul says faith is the substance of things hoped for, the evidence of things unseen, it's the *argumentum non apparentium*, evidence of things unseen.

Can you have faith, where everything is clearly seen? That question was asked of Pasteur. The man who asked it was a Catholic. He said that Pasteur, as a scientist, should see to it that all the Church teachings should be made rational. The answer to that is, if everything became rational, the Church would disappear. There are certain things that you accept without reason, and those are the things of faith. If reason could give you all the answers, you wouldn't need faith. Faith has to do with the praeter-rational or super-rational. In other words, it's a capacity for knowing that does not rest on reason, the assumption being that the sphere of reality is much greater than the field of rationality. That's one side of faith. The other — after all, faith is not simply a capacity to know — is this: the moment you know these things you are overwhelmed, you are animated with a confident expectation that something will come out of it, an expectation that because of faith we may again become just; the Lutheran would say: you know you are just. As a consequence of this — for faith cannot be idle — comes Love; love of God, that moves man to God through love of one's neighbor. You don't have knowledge. All you need to reach God and have that consolation people have been looking for, is faith.

Of course, how you get faith is another matter. St. Augustine would say: you pray for it. But whether you will get it depends on whether God, in his mercy, has decided to give it to you. Vulgar or popular Catholicism teaches, on a practical level, that, if you act right and you pray, you will get what you need. After all, according to the gospel, God came to save all of us. You will get faith, hope, and charity. These three things come to you from God as a result of Grace, a concept totally new in this world we are considering.

What is Grace? Many other things are different in Christianity, but always the difference is one of degree. The mercifulness of a Seneca and the mercifulness of Christianity certainly resemble one another, though quantitatively they are very far apart. And we all know that if you push a quantitative difference far enough you get a qualitative change. But in this one case, there is nothing similar elsewhere: Grace is something entirely new; and it comes to you totally undeserved — *gratia gratis data*, freely given. In addition, it restores, *gratia gratis data et gratum faciens*, making the human beings that have received this grace acceptable to God. Of course, of these three virtues, when you get to heaven, in the next life, only one remains. There is no room for faith, because you have the thing itself face to face. There is no room for hope, because your expectations are realized. There remains *caritas* alone. It is a pity, unfortunate, that this word "charity," in all languages, has come to be identified with alms giving, which is only a small phase of it, and a minor one. Charity should have retained its meaning of love. You can easily see how it got its present meaning. Love, of course, includes love of neighbor. If he is poor and you love him, you give him alms.

So: you move from faith and hope, to love of God.

Faith is really a pair of magnifying glasses. You take them off and everything is blurred; you put them on and everything is clear. It is a supplement to reason. But it is not only that; it also stimulates you on. As soon as you see clearly, as soon as this light that strikes the intellectual part in us, that creates a fervor in our will, shines on you, it makes you want a certain thing. And, immediately, the way appears: love. The desire is instilled in you for love of God, ἔρος φιλοσοφικός. Not desire in a narrow sense. The moment you have something that pleases, the moment you look at something with longing you are moved toward it by love. Aristotle speaks of it; and we took it up to the unmoved mover. In that context, it is still something seen; and seen, it arouses a desire, and what moves you toward this object of desire is love.

The love that comes from faith is something else. Here you see darkly, in a cloud perhaps, but you see a certain object, and you are enlivened by a very powerful expectation, a confident expectation, of reaching it. The other desire is different. If I desire a billion dollars — that's a kind of love too, isn't it — you can call it desire, but when you get up to a certain level, you have to change the word. Why not love? Because I would have no expectation of getting it. The expectation must be there. I could love to be Napoleon — I did once — but I didn't expect it and I never did anything about it.

Someone can always tell you that you put him there, this object of love. You can destroy all of this psychologically. The formula is very old. The usual one of the Sophists is: man built God in his own image. Not God made man, but man made God. That's the formula of the Sophists: man built God in his own image, then he forgot that he created him, and set him up on a high altar and knelt down and worshipped him. You can accept the formula or reject it, and according as you do one or the other, you are for or against religion.

Faith is the way to beatitude. Beatitude requires knowledge of God, requires philosophy. But there is another way: faith. The verification, the proof that beatitude is to be had by faith is found even on a low pragmatic level. How many people are there who get beatitude through faith? Are there people who are really happy through faith? There's the old lady in church, who takes out her rosary beads and seems perfectly happy; I wish I could have her faith, someone will say. Of course, there is always a certain amount of pride in saying that, because what that person means but doesn't say is: I wish I were as dumb as she is. The answer to that is to tell him how many people of superior intelligence have found satisfaction in just those things which seem foolish to him.

For a while people thought that everything could be dispensed with that wasn't faith. But then, all of a sudden, the demands of the intellect make themselves felt once more. People begin to say that they not only want to believe, but that they also want to know. They were people who wanted not only πίστις, but also γνῶσις. These people that wanted γνῶσις were the people who constituted that famous sect that almost shattered Christianity — it was perhaps the most dangerous crisis that

Christianity ever went through — the heresy of the
Gnostics. The struggle was fierce; but the heresy was
overcome, and a reaction took place. And that reaction
was, of course, very anti-rational. There are three words
that characterize this reaction. They are the three words
of thirty great volumes. I'm speaking of the words of
Tertullian, who said — and in various forms it has
reappeared throughout the centuries against the Gnostics
who say you have got to prove it rationally — *Credo qua
absurdum*; I believe it because it is absurd. You tell me
that it's absurd, and that's exactly as it should be. But of
course that too couldn't last. Crises followed one another; some were very serious. These things took a very
different direction in the East. In the West we find a
group of men, particularly in North Africa, who take up
a system that makes room for authority as well as faith,
for reason as well as for faith. St. Cyprian of Carthage
and others and finally, the great master of them all: St.
Augustine.

If I were to start to tell you merely the titles of his
works, I would run out of time. Of course, some things
about him you surely know already: that he is, in a way,
the philosopher of Christianity, of the Roman Catholic
Church, even though by Papal dictate the official philosopher is not St. Augustine, but St. Thomas. There are
many reasons, religious reasons, for that. Philosophically there is one great lacuna in St. Augustine — a lacuna
in the chain of philosophical thought. St. Augustine was
a man totally ignorant of the fate that philosophy had
undergone in the hands of the man who was perhaps the
greatest thinker mankind ever knew: Aristotle. He said
himself that all he knew of Aristotle was what is in the
Categories. And he said that he found it very, very
difficult, which can only mean that he must have had a
very poor translation. (He knew less Greek then than

when he was writing against the Pelagians.) In spite of
the linguistic difficulties, in spite of the bad translations,
St. Thomas rose to the Aristotelian level. He understood
Aristotle. But what is the message of these renaissances?
What is the constant problem? The ninth century renaissance; the Carolingian; the twelfth, thirteenth, and fifteenth century renaissances; it's a flow that increases in
intensity at certain moments, and then slacks off. These
moments take on certain characteristics but always, in
this long quest to recover what was lost of the civilization
of Greece and Rome, the question that arises in the
hearts of all these people when they hear of this world
that was so wonderful, in which philosophy was so great,
in which poetry was so beautiful, is: what's the use of
being a Christian? Part of the greatness of St. Thomas
was that he not only brought back Aristotle, but in his
commentaries and in his *Summa* he managed to build a
synthesis between peripatetic philosophy and the teachings of the Catholic Church. That was the grand gift of
St. Thomas. And yet, one can hardly say that St. Thomas
is an original thinker; and we have said already that St.
Augustine was so great that, if he hadn't of his own free
will put on the blinkers of Christian faith, he would have
reached heights not so much as dreamed of by the other
philosophers. He was checked; but checked as he was, he
launched all sorts of investigations, and placed before
the thought of man regions unsuspected.

But the question remains: why was not this great
thinker kept as the official philosopher by the Church?
St. Thomas is the official doctor of Christianity for the
Catholics; but St. Augustine becomes the official doctor
of Lutheranism. Or take that very dangerous movement
in the seventeenth century: Jansenism — Port-Royal,
Racine, Pascal; it is not only religious, for out of it came
the most brilliant literary group to come out of France.

Why did the Church speak out against it? Jansenism, according to the Church, was an exaggerated, misdirected Augustinianism. Or, there is the doctrine of ontologism in the nineteenth century. The ontologists took up the psychology of St. Augustine. How do we know truths, logical truths, mathematical truths? How do we know two and two make four? Or, practical truths: how do you know you shouldn't kill your father and mother? Well, you can give all sorts of pragmatic reasons, no doubt. But St. Augustine tells you that you grasp all these things with your mind and approach them with your soul, because all the time your mind is flooded with a light, and that light is God. If God stopped existing for a moment — which is an impossible assumption — your power of understanding would vanish. You would have a kind of arithmetic, like ducks or crows who seem to count. This is the doctrine of illumination, which is completely rejected by the Thomists, who put in its place the Aristotelian doctrine of abstraction. You have light, God is there; but instead of flooding you with light every time you enter upon a act of understanding, God has given you an active intellect. But that intellect only operates when the senses communicate to it what has passed through them — to be abstracted and elaborated. Against this conception of abstraction, you have the doctrine of illumination, which is a very attractive doctrine. You find it in a different way, which probably influenced St. Augustine, in Plato's *Republic* and the parable of the sun. This doctrine, taken up by some very distinguished thinkers in the nineteenth century, was called ontologism. The Church examined it, bishops assembled and condemned it, and there was one among them who was to become pope — Pope Leo XIII — whose contact with ontologism made him proclaim that the official philosopher should be St. Thomas. Not that St.

Augustine was not admired by this pope, but he could be misinterpreted. And the proof is the numerous heresies that have come out of St. Augustine. Nothing heretical has ever come out of St. Thomas.

There is nothing in this suggesting a relationship with the Modernist movement. Very bluntly and simply stated: the Modernists say that the important thing in religion is not the source but the accomplishment. Even if Christ had never lived, what is important is what Christianity has done. You have the Church, St. Augustine, St. Thomas, Dante, Raphael, the other great painters. This is all very beautiful from the point of view of sociology, no doubt, but the Church wouldn't stand for it. It was condemned by another pope — Pius X — a man to remember, because he was consistent. He was for peace and he meant it. When the leaders of France asked him to bless one of their corps, he refused. He would bless the forces of light, not of destruction. Of course, politically he was all off, but he wasn't supposed to be a politician. He was the Pope — a very pious man indeed — one of the noblest creatures to come across the world in the nineteenth century.

But all this has nothing to do with St. Augustine, who proved to be very dangerous for the Church. For example: you cannot reject as a Lutheran or Jansenist misinterpretation (it is too clearly present) the doctrine of predestination. Long before Adam was created, God knew that Adam would sin, and that from Adam's sin all mankind would be corrupted. And, regardless of any merit or lack of merit — out of that corrupt mass of humanity he picked out certain souls whom He would save, and sent them Grace, a summons; a summons of such irresistible force — irresistible Grace is the word he uses — that those so chosen have to be saved. They are not good, and therefore receive grace; they are good because God has sent irresistible grace. This is the doctrine of predestination. It makes it very difficult to have a Church, or even to see the necessity of Christ. God takes a short-cut. The Calvinists are for predestination. They used to say against the Catholics: what's the use of the Church? Everyone is predestined. The Catholics answered: then what's the use of Christ?

Some say the Catholics haven't explained or answered with sufficient reason. It's not a question of answering, but of the texts of St. Augustine, about which there is no question. First, certain people are selected, then they are summoned, and then saved. In other words, as he himself says in the letter to Simplicianus, why did Peter become what he became, and why did Judas do what he did? Why did God, who sent an irresistible summons to Peter when he was going astray, not send the same to Judas? St. Augustine says: I don't know; but I'm sure, I insist, that Peter went right and Judas went wrong because God had decided from all eternity that it should be so. He does no one any wrong: because all of us deserve damnation. That is the doctrine of St. Augustine, and there is no getting out of it. It's not that he first foresaw that so and so would go wrong, and therefore predestined him. No. He first predestined, and all else followed.

From this doctrine of predestination, we get St Augustine's entire political structure. God has predestined for salvation very few; the rest, the great majority, are predestined for damnation. They act immorally because they have no grace. They are all filled with lusts, desire for wealth, power and pleasure — St. Augustine goes through the long pageant of these desires — and their needs have called into existence the political state. The state is necessary because these people, with all their greed, with all their desires, would have exterminated

themselves. And therefore God, to prevent their exter-
mination, permitted — he did not create but permitted
— the constitution of states. The one advantage that the
state has is that it guarantees some kind of peace. And
peace is necessary so that those people may satisfy their
greed. That's what polity means, that's what a state is. It
is an organization of people who want to satisfy desires
more or less ignoble; and, in order to satisfy them so as
not to destroy one another they get together and form
a state.

In the state also are those few who are to be saved;
they have to stay there, they cannot form a state of their
own, because if all men in a state were such as these, you
wouldn't need a state. The state is like a hospital; if men
all got well, you wouldn't need a hospital at all. The state
exists because of the immorality of human beings; it is a
way of coercing people to be moral. If people weren't
immoral — if, taking the impossible, all people were
noble — there wouldn't be any need for a state.

So these people stay there. They are foreigners,
peregrini, *viatori*, in this city of the devil, this world of the
devil. And they will stay in the midst of this city until they
are called to return home. Who are they? God alone
knows.

24. ST. AUGUSTINE: THE SOURCE OF GREAT DOGMAS AND GREAT HERESIES

As we read *The Divine Comedy*, we find that Dante is learning, just as we are. His knowledge of Augustinian Christianity is clear early on, but it becomes quite impressive as we reach the closing canto of the Paradiso. Dante accepted St. Augustine, not only as the great thinker of the Catholic Church, but also of Christianity.

The fact is we find his doctrines as much outside the Catholic Church as inside it. He inspired Luther, for one. After the Council of Trent, the Church hasn't taken very kindly to St Augustine's doctrine of irresistible grace, absolute predestination, the complete enslavement of the will. The Church didn't pick it up, but Luther did. This part of St. Augustine's thought was tempered down after his death. St. Thomas did his best to pull the teeth out of it, without rejecting it. The Council of Trent entrenched that position, and Molino cut it to pieces.

We find Augustinian predestination also in Calvin. In other words, not only is he the greatest thinker for those in the Catholic Church, but also for those the Catholics would call heretics, from the earliest, from the first heretical disciple of St. Augustine: Wyclif. After him, there were a host of others. There was that very important heresy within the Church — people professing what they thought was pure Augustinianism — a group in France made up of the most enlightened thinkers and writers of the time: the Jansenists. And in the nineteenth century, again, there were some very religiously-minded people who accepted the extreme, the psychological realism of St. Thomas that insisted that you can't understand anything unless you have received the essential data through the senses. Dissatisfied with that, they returned to St. Augustine with a little bit of exaggeration. We do not understand things by abstraction; the grasp we have of things, the slight understanding we have, comes to us because of an absolute that operates in us. We don't see anything unless we see it in God; just as the divine *concursus* operates in all beings. What do we mean by divine *concursus*? It has come through in all languages. It used to be taught in the catechism; every child knew it.

Here is a tree, a house, a dog, myself. If God were to disappear, what would happen to this tree or this house, or myself? They would disappear, and I would disappear too. We exist only because the divine essence flows in us. The whole universe is kept in being, in action, in motion; all activity is kept up as a result of certain laws that operate — the laws of the heavenly spheres, of the elements. Each one is a particular case of an all-embracing, universal law. And this law — since the days of Greece, the law that governs the whole, first found in Heraclitus, before it passes on into Christianity and magnified by St. Augustine — is that, given God is good, all-knowing, unchanging, you have to grant providence. Because if God let things run in their chaotic course, he wouldn't be a good God, we wouldn't have the *summum bonum*. And if we grant providence, we have to grant the laws that constitute providence — those laws that operate in the stone, in the water, and that make fire rise, and operate in our reason. This multiple law is one in the mind of God; eliminate it and *solvet saeclum in favilla*.

Just as there is a *concursus* of being, there is a

concursus of knowing. We know because we know in God and because of God. It is hard to run this up to rival the Aristotelian doctrine, but there it is. In the nineteenth century it became a heresy ("ontologism") that made very much noise. The Catholic Church, since then, has decreed that future teachers in the Church be guided, before coming to St. Augustine, along safer paths mapped out by more sober thinkers. And since the man who was then a cardinal, who condemned ontologism, became a pope, seminarians have been guided in their studies along the lines of St. Thomas. For over a hundred years he has been the teacher of the Church.

St. Augustine is, of course, a theologian; but you can draw out of him quite an anthology of pure philosophy. What's the difference between a theologian and a philosopher? Why can't a theologian be a pure philosopher? Because a theologian is one who philosophizes, who operates within a particular frame, the frame of faith. But when St. Augustine lets himself go, he has the daring, he shows a power, an originality hardly to be found anywhere in the world. Fénélon is often quoted as saying that some day he was going to get together an anthology of philosophical thought out of the writings of St. Augustine, an anthology that was going to show that St. Augustine was an infinitely greater philosopher than Descartes. What is the famous thing of Descartes that everyone knows? *Cogito, ergo sum*; I think, therefore I am. Well, St. Augustine has it. Did Descartes get if from St. Augustine? He said he didn't; he said that he came upon it independently. That happens; look at the case of differential calculus, which was come upon simultaneously by Leibnitz and by Newton.

St Augustine *practically* formulated many of the great dogmas of Christianity. The Trinity was pretty much settled by that time; but he does take up the matter

twice in his life; he does break a lance against the Arians
(not Hitler's friends). What would cause St. Augustine to
encounter Arianism at this late date? It was settled,
wasn't it? What was going on? The Germans had come
down into the Roman world; and what they had just done
to Rome made him write a great book, *De Civitate Dei*.
They had sacked Rome — though not so thoroughly as
the Catholics did under Charles V. And when St. Augustine was about to die, the Vandals, the Arians, were
moving into his native Africa.

The dogmas I was referring to earlier were the
dogma of original sin, the dogma of redemption, the
dogma of crucifixion. St. Augustine said the definitive
word on each of these. He settled the three most dangerous ones; well, he didn't settle them, but he gave us the
materials with which to fight, on all levels, the Manicheans,
the Donatists, and the Pelagians.

What were the Manicheans up to? What drew
Dante to them? He was one of them. What brought him
to Manicheanism? Not the problem of evil. The older we
get, the more careful we are about saying things that
aren't true. St. Augustine was always careful, and the
older he got the more he insisted that there was one
voice always that he heard in his ears, a sentiment, a
name: Christ. Christ held him up. He didn't know it
when he was younger; he went on plunging into excesses, but all the time Christ was calling. He was always
indulging himself; while he was a student earlier, his life
was a round of self-indulgence. After all, it's pretty hard
to resist the lure of a mud bath. But he became aware
that it was a mud bath; he looked around, and with the
help of Cicero, he discovered the world of reason. And
here were the Manicheans who promised, or offered a
religion that sustained itself on reason. It's a claim that
always comes up — a religion that wants to be a science.

It promises that by working religious things out scientifically, religion will eventually reach the same results science has reached.

The scientist answers: why bother? It's already been done. Why do it over again? Well, the claim appealed to St. Augustine. But the real reason he picked the Manicheans, was that their reason promised to bring him in contact with Christ. Eventually he discovered that their reason would not do what it promised. And he saw also that in reality there was very little reason in their teachings, which were based on astrology. He is the first man to give a definitive and unanswerable criticism of astrology. After showing how senseless the whole thing was, he focused attention on the example of twins. He asked: how is it possible in the case of twins, to measure and account for the difference between them? He used the biblical example of twins that were born practically at the same time, and yet went on to live very different lives: Jacob and Isau. They were born not very far apart. Yes, said one of the Manicheans, but even an infinitesimal displacement in the circle would be sufficient to change the horoscope, even a difference of one-five-hundredths of a degree. And St. Augustine says: where is your instrument to measure such a difference? You can't even measure one degree. (They didn't have the instruments we have, of course.) But human folly continues. Even today, in this age of enlightened science, there are still benighted people who pretend to such knowledge. I would say to them — as he did — tell me what instruments you have to measure my horoscope. You would then find out how little they know. So, St Augustine explains, he rejected and became embittered against the hypotheses of the Manicheans, who, while putting forth the gospels and Christ, actually destroyed Christianity. They taught that there were two principles — not

one — a good and an evil principle. And they destroyed
the sacredness of the Old Testament by attributing it to
the evil principle. Why is the Catholic Church always so
insistent on maintaining the sacred character of the Old
Testament? On account of the Prophecies. It is the basis
of the whole theory of verification. The Catholic Church,
from the very beginning, has staked everything on it.
The Old Testament is the major premise in the syllogism
of which the New Testament is the minor premise. What
is foretold in the Old Testament is fulfilled, is brought
to fruition, in the New Testament. If you destroy one,
said St. Augustine, you destroy the other. I would say
that after St. Augustine, Manicheanism did not trouble
people in the fold any more; it survived in various
circles, and for a long time, but it was not a major threat
ever again.

Donatism was the heresy of North Africa. It is one
that we are apt to like in this day and age. It appears in
history in different forms again and again and is very
popular. It is the doctrine that affirms that the validity of
the sacraments depends on the moral condition of the
person who administers them. I say it's popular still,
because I myself have heard people say: I'm not going to
go to that church anymore, because the pastor isn't a
good man. The Donatists went further; the validity of the
sacraments depended not only on the moral condition
of the priests that administered them, but also on the
condition of those in the Church who received them. St.
Augustine says, how can we distinguish them? Who are
we to judge? How are we to find them out? The Donatists
called them *traditori* — those of the clergy who had
turned over the books, the records of the Church to the
Romans — called them corrupt, and the whole clergy
ordained by them, infected. There was only one religious group that was worthwhile, and that was the

Donatists. It was a form of Puritanism, which, in spite of its pride, had some attraction, and which was sustained not simply by theological aspirations, but, as in the Germany of Luther, by national aspirations; it became a rallying ground for nationalism. There were groups in Africa that were getting very tired of Roman domination, and they rallied around many ideas, some of which, certainly, came from the Donatists.

25. INTRODUCTION TO *THE DIVINE COMEDY:* THE LOVE POEM THAT LEADS TO GOD

Why is it called *Commedia*? It's not a comedy, like some of the dramatic works of the Romans. They knew those and they had theatres. Almost every Italian town could boast of a Roman theatre. Not all of them were uncovered, but most of them were. Surely Dante saw the one at Fiesole. But what went on in those theatres? How were the old plays presented?

They were read, recited. A person got up — he was called the *mimus*, the mime — and read or recited the comedy or tragedy. Dante's is called a comedy, not because it is supposed to be acted or recited, but because it begins sadly and ends happily. A tragedy ends unhappily; that's one aspect of it. For Dante, the example of a good tragedy is Virgil's *Aeneid*, it ends in death; the language is exalted (that's necessary also); the characters are public figures — whereas those of comedy are ordinary persons, and so on. They had no inkling of tragedy or comedy as we know it.

The word *commedia* had a special meaning; but, more important is what Dante was trying to do in this form. Several things have to be considered in this connection. Why did he write it in the vernacular, in Italian? Many of his other works are in Latin: *De Monarchia, De Vulgari Eloquentia*, and the *Epistles*. What is the advantage of a poem written in Italian? What is the nature of the poem, and the relation of that nature to the language? What is the origin of the idea of writing a poem of such a nature in the vernacular?

Dante describes *The Divine Comedy* as a love

poem. He said it was a sort of vision that came to him after he had wept over the death of his beloved Beatrice. But why write it in Italian? Was there a tradition of writing love poetry in Italian? Who started off writing love poems in the vernacular? The Provençal poets had done so, long before Dante. And from Provençe, before it went to Italy it went to Germany. As a matter of fact, in the twelfth and thirteenth centuries, in the age preceding Dante, it is in Germany that vernacular poetry reaches its greatest heights. The greatest of the German poets of that time is Walther Von Der Vogelweide. Germany had to go a long way before it found another poet like that. Dante didn't know much, if anything, about the poets in Germany; but he did know a great deal about Provençe. He knew the language, and amused himself with it. He takes his interest in it so far that he ends one canto of *The Divine Comedy* with quite a few verses in Provençal.

He wrote in the vernacular to honor Beatrice more or less in the way the poets of Provençe honored their women. He was in love, or pretended to be in love. In this connection, we have to guard ourselves from the very outset against something that has become most oppressive: the tendency to treat these great men as if they were ordinary people; to treat Plato, for instance, or Dante, or Shakespeare, as if he were one of us. If he were one of us, who the dickens would be interested in him? There are those who want to know how he lived, what he ate, whether he had some or all the vices we have. Who cares? God does perhaps, or the wife or husband, but no one else should. In any case, it's of no importance whatsoever whether he lives up to his theories or not. Let's keep that in mind in talking about Dante. We are not interested in what he did, but in what he said.

He pretended he was in love with this woman —

she was an historical woman, we know that. What exactly the relation was between them we don't know. Anyway, he wrote poems about her, and at a certain moment he put these poems together, he made a chain out of them, linked them together more or less in the Provençal manner, but with a modified strain, which was closer to the manner of the poets of central Italy. These poems, written God knows with what intention, were put under a certain yoke, each given a new meaning by linking them with a prose commentary. Together, they form a new structure — still a love poem, for love is still the animating principle of the whole collection.

But there seems to be a strange departure, an unexpected change of orientation when we come to that mysterious part that deals with Beatrice's death and Dante's affection for Beatrice after her death. The change indicates that Dante now looked upon love of mortal things, and particularly the love for what is physically most attractive as far as man is concerned, namely, woman, not as an end in itself, but as a point of departure, as a way, or a medium to something higher. A description of love of mortal things, in other words, now becomes an approach to the love of God. Not, of course, in the traditional way, as you find in St. Augustine, and everywhere else; not love of neighbor, which is not in reality love, but friendship (which is something else).

This approach to God — not through love of neighbor, but through love of a woman — is made possible through that characteristic of woman that attracts us: beauty. And here you open the floodgates to Platonism, to the *Phaedrus* and the *Banquet*. We spoke of the two halves of the Platonic world: the world of sense and the world of spirit, and the bridge between them that could be used, provided you are able to rise by climbing the rungs of beauty with the force of love operating in you. This is something new: love, not for the sake of the loved one in an immediate way, but love of a woman for the sake of God; not on the grounds of universal brotherhood, but because of the distinctive characteristic of this particular person. You don't love other persons in that particular way because they don't have that particular beauty.

Of course, Dante was not the first one to talk in this way. His century, both on the Christian side and the renascent humanistic side, looked with favor upon this general tendency as ennobling man and matter, by finding in both the imprint of the divine, the imprint of God. The way for the soul is through his creatures: *ad Creatorem per creaturas.* You get to God through the creatures He created, in the order He established. Meaning, that there is a multiplicity of beings in a scale of relative values. God gave man an intellect to enable him to discern the relative value of the various ranks of this order — the scales on the ladder. Most of us don't know when we move along that scale, whether we're going up or down. But these men knew when they were going up, because they kept their minds clear; and the way to keep the mind clear is to keep life pure. That, of course, is a universal postulate. You climb to God, therefore, by recognizing the stamp of divinity, the different amount of divinity stamped on his creatures. Some have more, and some have less. What kind of stamp should you look for? The stamp of the beautiful. It is a very Platonizing movement, a movement that is pretty general. It's quite a turn from the usual abhorrence in Christianity for matter. It's pretty hard for a Christian to get rid of the idea that sin lurks in matter; and yet this thirteenth century made quite an argument to the contrary. You find it not only in the poets, but also in the religious teachers. They cited St. Paul's invisible *Dei* — the invisible things of God can be known through those that are visible. You know how much was made of the fact that the Franciscans and St. Francis himself exalted the elements. You all must have read the great hymn of St. Francis. There he exalts the four elements; then the fifth, the quintessence through which he sees the beauty of the divine. At that point, he puts the poem aside — this is the legend — but after a while he picked it up again and said: "I've forgotten something." What he had forgotten to praise was death. Dante will take up all that.

This general feeling is there: a decided tendency against the traditional abhorrence for matter, against this Manichean survival. But perhaps "Manichean survival" is a bad choice of words, because in spite of what St. Augustine said in condemning abhorrence and despite what everyone else may say, it's really deeper than any religion. It's found at all times. It can be traced throughout the entire world; something inborn rather than cultural.

Dante was not the first to exalt women and the love of them in this way. The first poet to do so was Guido Guinicelli of Bologna, whose work is a little acorn compared to Dante's oak. But he was the first. He expresses that mysterious something, that mysterious attachment that is not friendship but love. If you don't know anything about it, if it's dead, I can't show it to you. It's like trying to define what fire is to a person who doesn't know. You have to say, finally, here, put your finger in it and you'll know what fire is.

The poets of Provençe had done that. They had exalted woman and love; love not as just a brutal desire, but justified as desire of possession, as exclusiveness. The difference between love and friendship is this quality of exclusiveness. The French would call it jealousy.

Jealousy doesn't figure in friendship. If it does, it is a very bastard kind of jealousy, and you had better do something about getting rid of it. In love, jealousy does have a place. So in Provençe *eros* has these qualities but it also has to do with ethics, with morals. You approach God through love of women. Of course, some of the things they said about the *gaia scienza*, about this science of love, don't exactly conform with the morals of the sermon on the mount; but, still, that's what they said, and it was, in a way, moral. The Italians, on the other hand, say that this love of woman is not simply a moralizing impulse; but since it is a light or splendor that comes from God, it should be used to give not merely ethical direction, but intuition, some sort of intellectual communion with the divine. It is a ray, this beauty; and if you follow this ray to its source, you should get, not moral improvement merely, but an intellectual attainment. In other words, through love it is possible to get what the philosopher attains through learning — the vision of God, the intellectual fruition of God.

These are the poets — in Dante's own expression — of the *dolce stil novo*, the sweet new style. That's what they are aiming for, all of them — including Dante. But in Dante there is a great deal more, as we soon realize. But why use this ray of beauty to climb back to the source, so that at the source you will catch not only beauty but all other values — why beauty and not *sapientia*? The Platonic justification in the *Phaedrus* is that the eternal ideas in the spiritual world, the idea of the true and the good, and the rest, all of these stay up there except one: only one comes down below to us and that is: beauty. Not *sapientia*. Not any of the others.

Dante realized that if he was going to reach that end he would have to do more than what had been done by those before him. He realized that if he was going to use this beam of beauty, it would have to be a beauty that is not corporeal, but which is grasped by the mind. That is pretty hard to take, isn't it? Plato and the rest of them shake their heads. *Το καλόν* is primarily spiritual not corporeal. Only in a degenerate way is it corporeal. It is only a deteriorated kind of beauty. In his love-mood (let's call it that), Dante realized this; whether it came to him as an artistic device or as a mode of consolation, it is there. His love poem stops abruptly at a certain moment; it comes to a sharp end because of the death of Beatrice. It continues in a mysterious way by the addition of a part that would indicate that Dante by this time had made this important realization: namely, that if he wants to go on, if he wants to follow beauty beyond corporeal beauty, he must learn to love a beauty objective to the soul. Instead of trying to console himself with the *donna pietosa*, he should reinforce his love for Beatrice, because in death she has become more beautiful than ever. Having learned this, he promises at the end to write a love poem for his lady more beautiful than anything the world has ever seen. He kept his promise and that poem was *The Divine Comedy*. For *The Divine Comedy* is a love poem — an ethical poem too, so far as ethics and love coincide.

What Dante does in *The Divine Comedy* is exactly what St. Augustine does in his *Confessions*. Why did Dante go to Hell? Some people say, he had many enemies and wanted to chastise them. But are we really interested in that? In his likes and dislikes? We're not interested in the vices, but in what he makes of them. Why did he go to Purgatory? To see the hopeful, the people he liked? And to Paradise to see his lucky friends? No, that's not it at all. If that were all, he has simply expanded on one of the many old accounts of journeys beyond the grave, just another *νέκυια*, that's the Greek word for it, like the νέκνια of Homer, or the sixth book of the *Aeneid*, or any of the 568 visions of more or less illiterate Christians reporting the sights and smells and filthy exhalations of hell. *The Divine Comedy* has nothing to do with that. What Dante is trying to do, what St. Agustine did in describing his vices and what happened to them is something else. Should you be good just for the sake of being good? Would anyone sustain this except a Sunday school teacher? You should be good, are good, so that you may enjoy the highest good, which is the fruition of God. St. Augustine describes in the *Confessions* that highest good, which is such that all other goods are as nothing.

St. Augustine wants complete satisfaction; he wants to find the good of the intellect. But there are all sorts of obstacles in his way, until the reading of certain books revealed to him the existence of realities, of goods that are not material, transcendent goods, the highest of which appeared to him as the God expounded for us in the sacred writings of the Old and New Testaments. That's what St. Augustine wants us to see. Dante sees it, with the help of the Neo-Platonists; he sees the supreme good and sees it as he should see it. He sees that everything we say is good here below derives its goodness and beauty from it. He sees that there is this God that does not need other things, but all other things need it, and are beautiful and good only because of it. But he's still in the position of the Arians.

How does St. Augustine become a Christian? Those of you who have read the *Confessions* know that having reached through the Neo-Platonists, Plotinus, Porphyry, this comprehension of the Father, of this absolute value, of the transcendent God, as seen from a mountain top, across a bush plain, emerging at a distance and altitude, he becomes confused. When he tries to approach, when he tries to cross this plain, he can't do it. He knows that the God is there, but doesn't know how to get there. Why? Because of his intellectual pride. Dante too will stress pride, almost in a kind of reverse Augustinianism. That pride now needs a transcendent, a metaphysical power to crush it absolutely and that transcendent power can come only from the God he has discovered.

How does he get that metaphysical humility that will pulverize pride? How is man redeemed? Mankind was corrupted through the pride of one man. *Eritis sicut dii.* Adam had that pride. He wished to become like the gods, and through his act all mankind was tainted. The love that should exist between God and man, that did exist originally, came to an end because of this act of pride of one man. That love has to be reconstituted, has to be brought back by annulling that act of pride. But how can that individual or any other, how can mankind annul it for all time? There is only one way. You need God. God has to become the anti-Adam. One man has to come to destroy all the work the other man had done. No single man except he be God could do it. That is the Augustinian doctrine. By His humility in taking on flesh and dying on the Cross, Christ reversed the whole situation created by Adam. The depth of humility corresponded exactly to the height of the pride. And matter too became an object of divine love; and that love, through the flesh of Christ, through the sacraments, was carried on to all mankind. Having seen God, St. Augustine finds the Trinity of Christianity — not by the *Logos*, not by the word merely, but by the word *incarnate*. From now on the *Logos* will never again be completely detached from the word incarnate.

This metaphysical humility is the humility of Christ in the incarnation, his becoming man, in God's taking on flesh — that flesh which was rotten and putrid up to that time. And that is the point that has divided the Christian Church, the East from the West: does salvation rest on the Incarnation or on the Crucifixion?

The act of self-vilification, of humiliation was so great that it annulled, cancelled off all the evil of that act of pride that had been committed by Adam. St. Augustine felt sharply the necessity of that metaphysical humility, for he always has before his eyes the terrific obstacle of pride, his own intellectual pride. As a result of this humiliation, love was established — love of man for God and love of God for man. And that love of God, according to Paul and St. Augustine, and all the rest of them, is the Holy Spirit. Humility he found through Christ, and love through the Holy Spirit. For what is the Holy Spirit if not love — the love of God for the Logos, and of the Logos for God. That's what St. Augustine is trying to do in the *Confessions*, to show that in his desire to reach the lode-star he solved one problem after another; and as a result of his experience he was able to reach, by the grace of God, the Trinity.

How does this apply to Dante? *The Divine Comedy* too is a confession, even though the transgressions which Dante confesses are very small compared with those that you find in St. Augustine. Dante is more concerned with the confessions of others. He starts, he tells us, almost dead, morally. And at the end of the *Purgatorio*, after he has been bathed in the water of Lethe, when he is asked about his sins, he says he can't remember them (drinking the waters of Lethe made him forget). And, how does it end up? What is Virgil's role? Or, first let's ask: what was it that turned St. Augustine, that carried him away from a life of indulgence? It was a book by Cicero. But Cicero goes so far and no further, and so does Virgil for Dante. But eventually all this is but a way of showing how a man, because of an inborn desire, because of a love for the beautiful, and as a result of all this, reaches God; but a God which is not something to be grasped simply with the mind. The vision of divinity is not only an intellectual vision, but something that you can grasp with your whole being.

APPENDIX

*The following four lectures were given by
Professor Henry Paolucci at the request of both
Dino Bigongiari and President Butler of Columbia University, when Professor Bigongiari was
forced by illness to take a brief absence. They
expand on Aristotle, reinforce what had been
covered, and prepare the way for what follows.
They have been inserted here, rather than in the
text itself, so as not to interrupt Bigongiari's
sequence and to avoid introducing a new voice
(though equally impressive).*

(HENRY PAOLUCCI) ARISTOTLE'S POTENCY AND ACT: VIRTUE AND THE GOLDEN MEAN

The question has been raised: what is it that makes potency become actuality; what is it that makes a stone press toward the center of the earth; what is the power that draws the man out of the boy? Or, to put it more generally, what is the force that makes primal matter, which is potentiality pure and simple, a shapeless chaos, what makes matter take on shape, become something in particular — such as we call the elements, compounds, plants, animals, and so on.

There is a force, a principle, says Aristotle, that works all this out, that makes it all happen. We know some of the names of particular manifestations of this force. We say it is the force of gravity that makes a stone fall; and a corresponding levity that makes the lively flames of a fire shoot up. There is a law in water that makes it seek its own level. And science, of course, from the very beginning down to the present, has sought to identify the principle or force behind all phenomena, all physical change — and to express the whole thing in more and more compact formulas — the goal being, to find the one formula that accounts for all change, all motion, all development.

That was the first object of the naturalistic philosophers, Thales and the rest: to find the one principle or substance or force that would explain all phenomena. There were two opposing poles: the *eleatic* and the *heraclitan*: the one holding that the only reality is *being*, fixed and immutable, that anything else is only appearances — which, of course, explains nothing; the other,

Heraclitus, holding that there is only flux, nothing abides, except that the laws of flux, strangely enough, seem to abide. The problem, thereafter, is to account for the abidance of the laws of change, as well as to account for this visible, sensory, materiality of the world. The most famous, Democritus, rationalistically and materialistically posited the hypothesis that there are both laws of change, as Heraclitus said, and something that abides materially. There are atoms, or matter; and there is motion of atoms in space according to calculable laws of motion. For men concerned with the qualitative rather than with the quantitative, however, this would not do: this mere skeleton could not satisfy.

Out of Socrates — rather than out of the naturalistic philosophers — came the main development of Greek thought. The Platonic position was: you have an intelligible world, which is the only true world (reality), and in between that reality and complete non-being you have semi-reality, the world before our eyes, objective to the senses. The problem was exactly the one we are raising now: how to account for this world before our eyes, with all its colors, sounds, odors and so on, with things that grow and change, and live and die; and this includes, of course, man and his civilization. How do you account for it? What is the force that makes all this be what it is? We see it coming into being and passing away, we see the stars rise and set, one generation born and grow and die and another succeeding it; we see all this: how do we account for it? Plato's answer was: imitation, participation. This world is what it is , does what it does, including man, by participation in the being of the realm of ideas. And Aristotle observes: Plato used the word, and gave an extraordinary glimpse — poetic glimpse — into what it might mean; but he left for others the task of stripping the poetry away and getting at the solid core of it, if it has any solid core. In trying to work out what participation could possibly mean in precise language, Aristotle was constrained to scrap the whole scheme of transcendence, he threw aside that whole world of a multiplicity of ideas, except for one — the highest — what Plato called the idea of the Good. There is something fixed, unchanging, apart, that accounts for all of this. There is something for science to know — whether you want to call it the principle of universal gravitation, *id quod est*, the one substance as Spinoza called it, or anything else. In other words, Aristotle held that science is not in vain. There is something that is fixed even though scientists come and go, even though it takes years, centuries to explore it, there is something to explore.

Aristotle takes this idea of Plato merely as an hypothesis, and then he asks, very scientifically: how is this idea, this principle present in the world around us? He frames the hypothesis in the form of questions, an interrogation of the phenomena, of nature. Is this principle something in itself, isolated, existing entirely apart from this world? Or is it present in the world, rather like Heraclitus says, as the order among the parts? Let's begin by assuming it is both. And Aristotle, who rarely makes use of analogies, here introduces one. He says: let's compare the situation to that of an army. At the head of the army you have a general who gives the orders. He has the orders in himself; the orders issue from him; but when he has issued the orders, then what is in him passes also into the body of the army. So you can say, when you see an army on the march, breaking camp and going into battle: everything they do, they do because of orders coming from the commander-in-chief, who is the source of all order in the army. And, you know that, in an army, although the order is one when it comes from the commander — say, he gathers his chief aides at his headquarters and says, tomorrow we break camp and

set out for such and such a place — these chiefs who hear
him have certain potentialities; when they receive this
order, which is one, they break it down into many parts.
They give different commands, particularized commands
to their subordinates, all the way down the line, until the
whole army with all its equipment, guns, tanks, animals,
privates, sergeants, lieutenants, majors, everybody is set
in motion. Everything is moved or moves itself according to its potentialities. Ammunition, food, and other
equipment will be crated and carried, for such things
cannot move themselves; horses and other animals will
be led and the military personnel from the lowest rank-
ing to the highest, will move themselves according to
their potentialities, as members of the army, each with a
predetermined degree of freedom and responsibility.
You have all this variety of motion, but it results from a
single command. All this multiplicity is made one by
order. That's Aristotle's analogy, in somewhat greater
detail.

Let's apply the analogy to the natural world of
elements and compounds, plants, animals, men, and
whatever else there may be. We have the hypothesis; let's
test it. Aristotle says, just as clearly as any empirical
scientist, that the test is in observation of the facts, for
with a true idea the facts harmonize, whereas with a false
one they soon clash. So he says: let's see if there is any
kind of order in this multiplicity of things, like that
which we find in an army. Do things move, change,
develop here at random, haphazardly, or are there
definite potentialities? Obviously there seems to be
potentiality. For example, if we take a rock in our hands
and release it, it won't move in any direction, sometimes
this way sometimes that — it always falls toward the
center of the earth. And the same is true of seeds. An
acorn is potentially an oak; if it really is an acorn, if it
grows, it won't become a cherry tree even though planted

in the same ground as a cherry tree. One might say it is the very idea of stone that it should fall, and the very idea of an acorn that it should grow into an oak. But from an Aristotelian point of view it would be better not to use the word idea, for, after Plato's use of the term, "idea" has come to mean a motionless unchanging entity, and here we are concerned precisely with motion and change. The word that Aristotle uses is *form* — or better still, *nature*. It is the *nature* of things that makes them pass from what they are potentially into what they are actually.

This force of nature is one in itself, but its power fans out; all things respond to it according to their potentialities, just like the various parts and members of an army respond in their different ways to set into motion a single command from the commander-in-chief. Aristotle observed the various things of the natural world thoroughly to determine their characteristic acts; he distinguished the natural sciences, even as they are distinguished today. Often, if you question a student of science, say, a physicist, or a biologist, if you ask him what it is he is studying, he has a hard time telling you. Does a physicist study what things actually are? Many physicists think they do. But the best of them know what Aristotle first taught, that physicists take things as they are for granted and study not their being — not what they really are — but their motions and rest, their alterations. So too, the biologists take things as they are for granted and study merely how things grow. A biologist or physicist may be interested in *being* as such, but that surely cannot be studied by the methods of biology — it is something that comes after physics (to make a pun). The science of *being* as such is still called by the name it took in the corpus of Aristotelian writings: *metaphysics*. But what we want to consider next is the operation of nature in man.

We know that man is made up of elements, compounds and so on; but he is not a man because his body is compounded of elements, nor because he can nourish himself, feeding on material things and making them materially a part of his own body as a plant does — growing, reproducing, expelling wastes. He is not a man because he can receive in himself the shapes or images of things without the matter, nor because he can experience pleasure and pain in sensory contact with particular things, nor because he can see to enjoy pleasure and to avoid pain. If this were all, you could not yet speak of man. What alone distinguishes man from other animals — he is an animal, of course — but what alone distinguishes him is his capacity to think. Man is a rational, mortal animal. Just as in the ordinary animal the plant function of self-nutrition is animalized by sensation (the animal not only eats but "sees" about eating), so in man what there is in him of animal is humanized by his thinking about it. You can think of reason as a kind of seed planted in an animal. The seed grows by absorbing the animal nature a little bit at a time until all that is animal shall have been humanized. At first the seed is nothing in itself, but gradually the animal substance is thought out. Animal sensation, imagination, memory — animals have all these faculties — when thought out or are being subjected to the control of reason become human intellect; and the animal appetites, or impulses — the desire for sensory pleasure. The pleasure of eating, of sex, and so on (and some animals have them all, all the passions — love, hate, friendship, and take delight in bodily motion, some take delight in the care of their offspring) — the animal impulses, when subject to reason, when they are thought out, become human will.

In other words, animals have apprehensive and appetitive faculties. Man has the same faculties, but with something added that gradually transforms them. Reason working in the apprehensive faculties — sensation, imagination, memory — makes them intellectual faculties, capable of all the things men are proud to do: man's right to knowledge. If reason is not added to the animal apprehensive faculties there is no science, no universities — all you can have is what happens in the cages where psychologists experiment to show how intelligent animals are. The difference between the intelligence of animals and the intelligence of man is roughly the difference between what the animal in the cage does in response to the psychologist and what the psychologist does for himself. If the animal had reason, and the psychologist did not have reason, the two would change places — the chimpanzee or the rat would be studying the conditioned reflexes of the psychologist.

So: man is an animal that reasons. Like other animals, man wants not to be vexed by bodily pain; he wants not to be disturbed inside by unsatisfied physical desires, and he seeks to avoid being disintegrated by death; yet his nature is such that he cannot avoid those things instinctively but must think about them. Reason, working in the apprehensive faculties, results in intellect; and working in the appetitive faculties results in will. These distinctively human faculties have distinctive ends. The intellect has no choice about it, any more than the eyes have a choice, or the ears: the eyes can't smell or hear; sight has a definite object, color, with light as the medium. Hearing has a definite object, sound, with air as the medium. So with the animal appetites. Thirst has a definite object; it can't be satisfied with bread; the sex appetite has a definite object, and so on. The intellect also has a definite object, and that object is true knowledge. Will also has a definite object, and that object is to satisfy what is willed, and that satisfaction is called happiness. Therefore, because man is a rational animal, because he has an intellect and a will, one can make, with regard to him, the two famous statements that have been quoted thousands and thousands of times from Aristotle: All men, by nature, desire to know; and all men, by nature desire to be happy. There is no choice in the matter. So long as they have intellect they must desire to know; so long as they have will they must desire to be happy.

All of this leads to Aristotle's *Ethics*. The difficulty in man that makes of his life a problem, an ethical problem, is that, although reason is supposed to control the animal appetites, the latter for some reason or other, get a head start. Reason matures slowly while the animal appetites are unfortunately already quite mature in infancy. Why this is so, or how it came to be, is a knotty question; yet anyone can easily verify it for himself. The fact is that a child entirely undisciplined by adults has only to see something or feel something that pleases it to be carried away by the force of those passionate appetites which Plato compared to a pair of powerful horses. Newly-born babes yearn for the gratification of sensuous desires and readily give vent to anger when that gratification is interfered with or denied. Unless adults, in whom reason has matured to some extent, curb these passionate inclinations of the young, sensuous gratification and anger at interference may become habitual; and the consequences may be that maturing reason itself, instead of mastering the passions will be overcome by them and made to serve. And, Aristotle says, what happens then is that the child, when he grows to maturity, is apt to be more savage and brutal than the wildest animals. For reason is a mighty weapon; armed with it man can pursue the indulgence of his sensuous appetites — sexual desire, hunger, thirst — into regions of intense gratification completely closed to other animals; and he can carry his capacity for venting anger . . . well, you all know what an angry man can do with the instruments that reason has fashioned.

Of course, there have been people who have said that the intelligent pursuit of pleasure, of sensuous gratification, is the whole purpose of human life — there's where man finds happiness. Plato has recorded the views of people who believe that; later they were called Epicureans, although Epicureus himself taught something a bit more refined. At the opposite extreme are those — some exaggerated Socrates, Cynics, and later Stoics — who held that pleasure has nothing to do with the true end of man; it may be present as an accompaniment, but the true end of man is to live entirely the life of reason; to crush and uproot the animal appetites, which are only an interference. This is a natural development — exaggerated of course — of the Platonic notion of the soul being imprisoned in the animal body.

Aristotle rejects both these extremes. He rejects the idea that man is some kind of an animal whose end is merely to satisfy his sensuous appetites; but he also rejects the notion that the body is a prison. The rational soul of man, by nature, needs to rise to the truth; but it must deal with the body first, and not in a tyrannical way. For to control the body is not an unfortunate necessity; it is in fact the primary good of man, as man. Man is neither a pig nor an angel. He is most completely human when he has thought out, rationalized his animal needs — what to eat, what to do about the sex appetite, and so on. So that the rule is, neither to let the appetites go their own way nor to crush them, but to moderate them, control them. See to it that you don't eat so much that you cannot satisfy your other needs; that you don't get so angry that it upsets your stomach, but that you can get angry enough to defend yourself when necessary, and so on. That is to say, man is well off as man when he keeps a mean between extremes of excess and defect. The appetites must neither be over-indulged nor starved.

This is the famous moral doctrine of the mean.

But — you won't get very far if every time an appetite makes itself felt in you, reason has to explore the matter, make up its mind what the intelligent course of conduct should be. As a matter of fact, if, in the case of an infant, we were to wait until its reason made up its mind, we'd have to wait years, and by that time the child would have gotten into the habit of doing all those things you hear mothers telling them not to do — and many other things besides. So, there has to be training. Unless a child is well-trained to begin with there will be serious difficulties later on. It's hard to break habits, even if you who have them want to break them, because what is habitual you do without thinking and, because easily, with pleasure. To break bad habits requires great effort and causes considerable pain. The best thing, therefore, is to train children to do habitually what they should; then they won't have to think about it, they'll take pleasure in it. And their reason will have a head start; as grown-ups, they will be able to apply reason and train themselves. But always the end is to do the thing easily and with pleasure. Only then can it be said that a man is well off, or virtuous. Merely to restrain yourself is not enough. Say you've decided that drinking is bad for you, it ruins your health. You've been drinking too much and you can see where it will lead; your wife, your children will suffer, etc. So you give it up. You don't drink. But you have a great appetite for it, you would like to drink. You can't say you're a happy man. Only when you no longer have to restrain yourself, when you do it easily and with pleasure, when it delights you to do it, are you happy. In other words, it has to become a good habit. That's what virtue is.

All of this has had a lasting influence — even though Christianity couldn't possibly take over the doctrine of the mean. After all, what Aristotle calls an extreme — and therefore immoral — in Christianity becomes the very height of saintly morality. Dante in his account of the sins treats only one of them in the Aristotelian manner, as a pair of extremes and that is avarice and prodigality. The mean there is virtue; but the same thing is not true with lust and the rest.

But there is more to the Aristotelian concept of moral virtue. The development of moral virtues is not an end in itself. Man, as we said, by nature desires to know; and the development of moral virtues is a means whereby reason, released from the task of directly controlling the animal appetites — it has left good habits as its lieutenants — is free to think of itself, of its own ultimate end. It has thought about the objects of the animal appetites; now it can think about its own object and the life of thought. The ultimate end of man, attaining the happiness of virtuous living, is to arrive at the life of pure reason, contemplation of the highest truth. In the end, we get back to Plato after all. Thought, reason is all wrapped up in itself, and the body is left behind. Well, Yes and No. This life of contemplation, Aristotle tells us in the tenth book of the *Nicomechean Ethics,* is not, strictly speaking, the good of man as man.

So you see, this is not the ultimate human end or good. If it were, says Aristotle, all men might attain it; but in fact how many can? How many have the leisure or the desire to go through the study it takes to elevate the mind above the needs of the body? And that is only the beginning. Only some few, those whom the gods especially bless, get a glimpse of this high vision which makes man for a moment like unto God Himself. The rest of mankind? Well, they do what they can and there is the human happiness of the virtuous life, attainable by all, potential and capable of giving — with a little luck — true happiness.

It is a very reasonable system; really practical, not

aiming excessively high as the Stoics do (and there have been very few Stoics) and not aiming too low, but hitting the mark.

Of course, that vision of a higher happiness is saddening too. Few can come near it. In the Hebrew world, not long after, there comes a great longing for another kind of mediation — not philosophic reason, which only a few can attain, but something which is given to every class of human beings, from the highest down to the lowest. Reason does not take you to that divine end; faith does. Faith, as the Jews said, in the coming messiah.

The ethics of Aristotle are reasonable and beautiful in their way. But it's all up in the air, isn't it? Man is never isolated that way, has never lived thus wrapped up in himself. To the two famous quotations already quoted — all men by nature desire to know; all men by nature desire to be happy — we have now to add a third, not less famous: man is by nature a political animal.

(HENRY PAOLUCCI) ARISTOTLE'S *ETHICS* AS THE PREMISE FOR THE STATE

A general idea of Aristotle's *Ethics* is important for an intelligent appreciation of *The Divine Comedy*. One hears a great deal about Renaissance Humanism, which is alleged to have begun with Petrarch; then (we're told), the ancient world began to live again. But when one reads Dante — who was certainly no rebel against the so-called Middle Ages, as Petrarch was, Dante who acknowledged the leading schoolmen to have been his masters — we find in him far more of pagan antiquity, of the substance rather than the empty form, than in the great majority of the so-called humanists. Obviously, what Dante received was present in the generation that taught him, and they in turn received it from others before them. So there must be some lines of continuity, or, as the historians say, some earlier renaissances than the literary and artistic renaissance of the period after Dante. We have learned enough about the rich content of pagan culture to indicate how much of it was alive for Dante. The pagan ethics of Aristotle — thoroughly pagan — were certainly available to Dante and the schoolmen of his era. It is strange to find that Aristotle, who is far more removed from the spirit of Christianity than the Platonists or the Stoics, should be identified in the minds of some people with traditional Christianity, that many think of him as some kind of Roman Catholic. Of course, if the Roman Church had acclaimed, say, John Dewey, or Benedetto Croce, as it has acclaimed Aristotle, people would say, "at last the Church has become open minded." Well, it took a lot of open-mindedness to take in Aristotle, who is a far more formidable challenge than either Dewey or Croce.

The *Ethics*, as we explained earlier, centered about the form of man, and the response of man to that general principle that moves all things — elements, plants, etc. Man is an animal, but an animal with reason. Reason, operating on the apprehensive faculties which he has in common with the other animals — namely, sensation, imagination, memory — results in intellect; reason operating on the appetitive faculties, results in will. These distinctively human forms of the apprehensive and appetitive faculties have distinctly human ends, namely: knowledge and happiness. All men by nature desire to know. All men by nature desire to be happy. Man's happiness consists in the satisfaction of both appetitive and apprehensive needs; his body as well as his mind must be satisfied. And our conclusion was that he attains the good life if he satisfies his bodily animal needs in such a way that his mind is free to pursue knowledge, although the rationally controlled life of moral virtue, even without contemplation added, is a true human good.

The life of contemplation belongs to a higher level. Few attain it — yet, Aristotle says, it should be sought as the absolutely highest good. He believed that the free use of knowledge or the fullest fruition of knowledge of the truth is the highest good of man, even though few could hope to attain it. It is a sentiment somewhat like that of the bicentennial theme. The greatest interference with that right is that most men have to work at more menial tasks to keep a few in the universities, and from time to time it becomes necessary to send brave young men to war to defend the common good. In other words, sometimes even the right to knowledge has to be sacrificed for the safety of the nation. Aristotle puts it in a different way. First, all the other needs — economic, political and military — have to be satisfied before anyone can begin to enjoy the privilege of the pursuit of knowledge. In other words, ethics, which concerns the good of the individual and aims ultimately at full fruition of true knowledge, is a function of politics. To the two statements of before — all men by nature desire to know, and all men by nature desire to be happy — we add a third, not less memorable: Man is by nature a political animal. That means, according to Aristotle, that it pertains to the very form of man, to be associated with his fellows in political organization.

What are the alternatives? One has been mentioned repeatedly: the opposite of "by nature" — "by convention." The Sophists argued the matter, as we can read in Plato's dialogues. There we learn the various notions about the state. States are formed, with their police powers, by the few strong or rich enough to impose their will upon the many weak or poor. But this doesn't always seem to be the case. Sometimes, the opposite seems true: the many weak pass laws on their strength of numbers, to control and restrict the exceptional person. But the fullest statement, later provided by the Epicureans, is that the state is a social contract, entered into for personal utility, by persons who, if they could, would enjoy imposing their will on all others, but who fear that others may get the best of them. So, each one says, I'll agree not to try to impose my will on you if you agree to do the same. And the validity of this contract, since it was entered upon for utility, is maintained by utility; if you feel you are no longer getting your share out of it, you break it if you can. And, of course, any time you feel you have strength enough to impose your will on the rest, you will surely have no compunction about attempting to do so. If you only entered it because you feared some harm, surely you will break away if you no longer fear.

That is the notion of the conventional origin of the state. Socrates apparently accepted it in the *Crito*, though he defends it as sacred, once it has been established. Older in the western world, and contemporary in the eastern world in Aristotle's time was the notion of the divine origin of the state. The king is appointed by God to rule; this was the notion, already greatly decayed, that the Sophists rose against. The laws, if not the rulers, were said to be of divine origin; but the Greeks, who secularized everything they touched with their thought, secularized the laws and we have seen in the period of the Sophists the final phase of secularization.

Against these two conceptions of contract and divine establishment, you have the systematic working out by Aristotle of the theory that the state is by nature: that, just as there is in man, in the fetus, something that will make him able to reason and desire happiness, there is a potency that will make him want to associate with others in organized society.

To say that the state is *by nature* means that two conditions must be met. Nature, first of all, is never wanting in necessaries. If a man is intended by nature to pursue knowledge, nature will see to it that he will have the necessary means: so, if the state is by nature, the necessary elements will be provided. Second condition: nature does nothing in vain. If man has a political instinct, a state will be formed. His gregarious desire will not be in vain. If the state were conventional, there might be people without social and political organization. You could imagine Epicureans living in ivory towers, deciding whether they should join up or not; but, not if the state is by nature. Then all men will be found to be members of organized society. And, if they are not, they won't be men. They will be something either lower or higher than men, beasts or gods.

Nature provides what? A multiplicity of people,

with a diversity of capacities; people suited by nature to perform the necessary trades. There are people incapable of working, delicate children who grow up to be doctors, lawyers, teachers; if all men were like that you could not have a state. Similarly, there are natural soldiers, natural workers who have not the temperament for study; if the family tries to force them, they get a nervous breakdown. Nature provides every kind of person necessary for the constitution of a state: including, Aristotle says, natural slaves.

(HENRY PAOLUCCI) THE GREEK HERITAGE

This rapid review of the culture of pagan antiquity is meant to equip us for reading *The Divine Comedy* somewhat more meaningfully than we might otherwise have been able to do. There is much more of the classical heritage that has a bearing on Dante, but that will come up as we examine the text and what is reflected there. So far we have touched on the substance of Greek thought, the *sine qua non*, the minimum necessary for approaching Dante intelligently. There are other ways of approaching Dante, but, if you can't read the original text then it would be better to leave the esthetic appreciation aside and confine yourself to the intellectual content. And to enter intellectually into the poetic world of *The Divine Comedy*, you have to be familiar with pagan culture because that world of the greatest of Christian poets is, after all, almost two thirds pagan.

Here we will try to sum up the Greek heritage as Rome received it, to touch upon the peculiarly Roman contribution to that heritage, as it was passed on, and to indicate the way of entry of the Hebraic current. For, it is the civilization or culture of all three — the Greek, Roman and Hebrew people — that runs together to form the basis of the civilization of the Christian era. The seed of Christianity was planted in such soil. It drew its nourishment from the Greco-Roman-Hebraic *milieu*. Other seeds were planted in the same ground and grew. But, as we said in connection with Aristotle, it is what is within the seed itself — the inner idea or form or nature — that determines what will grow out of it. Two different kinds of seeds planted in the same soil, drawing in the same nourishment, do not become similar trees. An acorn grows into an oak, although feeding on the same soil as a mustard seed. It isn't the soil that makes the specific difference, yet without soil there would be no growth. Christianity, was in fact the result of and grew out of its original seed, nourished by the culture of the Greek, Roman and Hebrew people.

How can we sum up the Greek heritage? What is it that we owe to Greece? Well, surely nothing of what we take seriously as religion. The peoples of the western world — there can be no question about it — have received their serious religion, their ideas of the hereafter from oriental lands. But, in the words of Hegel, the here and now — the living present, science and art, and all that which satisfies our spirit and confers upon it dignity and ornament — has come to us from Greece, either directly or indirectly through Rome. When we are unhappy in the world, when we are pilgrims in it, wandering far from home, we often look longingly for the light of the East; but when we have come to feel at home in our worldly circumstances, when we cease to be strangers and become citizens, it is most often to Greece that we look for enlightenment. For it was in Greece that men first put aside all discontent and took possession of the world, shaping and reshaping it according to their pleasure. Of course, the Greeks also had a religion, the substance of which they inherited, as they inherited the rudiments of their entire culture, from Asia. But, with that religion, they did what they did with all other things their thought touched: they humanized it, or secularized it. They gave their gods a history and made that history a part of their own spiritual evolution. As the gods came out of nature, and nature out of chaos, so the peoples of Greece, with their heroes, institutions and customs, arts and sciences, evolved from the gods; but the final result of that evolution, the glorious civilization of the Greek city-states, far surpassed in excellence the powers that made it. Their historical function accomplished, those powers would have sunk back into chaos and oblivion if the poets and sculptors of Greece had not given them as much immortality as men have power to give, by making them embellishments of the city of man, embodiments of idealized humanity. What other real significance their gods may have had, the Greeks have hid from us, and from themselves also, in mysteries that have remained mysteries.

Fixing their gods in the world of art, the Greeks displaced them everywhere else. Divinity was put aside first of all in the explanation of natural phenomena. The movements of nature ceased to be interpreted as the effects of the actions and interactions of beings in whom whims and reason and passions operate very much as they operate in man. In this rejection of anthropomorphic explanations lie the beginnings of western science and philosophy. The beginnings were crude with movements and changes of nature explained as the effects of a qualitative transformation of a single substance, itself objective to the senses. But soon the explanations were brought up from the purely empirical, to the level of thought, expressed in terms of laws based on quantitative, numerical relationships. The Greeks went a long way in this direction. The historical ignorance of modern science has for a long time prevented us from seeing just how far they really went; but at a certain moment they stopped. The race of men that had humanized the gods could not content itself with a dehumanized science. Science was not rejected, but man had somehow to be brought back to the center of things. Such was the commandment of the humanized oracle at Delphi for Greeks who seek after wisdom: before you try to know anything else, know thyself.

But the study of man among the Greeks also

involved, in its beginnings, the rejection of divinity, or, at any rate, rejection of divinity in the form in which it had first appeared among them. In the practical sphere the Greeks very early stripped the temples of organized religion, of authority over the basic social relations and activities of men. They took out of the control of the priestly hierarchy the institution of slavery, even as they later secularized the law, transmuting *Themis*, law by divine command, handed down charismatically, to *Nomos*, the laws passed by men. In the same way they took drama, medicine and deposit banking out of he dominant control of the temples and turned them into individual enterprises.

But for a long time the temporal authorities charged with maintaining law and order took care to guard against subversive criticism, the popular beliefs which ascribed to the laws and customs of Greek civilization a divine origin. Not until the period of the Sophists, when the public reticence of the wise was broken, when learning passed into the streets, were the gods stripped of this last privilege and swept utterly away. Xenophanes, you recall, at the very dawn of Greek thought had said: "if oxen or horses or lions had hands and could draw with them and make works of art as men do, horses would draw the shapes of gods like horses, oxen like oxen, each kind would represent their gods' bodies just like their own form." Later, Critias explained that gods were invented for public utility. In the beginning, he said, men lived like beasts, in violence and disorder. Then they made laws for themselves so that insolence might be held in check, and offenders punished. But, he added: although the laws kept them from open deeds of violence, men went on doing them in secret; and then it was that some clever and sagacious man first invented for mortals the fear of the gods, so that there might be something to frighten the wicked even though their acts or words and thoughts were secret. But always, when men say that the divinity owes its existence to the needs of men, they invariably mean also that much of the need is gone and that the gods must go with it. They mean that it has become possible to guarantee the safety of the social order without the help of the gods. They mean that the inventors of the utilitarian gods are working on a new and better invention. At any rate, that's what the Sophists meant when they dismissed the gods. The gods, they said, were invented to solve certain problems; it seems to us that if we reconsider those problems in their barest essentials we ought to be able to work out or invent any number of better solutions.

Protagoras marks the completion of this secularizing process. He says, we must speak out clearly and honestly, and not veil our thoughts in myths and fables as the old teachers used to do. Let us proceed scientifically. Let us accept no laws or customs, no standards of right and wrong behavior, no principles of justice as valid and fixed, until we have subjected each and all to critical investigation. If they can withstand such scrutiny we will accept them: if they cannot we will reject them and find or make something better. In any case, thinking man, indeed, each man for himself, must be the sole judge and measure of things — of things that are, that they are; of things that are not, that they are not.

This critical position is never lost by the Greeks; Socrates subjects the laws to the very severest rational criticism, in the *Crito* and elsewhere. He finds that the laws of organized society, the authority of temporal government, stands to reason. He says, whether the laws are God-given or not, whether they are by nature or convention is irrelevant in assessing their validity. Whatever their origin, one is bound in duty to submit to their authority and respect them as authoritative, even if they are badly administered, even if the price for the individual is death. Socrates, as you know, accepted this judgment about the laws and died to prove how seriously he meant it. Then Plato turned the argument around and said: the purpose of man is to rise to knowledge of the truth, but he needs organized society to live at all. What he must do is try to organize society in such a way that all classes contribute to the elevation of some men to the highest reaches of thought. Then these men will return and help govern so that other men can in turn rise to those heights. Of course, states don't usually operate effectively toward that end. The only chance of their doing so would be if by some happy accident a philosopher were to become king. But Aristotle turns that around again and says: you don't have to wait for a happy accident. Nature provides. The ethical scheme of Plato is exaggerated. The good of man is attainable with states as they are, for that good consists in a rational control and intelligent enjoyment of the good things of the body as well as of the mind.

All of this, from Socrates through Plato and Aristotle, is really the evolution of a grand defense of the civilization of the Greek city-states, on rational grounds. That civilization was certainly worthy of defense against the individualism that had undermined its religious basis. Here was a rationalistic or naturalistic justification. The ultimate object of the state for Aristotle as for Plato was to make possible the pursuit of knowledge and the free use thereof. The state is, or should be, a great training school preparing individual men morally so that the society as a whole can attain its high end, which is to know actually all that it is potentially capable of knowing, from the lowest order of things knowable to the highest. Obviously, this is not a task for a single individual, nor for a single, or a few generations of men, but for the whole society taken together. But of all those who live under the restraint of the law and education, not very many attain real moral virtue, doing willingly and with pleasure what they ought to do; and of these, it is only a rare individual who raises himself for a time to the ideal *biós theoretikòs*. What of the many, then? What of the poor majority who have to work and sweat, the mass of slaves and laborers — what do they get out of life? Nothing worth anything, unless they grant the truth of the organistic conception of society, admitting that all its members really constitute a single body. Just as in our own individual bodies, which are made up of many members, the eyes do not see for the eyes only, but for the whole body, the hand does not move for itself but for the whole, as it is in society. When an individual, howsoever lowly his function may be in society, feels himself to be a member of the whole, he shares in its highest achievements, even as a lowly private has his share of elation, sometimes even greater than the commander's, in the moment of military victory.

   That's the culmination of the rationalistic defense of organized society — of their own way of life — undertaken by the Greeks after the Sophistic critical enlightenment. But what happens to the Greek world in the post-Aristotelian period? Even as Aristotle was formulating his grand apology for the Greek humanistic man-centered way of life, demonstrating the naturality of the philosophic and social ideals of Greece, the political and economic foundations of that civilization were crumbling. The Greek city-states, judged according to the Aristotelian definition of statehood, had, in fact, already ceased to be true states, for they lacked military and political power to guarantee their independent existence. To protect themselves from destruction by Persia, they had been constrained to sacrifice all but the most superficial semblances of self-rule in submission to the sovereign might of Macedonia. The situation was very similar to what is happening in Europe today. The states of Europe, after centuries of independence, after fighting one another, but because they had the strength to fight building up the glorious thing we call European civilization, now have to unite. Why? Because they have turned over a new leaf? No, there is a great enemy, like Persia was for the Greek city-states. Europe has to unite and take orders from the real sovereign power, which alone has the power to match the mighty nation of the East. People like to say, this will give new life to Europe; but the opposite is true. People huddle together when they are weak, not when they are strong. If the European merger succeeds, it will mean that Europe is finished.

When the Greek city-states were united under Aristotle's great pupil — Alexander — it meant they were finished as political entities of any significance. Often the historians tell us that Greece's submission under Macedon was really a conquest, for thereafter the culture of that people became the legacy to the entire Mediterranean world. But the world's cultural gain, nevertheless, was no gain for the Greeks. Alexander's policy of securing conquests by colonization drained the Greek city-states of their manpower. At home, under foreign domination, the old patriotism was almost completely suffocated; while in the colonies young Greeks far removed from the sources of their own culture, and in intimate daily contact with the cultures of the conquered peoples, even as they Hellenized these peoples, themselves became less Greek. In time they ceased to be as convinced as they had been of the distinctiveness and superiority of their own culture. Differences between Greek and Greek were emphasized as never before, and conversely, the traditional antithesis of "Hellene" and "barbarian" was more and more minimized. That is to say, the social instinct that had united the Greeks culturally became divided against itself, reverting into its abstract components, tending toward social atomism on the one hand and toward a broad and undiscriminating humanitarianism on the other. In a well-ordered society these antithetical inclinations operate together, the force of one checking the force of the other. Only with the loosening of the bonds of civilizing society are men's minds drawn to extreme positions, some to cultivate a one-sided concern for the particularity of the individual, others a one-sided concern for his universality.

The Epicureans and the Stoics, respectively, were the champions of these two abstract extreme positions in the post-Aristotelian period. With the Epicureans, all values are reduced or subordinated to personal pleasure; with the Stoics all things are subordinated to personal virtue. Epicureanism, you recall, puts the accent on self-interest; yet it is interesting to note — and we did in connection with Aristotle's politics — their pursuit of individual pleasure ends in a very attractive, liberal social contract. Stoicism posits the unity, the universal brotherhood of man, yet moves rapidly and heroically to the position that the wise man does well to take his stand alone, if necessary, against the entire world.

Both these positions, that of the Epicureans and the Stoics, are dogmatic positions, propped up with a semblance of logic and physics. Really, all they amount to is an abstract intellectual refuge from the very concrete miseries of life. When men feel that they have no real honest-to-goodness country to be proud of, either because the country is impotent or they are, they start talking on the one hand of the atomistic uniqueness of the individual apart from the general mass of the nation; or they start talking vaguely of internationalism, the universal brotherhood of man as something higher than the nation — though their notion of humanity is never concretized. They love humanity but not the portion of humanity that tried to exterminate a race, or to enslave others, etc. They love humanity but really only that portion of it that vaguely thinks like they do. If they tried to really act together as people who think along the same lines, they'd have to form a nation, for a nation is the only effective form in which people can act together on anything.

When you have extreme views like atomistic individualism and indiscriminating vague humanitarianism, there is always a profound frame of mind underlying it all: namely, skepticism, agnosticism, doubt. If doubt is overcome, action follows and the extreme positions are necessarily abandoned. Well, doubt, skepticism, which is the third great movement of the post-Aristotelian period, really dominates the rest. Gradually, almost no one who thought at all held anything for certain. The Skeptics raised pretty much the same sort of questions the Sophists had raised, but now there was no Socrates or Plato or Aristotle to stand up against them. The Epicureans and Stoics were holding dogmatically positions which were rationally untenable, mere fragments of the great Aristotelian system. Often you found men were at once Epicureans and Stoics — a little bit of both, with more than a touch of skepticism thrown in. The result was what the manuals call eclecticism. And this was the form in which the Greek cultural legacy was passed on to Rome.

Like all great nations as they rise to power, Rome was at first indifferent to the subtleties of ethical problems. They had a ready and sufficient answer to all moral questions, and it was simply this: what advances the cause of Rome is good; what hampers that cause is bad. At first there was general resistance by responsible persons, to the penetration of Greek refinement and culture in Roman life. The great elder Scipio — not the one who destroyed Carthage, but the older Pontifex

Maximus, Scipio Nasica — warned the Romans against pursuing the refinements of life, that it would be their ruin if they did. He went so far as to oppose Cato strenuously when the latter called for the destruction of Carthage, pointing out that fear of a great rival was the only thing that could serve to keep their great nation from becoming corrupt. While the enemy is there, some discipline is possible; money is not all going toward making life comfortable, insure pleasures, etc. There are expenses for defense; the need for physical training of soldiers. Remove the last enemy, make yourself the undisputed masters of the world, the one greatest power, and you will yourselves become slaves of vice. If you think you're badly off when you're at war, wait until you see what happens when the victory party begins: there will be political rivalries, bribes to veterans to get their backing, splits in party allegiances. Well, as you know, Carthage was destroyed: Rome became what the U.S. will be, if it finally eliminates the one source of all our fears and troubles. And what the old men had warned about happened.

Oh, it was a great day for the populace — eat, drink and be merry — the highest standard of living in the world, bigger and better pleasure houses were built, theatres, boxing arenas, big bonuses were given to the veterans. But the pleasure of the populace was procured at great pain to others — cities and communities reduced to utter ruin; hundreds of them, combatants and non-combatants, slaughtered, left maimed, while the victory hung in the balance. You have only to think of what we could call "reparations" exacted from Egypt to keep the grain pits of Ostia filled, so that the Roman populace might be fed by governmental bounty. The peoples of Egypt were reduced to beasts of burden and often worked to death in the fields. To this very day, that land and its people show the awful consequences of Roman exploitation. But at least those people have somehow survived, unlike the nations of Indians at whose expense our glorious nation grew.

In the hey-day of victory, the desire to know was no longer resistible. The Romans began to seek out Greek learning; learned slaves were employed at home as teachers. Romans also began to travel or send their sons to Greece itself to pick up cultural refinements to the extent that befits citizens of the mightiest nation, with the highest standard of living in the world. And the culture they picked up was eclecticism, made up of bits of Stoicism, Epicureanism, and Skepticism.

Epicureanism soon made its way everywhere; but as it did not go well with public policy, it was usually practiced privately by the upper classes. Stoicism on the other hand, went well superficially with the Roman world dominion. Stoic humanitarianism was taken up as part of the official propaganda, and many Romans seriously clung to the idea as a program for Roman influence in the world. What Rome was doing — what every great nation does, or claims to be doing when it rises to worldly leadership — is summed up by Virgil in the beautiful lines; where he says Rome's art is to secure law and order in the world:

> to make all knees to sacred peace be bowed,
> to spare the lowly and pull down the proud.

The last line, in Latin — *parcere subjecti et debellare superbos* — is the equivalent of our own favorite expression: stop aggression and help backward areas.

What actually happened was pretty sickening: the poor people all over the world became aware of mighty Rome only because they were sick with envy, even as the lower classes in Asia and Europe have a confused admiration and envy and hatred for us on account of the prosperity our military might has brought us. Of course, the situation was somewhat more intense then, espe-

cially as you get into the first century BC. The ancient
historians themselves have left us the picture repeated
by St. Augustine; and modern historians, by and large,
have agreed that the old accounts are pretty accurate.
There were noble ethical precepts; but, as always, they
affected only a few. The mass of men throughout the
empire and especially at the center were restrained only
by fear of the law which only too consistently winked at
and even encouraged them in the indulgences of their
vicious pleasures. The traditional religions, as practiced
popularly, were no restraint, but rather the occasion for
the wildest excesses. It was generally true that those who
had not the means burned with envy. Certainly, Rome
had known better times, when its citizens were capable
of restraint, when public-minded men taught well the
duties of men. And men began to hark back to the good
old days before all this juvenile delinquency, corrupt
politics, extravagant pursuit of pleasure took hold —
changing wives as if they were concubines.

Especially among the thoroughly Hellenized men,
those who really felt the sadness of the fall of Greek
civilization, the talk about the self-sufficiency of man
began to seem like so many empty words. All men do is
talk sweetly; but what they do the minute they get the
chance is — well, what we see them doing when there is
no effective police and legislative discipline. If only we
had men like those of earlier times!

As they looked around themselves, at their situation, at so much that could not be remedied, they
reflected: if all there is to life is to enjoy it, what a
wretched thing life must be for those who can't enjoy it
— the deformed, the sick, those who are blind, the weak,
the aged. And what if you never manage to get a
comfortable living and end up living in some cellar or in
a dingy, furnished room on Morningside Heights, when
you're old, surrounded by gibbering young students.

Friends die, loved one die, what is the meaning of the whole thing?

Men began to think of the old days, even of some sort of golden age, way back. Of course, there had been the democratic theory of progress, from crude animal beginnings to the glorious present. But it was hard to persuade oneself that humanity was really progressing. Technical scientific progress, yes; but moral progress, no. Perhaps the two views are complementary. Perhaps the more we acquire means to get on in the world, the more miserable the world does become for us. It was something like our situation — material prosperity, great strides in medicine — but the mental hospitals are full, more and more peoples insane or exhausted mentally, sitting in the midst of plenty with their heads hanging glumly between their knees, their eyes bulging, staring helplessly.

And after this life, what? The heroic personalities of pagan antiquity, the old warrior class of Homeric times, the political leaders of the Periclean age, the sages of the Alexandrian and post-Alexandrian period, the great military heroes of Rome, might have indeed felt their lives justified in the very fact of their existence. But what satisfaction could individual existence be to subject peoples, defeated peoples, slaves, wretched peasants? What was promised them after death, by their sages and poets? Oblivion, or worse, a "*shoel* or Hades, a condition eloquently described as worse at its best than the least desirable existence under the face of the insufferable sun." The lowly had always felt the miseries of the burden of life; when the upper classes began to be downcast, they gave a voice at least to that deep-rooted discontent. This discontent took the form, everywhere in the Mediterranean world, indicated by the word *soteria*. It was very vague, but you get it surely in the pagan sibyls, even in Virgil; and of course, in the East it's most powerful. The Greeks and Romans began to listen eagerly to anyone who claimed to possess secrets or mysterious truths, or who practiced strange rites which enabled them to share, they claimed, in the true full-blooded immortality of the gods. Some of the groups were very exclusive; those that sought proselytes had so-called mysteries that appealed to sensory appetites. The Greco-Romans had enough such rites of their own.

But one people, the Jews, appeared to have a real *Arcanum*, which they jealously guarded, as well as a rigorous moral code which they strictly kept. They were scattered about, like the Greeks, but managed to keep their distinctiveness. They proclaimed the worship of the one true God, and it was their duty to call all peoples to Him. And it was a religion distinctly superior to all the rest in the near east and around the Mediterranean. In contrast with Hellenistic culture it demonstrated itself to be a truly philosophic religion, *the* philosophic religion. Later, as we know, Philo — the Jewish Platonist — showed by allegorical interpretation how consistent with Greek thought the Jewish scriptures were. *Deuteronomy 6:5* of course gave such an exalted idea of the relationship of man to God that it thoroughly transcended anything else in the world of the time. "Thou shalt love thy God, etc." But there were other passages, like *Leviticus 19.18*.

The Jews had a two-fold mission. This of the *diaspora* — to call all the world to the one God — was attractive but itself was Hellenized. At home there was another emphasis: the awaited *soteria* — salvation — in the form of a Divinity-sent king that would subjugate the world for the advantage of the Jews and return their homeland to them. This the Greek-Romans couldn't stand. It was not for such a God-sent sovereign that they longed. They, who had been nourished on thoughts of man's self-help, who had experienced the self-confidence of philosophic enlightenment, who had stormed Olympus and humanized the gods, were unwilling to succumb.

Man had somehow to keep his place. He had somehow to have a hand in his own release. But how insufficient were his powers! Still, what had he not tried; from the Sophists' schemes down to the wise men of the Epicureans and Stoics and Skeptics, and the Imperial system!

Nothing could be done in isolation. The wisest said it must be done in a political order; but suppose that fails, or you can't give yourself to the organistic idea? Work for some vague notion? What does it mean to pursue happiness, to build up temporal government? Perhaps it's just as well that we quit; let God come down and crush us with his omnipotence; let him put a stop to these atomic stock piles, the guided missiles, with his omnipotence. Throughout the Roman world there is this vague desire. But what will happen to man? He is nothing in the hands of Zeus, Jawal. What of the spirit of Prometheus, who, for man's sake, was bound to the rock, his liver gnawed by vultures? Must we be Jews and throw out this whole Greek quest of man to do something, to make something of ourselves?

Then out of Tarsus came a Jew who knew this pagan mentality and brought them an answer to their deepest longing, and to longings deeper still, of which they were not yet aware. He brought the answer in two words: Christ crucified. Salvation has come, eternity has passed into time; the divine has become human.

What is the evidence? Have there been signs? For the Jews, who require signs — says the Jew of the Pharisees — there have been signs: the blind have seen, the lame have walked, the dead have risen; and for the Greeks, there has been wisdom. But it is neither signs nor wisdom that we preach. Signs alone crush humanity, wisdom puffs it up.

In Christ crucified you have your Prometheus nailed to the cross, but He is also omnipotent God. He is the Moses of the Jews and your Socrates. He is *Deus-homo*, who by His humanity does what the Greeks would do for themselves; and by His divinity does what the Jews would have done for them.

Who can believe it? It is a mad dream. Consider the absurdity of it. The man says: I am the way, the truth, and the life. Men have tried so many ways to reach happiness, but they want it to be a true way. He says, I am the way; follow me and you will see the truth. And he leads his followers finally up a hill, and they are invited to see the truth — what truth? They see this miserable Jew beaten, spit upon, scourged, crowned with thorns, nailed to a cross, with a few friends mourning nearby and a crowd jeering. Even the thief beside him on another cross jeers. Give us signs, you're supposed to be such a big shot: climb down from the cross. But he didn't come down, he just hung there and bled to death. And before he died, he cried out saying, among other things: My God, my God, why has Thou forsaken me! And his disciples have dared to record those words for all to read.

This man dies in this way. This is the truth; but He would have us believe that in that death there is everlasting life. Who can believe such a thing? Surely no one can, not of his own will, not with his own reason. He said it Himself, while He lived, to those who followed Him: you have not chosen me, I have chosen you. He also had said He was the way to God; none can come to the Father in Heaven except through Me, and then added: No one can come to Me unless the Father drag him to Me. Drag him? Yes. But how? Bodily? As an unwilling draftee is dragged into the army? Or like that great magnet of a God of Aristotle draws all things to it? No. It drags by overflowing love, a love comparable to the all-compelling force of truth. Man is dragged to God by a compelling love just like the man who loves truth cannot be made to lie.

(HENRY PAOLUCCI) THE FALL OF THE EMPIRE AND THE NEW RELIGION

Those of you who have read *The Divine Comedy* and, better still, those of you who have read Dante's *De Monarchia*, his treatise on the necessity for world government, know what his ideal was. The treatise has gained new popularity in recent years because, as a recent translator has said, no one today can read the work with indifference. His ideal, Professor Herbert Schneider of Columbia, says in his translation of the work, seems intensely relevant and practical today, even though it may have seemed irrelevant and antiquated in Dante's own time. It was by no means original at the time; as a matter of fact it was already centuries old; Dante was one of the very last to uphold it. At a time when the modern plurality of sovereign states was just coming into being in Europe, he dedicated himself, all his energies, to the hope of reestablishing political unity as world government; and he argued that, unless there was efficient world government, a power that could settle international disputes and enforce peace, it would never be possible for men to attain any real happiness in the world — adding that it would surely be next to impossible for most people to live righteously, because so long as there is a plurality of states, men can never be properly educated to overcome greed and lust and criminality.

Let us say that a nation is getting along fine, materially and spiritually. There is genuine order, good citizenship, people respect one another, they are morally and religiously trained, so that crimes fill them with abhorrence: all the wildness has been civilized out of them. What happens? Another nation begins to make trouble. The peaceful, well-educated nation has to go to war; the youths have to go out, kill people they don't know; some have to spy, enemy spies have to be sought out and humiliated; and the blood lust comes back and so on. And what happens in the defeated nation? The war party and its followers are thrown out, all the enemies of the old regime are freed, the criminals who would have been in jail as enemies of society are now freed or escape and begin to cooperate with the enemy. It happened in the Second World War: the criminals in Italy came out to meet the allied soldiers, gave them the big welcome. The better people in all nations, those who love their country, never rejoice when their county is defeated, even if the regime was a bad one; you can't turn a defeat into a victory by siding with the enemy. Apart from all else, the enemy won't let you. When it comes time to making a treaty of peace, you're going to be dealt with as a defeated nation, even though you protest that you were always hostile to the regime. Well, these criminals come out with their lists of so-called war criminals — the fascists, for example. They would say things like: "they put me in jail six times. I've always hated the fascists." I met one of these — I met many — but I asked this particular one, why the fascists had put him in jail. I found out — not from him, but from the authorities — that he had been put in jail once for stealing a woman's purse in Church, another time for breaking into a dry goods store, and another time for raping a young girl. But he hated the fascists, and he was very anxious to divulge their names. Of course, the allied soldiers (in this case, it happened to be a battalion of Canadian troops) had welcomed his cooperation, and had actually installed him as the representative of their authority in the village where he had committed all those crimes. Wars are like that; in defeat, at least for a short time, everything is turned upside down. Even on the victor's side the disturbances are great. Dante himself had in his own lifetime experienced the disorder as it works itself down from the top to the very bottom. He says, echoing a biblical phrase, that in his native city, in consequence of the international situation, it was party against party, neighborhood against neighborhood, house against house, brother against brother in bitterest conflict.

For Dante, the only solution was to have world government — one supreme governing body, a real United Nations with truly sovereign power, which would have rights over the entire world, would have no outside rival. He was very realistic, you see. He didn't believe two great nations facing one another were a guarantee of peace: two nations facing one another are as much a guarantee of war as they are of peace. It is better to have a plurality of nations, but all of them members, subordinate to a world government that could not be greedy because it had everything. Therefore, having all power, it could act rationally and apply reason to the difficulties between the nations. He supposed, and no doubt he was right, that a nation that has national interests will pursue them; and that when various nations each pursues its own interests, wars are inevitable. But, if you have a governing body that has no supreme rival, no possible competitor, you will have a situation where greed for power cannot be a motive. You will have a real United Nations (not like this one in New York); today's United Nations is not sovereign. The United States and the Soviet Union, particularly, have not renounced even a bit of their sovereignty, and indeed are so constituted that the law forbids them to do so.

If, says Dante, we can have such world government with real sovereign power, we will be on our way to curing the ills of mankind, and men will be able to attain the goals which they are supposed to attain.

We have discussed the progress of philosophic thought and the applications of philosophic teachings according to our moral and intellectual capacities, to the attainment of that goal. We saw how under critical examination of the nature of things, of the condition of man in society, the pagans or at any rate the best of them, came to the conclusion that if man is to exercise his intellectual faculties satisfactorily, if he is to satisfy his desire to know and his desire to be happy, he can only hope to do it through organized society, as a member of a political body, a state. The success of the whole will be the occasion for the success also of the individual. We also noticed what happens when a state is overcome, when it fails. Men feel like atoms then, all different, but by the same token all alike. It is at such a point that the state ideal of one world, all mankind united under one law in one ideal state, becomes popular. The Roman state we noted, as it expanded, took up this ideal as official propaganda; from now on there would be no defeated nations because there would be no more wars. Rome would enforce the habits of peace on all the world,

> Make all knees to sacred peace be bowed
> Upraise the lowly and put down the proud.

Dante quotes these lines in praise of Rome, and goes so far as to say that in its whole history, the human race was never so well off temporally as under the pagan Roman Emperor, Augustus, for whom Virgil wrote those lines. The world had found the way to attain worldly happiness by the use of man's natural powers. And of course, this effort, according to Dante, was crowned by the birth of Christ, under that same emperor. The crowning of Christ is a crowning of the efforts of man, making possible the attainment of an even higher goal than that of worldly happiness. That's Dante's attitude.

The pagans had worked things out with their worldly
wisdom: with their prudence, the moral means for
improving the lot of mankind; with temperance and
courage, the political means for attaining the ultimate
goal: justice. With Christianity three spiritual virtues are
added to these cardinal virtues and man is thereafter
equipped to attain his two-fold happiness, in the present
and in eternity, providing he lives according to those
virtues.

Well, as we have had occasion to observe, Christianity didn't initially present itself as a crowning of the
achievements of men, but rather as a means of relief or
salvation for men in their failure. The original message
of Christianity was: instead of trying to be happy on
earth, hope for happiness in a world to come; instead of
relying on human wisdom rely on faith; instead of living
by political ties, with some men dominating others, live
by ties of charity, serving willingly, lovingly, without
having to be coerced. In other words, Christianity presented its virtues initially as the antithesis of the ways of
the world. There are indeed two ends for mankind, as
Dante says, but men must follow one or the other, not
both. Of course, Dante wrote early in the fourteenth
century. Fourteen centuries is a long time; the United
States, as such, is just above two centuries old, and
already there have been great changes in outlook. One
of the tasks in studying the backgrounds of *The Divine
Comedy* is to attempt to account for the change that made
possible such a conception as that of Dante — a harmony,
as we have learned to call it, of worldly and heavenly
ideals.

This ideal, is of course central in *The Divine
Comedy*; it is really what the whole poem is about. All its
wealth of content is built up around this theme: men are
not attaining the two goals they are supposed to attain,
and Dante writes *The Divine Comedy* to show, and to

make his readers feel, what a terrible thing this failure is, to explain the cause of the failure and to point out the remedy. In the course of the development of the poem, he reviews the achievement of ancient pagan culture — philosophy, ethics, politics — he reviews the contribution of the Romans, especially in law and political organization, and, of course, the history of the Church, from its founding by Christ down through his own day, paralleling that with the history of the Holy Roman Empire. Both the Church and the Empire had just suffered great defeats, practically in Dante's own lifetime, so that he is able to say that neither one nor the other is functioning. He wants his readers to understand why; and also what must be done about it.

From the very beginning, Christianity understood itself to be the answer to all the needs of the world, come in the fullness of time, to the Jews first and then to the rest of the world. And it was an answer not for the scribes and philosophers alone, and not for patriots, surely, who would seize their happiness by force of arms. It answered the needs of all, but all must first become conscious of the needs to hear the answer. Those whom the world had rejected, who were destitute of all things the world glories to possess; those who labored and were heavy laden heard the call most directly, for they most urgently felt their needs. Among the Jews. the first disciples were very lowly men. Klausner, the great Hebrew scholar, Max Radin, and also the author of the article on the so-called common-man in the *Encyclopedia Judaica — Am-Ha-Aredz* I suppose is the Hebrew word — agree that the preaching of Jesus attracted the lowly and the uneducated who resented the attitude of the scribes and the Pharisees. To read well was very essential for right living among the Jews; and it was also necessary to be rather well off financially in order to comply with the requirements of Jewish Law that covered every aspect of life. It was all a great burden for the common man: to live righteously, he had to depend on the learning of others; and they had to make great financial sacrifices to meet the dietary and ritualistic requirements of which he was largely ignorant. Here now came a man who met them in their lowliness and misery, who made the burden of the low much lighter — not so light as some modern Jewish reformers have made it, but much lighter than the orthodoxy of his time. All the early disciples were of course Jewish. Jesus is reported to have said many things to the effect that his mission was not restricted to the Jews. But He himself, in His lifetime, actually confined all his work to the Jews or at any rate to the Semitic people.

Obviously he could not be accepted by the Jews as a nationalistic hope. It is not to be wondered at that the learned leaders of the Jewish people should have re-jected this Messiah, about whose birth there had been more than a suspicion; who was impudent toward his betters, who led a politically insignificant life, who died a scandal to his disciples and to the Jewish nation generally. If His claim to be the Messiah were true, why did He not give a sign for all to see? Why did He permit Himself to be humiliated and mocked by the Roman soldiers? But it was, from beginning to end, nothing more than a pathetic farce. Judaism could not, as Klausner puts it, rest its future existence upon such a foundation. Not that they were not still longing for a Messiah: on the contrary, the leading thinkers of a few decades later supported the messianic claims of Simon bar Kosiba; but the latter was a heroic personality, fit for the role, even though his mission was soon aborted and the messianic hopes shattered once more.

As among the Jews, so among the gentiles, only the very lowly were attracted at first. Paul boasts about it. There are not many wise or mighty or noble among those who are called. God has chosen the foolish things of the world to put to shame the wise, the weak things to put to shame the strong, the base things, things that are nothing to bring to naught things that are worthy. Roman authorities only very gradually became aware of the existence of these Christians. At first they seemed to be but a part of the Jewish community. When the nationalistic homeland of the Jews became hostile to them, they went into the *Diaspora*; always to the Jewish centers, where, as we saw, there were already a lot of God-fearing pagans. Those God-fearing pagans attached already to the Jewish God without, however, having abandoned their nationality to become Jews, with circumcision, were of course the source of the first gentile converts. The Roman authorities began to become aware of this new group on account of the opposition of the Jews who did not accept Jesus as the Messiah. The Christians were denounced as subversives. We all know the situation with Jesus Christ Himself. He is denounced to the Roman authorities for claiming to be a king. Caesar is the only king; if this man claims to be king, He must be a plotter against authority. Pilate — the skeptic, who no doubt was also a Stoic publicly and an Epicurean privately — shrugs his shoulders and asks Jesus: what is truth? and if he is indeed a king. Jesus says: My kingdom is not of this world. If it were of this world my followers would have fought to keep me from being arrested. You remember, Peter pulled out his sword when the guards came and actually cut off the ear of one of them before Jesus stopped him and warned him that those who take up the sword shall die by the sword — meaning, a society that defends itself with military power and all political societies must, will inevitably perish by the very means with which it defends itself. The followers of Christ therefore must not have regiments. You may remember the remark of Stalin when he was asked what he thought about the Church as a power against him. He said, how many regiments does the Pope have? Well, Christ gave the answer to Peter long ago: He who takes up the sword shall perish by the sword.

Later, the charge against the Christians was always sacrilege and *lese majesté*. The two charges are really one. The Christians were required to make a sacrifice to the *daemon* or divinity of the Emperor. This *cultus* of the reigning emperor constituted nothing more than a pledge of allegiance to the authority of the state, a pledge to subordinate one's private interests to the higher interests of the state, should the two ever be in conflict. It was nothing more mysterious than the pledges of allegiance exacted from their citizens by modern nations. A man cannot refuse to pledge allegiance, to give an oath if his country demands it, unless he has already sworn allegiance to another state. Foreigners from far-off lands not subject to Rome, were exempted from such oaths, and the Jews, after long struggles, had also won that right. They refused to worship; and the Romans, to avoid unnecessary trouble and because the Jewish communities scattered throughout the world were useful, allowed the Jews this exemption, on the grounds that the Jews in a sense constituted a foreign nation, with a homeland, and laws and so on. And while the Christians were regarded as a sect of the Jews, they enjoyed the same immunity. But as they began to distinguish themselves more and more from the rest of the Jews, they lost this immunity. They professed to be different from the nationalistic Jews. They had no distinctive fatherland anywhere in the world. Then why, while they lived in the Roman Empire, did they refuse to pledge allegiance to it by sacrificing to the divinity of the Emperor? The Christians, of course, insisted that they were not subversive, that their kingdom of which they spoke was not of this world. They cited the words of St. Paul on obedience to civil authorities. Some of them even began to point out to the enlightened emperors that their increase corresponded to the increase of the Empire; that Christianity was a benefit to the Roman state. But, of course, there were the gloomier Christian views, such as you find in the *Apocalypse* of St. John.

Only gradually did the public-minded pagans become aware of the true Christian attitude: that the Christians were setting up a spiritual cosmopolitanism against the political cosmopolitanism of the Roman state, and that they were hammering away precisely at the point where Roman cosmopolitanism had to acknowledge the existence of a wall. The Christians began, first of all, by breaking down the barrier between pagan and Jew. They presented themselves as a third people; the expression appears again and again — a third people in whom Jew and gentile would be united. No female or male, no slave or free, no distinctions whatever. What Rome was attempting to do politically, the Christians were obviously attempting to do religiously. And the high-minded pagans — when they realized this — criticized the Christians all the more severely.

Celsus first criticizes them for the kind of people they call together. Instead of bringing in nice people, they invite the worst. Just what you need for a band of robbers! More important, he criticizes the attitude of the Christians who despise this world but continue to live in it and love another world in which, however, they don't live. Celsus charges that it is indecent for men to have such an attitude. One or the other. If you stay, obey. Otherwise get out. What Celsus really means is: why take your religion so seriously? Make the public gesture, and all else will be forgiven.

Tertullian was a contemporary of Celsus and though he didn't actually answer, he discussed the same questions from the Christian side. Everybody knows his

famous expression: *Credo quia absurdum est.* He also
asserted that nothing is more alien to Christians than
affairs of politics. Those who say the Christians are
subversive, he points out, should consider their numbers: they are far greater than any of the alien tribes that
give so much trouble. If they wanted to, they could really
upset things. That's proof enough that they have no such
subversive ambitions. Then he makes that famous statement: we are but of yesterday, yet are everywhere.